NORDIC RUNES

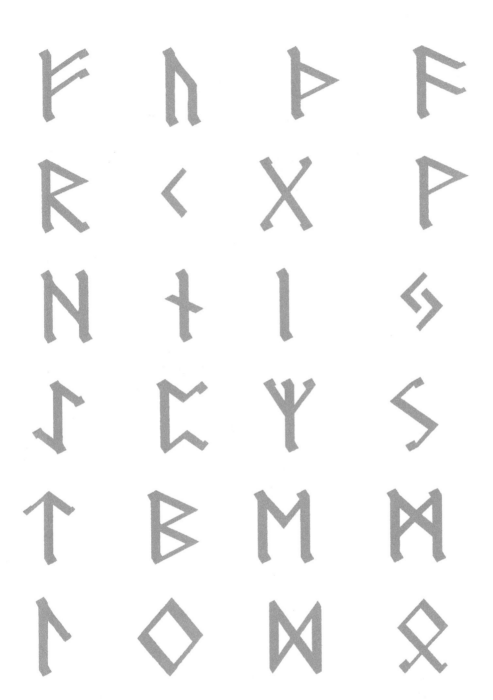

The Elder Futhark Runes

NORDIC RUNES

UNDERSTANDING, CASTING, AND INTERPRETING THE ANCIENT VIKING ORACLE

PAUL RHYS MOUNTFORT

Destiny Books
Rochester, Vermont

To my son, Finn, the brave-of-heart

Destiny Books
One Park Street
Rochester, Vermont 05767
www.InnerTraditions.com

Destiny Books is a division of Inner Traditions International

Library of Congress Cataloging-in-Publication Data

Mountfort, Paul Rhys.
  Nordic runes : understanding, casting, and interpreting the ancient
Viking oracle / Paul Rhys Mountfort.
    p. cm.
Includes bibliographical references.
  ISBN 978-0-89281-093-2 (pbk.)
  1. Runes--Miscellanea. 2. Fortune-telling by runes. I. Title.
  BF1779.R86M68 2003
  133.3'3--dc21

                                        2003001579

Printed and bound in the United States

10 9 8 7
Text design and layout by Priscilla Baker
This book was typeset in Times with Mason as a display typeface

CONTENTS

PREFACE

*N*ordic Runes is a companion volume to my *Ogam: The Celtic Oracle of the Trees* and is a similar guide to the earlier book in that it presents a fully functional system of divination based on ancient and authentic materials. Along with an upcoming work, *Tarot: Oracle of the West*, it forms part of an oracular trilogy that seeks to show that the meanings embodied in the divinatory systems of the ancient Celts and Norse, and of wider western European cultures, with their profound pagan resonances, are far richer than has previously been suspected. Within them we find embodied the primary images, teachings, and techniques of the Western Mysteries. At the same time, these books are intended to be workable, practical systems of divination, and in this *Nordic Runes* is no exception.

The spell the Runes cast both in the collective imagination and in our individual lives through their use as tokens in divination, magic, and creative visualization is a powerful one indeed. This—at first sight simple—set of signs expands almost infinitely upon acquaintance to reveal an entire system of magical correspondence and lore. Its oracular signs form a network of pathways no less potent than the Hebrew alphabet does in kabbalism, which has long been a mainstay of Western occultism. As the pages ahead reveal, the Runes contain a blueprint or road map to the Northern Mysteries, and, above and beyond their fortune-telling role, a kind of initiation into a profound cultural tradition. By using the Runes, the reader can not only access this unique wisdom tradition but also participate in its contemporary revival.

A few technical matters need to be addressed to help the reader to navigate the pages ahead with the maximum of ease. The first involves the use of archaic names and other terms. While I have carried over the use of accents from the original Old English, Norwegian, and Icelandic sources, I have (with some regret) not included letters from these languages that do not occur in modern English. To make the mental leap from Odin to the native representation of his name, Oðinn, may not present too much of a problem, and with time Þórr becomes recognizable as Thór, but less familiar terms place unreasonable demands on even the most reasonable reader. However, I have made an exception to this with the titles of poems, sagas, and tales, which seem to me to deserve special treatment; English translations for these follow in parentheses. Another source of confusion may be caused by my selective use of capital letters for the same word in some contexts but not others. As a rule, I use the phrase *the Runes* to refer to the Elder Futhark alphabet used for runic divination, but *runes* for the individual letters and more generally for the other rune scripts that existed in centuries past. I also use lowercase to refer to historical forms of paganism, while contemporary Paganism is given a capital *P*, to draw a distinction between early beliefs and their modern revival. Finally, I follow modern scholarly convention in replacing the outmoded terms B.C. and A.D. with B.C.E. (before the Common Era) and C.E. (Common Era), for obvious reasons.

I would like to thank all those who made this work possible, especially my partner, Claire, and our son, Finn, for their patience, support, and inspiration. Of those who have contributed to the present work directly or indirectly, I would like to acknowledge my mother and father for help and support along the way; the Downey brothers and their extended kin, especially Kirk and Shane; and the indomitable Rhys Hughes. Salutations to Wilson and Margaret Harris for encouraging me in my researches, to Elaine Sanborn and Jon Graham at Inner Traditions for their fabulous enthusiasm, and to that maker of talismans, Paora Te Rangiuaia, for holding the manuscript in magical trust. To Cian MacFhiarais and the other members of the Coven of the

Triple Moon, my sincere compliments. Finally, every writer should have a home away from home: My thanks go to the Lazy Lounge Café, a wayfarer's house and safe haven that faces the sea to the north and south. May its owners, Nick and Pat, enjoy the favor of the gods for their generosity of spirit.

THE ORIGIN OF RUNES AND HOW TO USE THIS BOOK

This book is a complete guide for those who wish to draw on the well of practical and esoteric wisdom embodied in the ancient Runes. It provides the necessary tools for interpreting "the runes of good help" and the teachings from the Norse wisdom tradition on which they are founded. Having come into prominence some two thousand years ago, the twenty-four runestaves of the ancient Elder Futhark alphabet are more relevant to us today, at the dawn of a new millennium, than ever before. Like the images of the tarot deck and the hexagrams of the I Ching, Runes are profound keys to personal empowerment, self-development, and spiritual awareness.

The Runes are native to traditional northern European cultures. They have deep resonances within the pagan Norse world of high gods and goddesses, elemental forces, giants, dwarfs, warriors, and wizards that inspired, among others, J. R. R. Tolkien in the writing of his fantasy fictions. Ancient tales tell of their discovery by the magician-god Odin and their use in magic and divination. This last, predictive use of Runes continues with us today, in guides such as this. It is, however, the contention of this book that the twenty-four runes of the Elder Futhark are more than mere fortune-telling tokens: they are a potent key to the rich mythological heritage of the Norse world. As we will see, each stave (individual rune) evokes a set of tales and correspondences in ancient Norse myth; they encode a set of profound

1

teachings, an entire wisdom tradition. These teachings, moreover, have a universality and a timelessness to their insights, messages to impart that transcend their northern European origins. To the runecaster, the runic system is a magical mirror of symbols that, through the act of consultation, can be turned to in order to reflect the nature of a situation and offer counsel or guidance.

To *divine*, in the original sense of the word, is literally to discover higher insight, the workings of fate, or the "will of the gods," as it applies to our lives. Divination systems like the Runes are based on sets of meaningful signs, omens that we "randomly" choose and interpret for their personal message to us. But how could such a procedure possibly work? The traditional Norse answer would be that in the Web of Wyrd (fate, destiny), all things and events resonate in a profound and luminous way and that Runes faithfully record the signature of the energy movements underlying our own unique fate path at the moment of consultation. The scientific rationalism of the West generally does not admit that events that are not causally related can have an underlying connection, but the idea is no longer disreputable even in scientific terms, for the notion of randomness itself has increasingly been subject to scrutiny in modern times. In the 1950s, C. G. Jung introduced the concept of synchronicity, which he described as "meaningful coincidence," and some quantum theoreticians have supported his conviction that "chance" events not physically or causally linked may nonetheless spring from a deeper ordering principle. For all its chaos, we are now entering an exciting time when modern science and ancient magic can at last meet and come into dialogue.

In the ancient world, divination was, of course, attributed to the activity of gods and spirits. Whether we regard such entities as real or metaphorical, it is vitally significant that in northern Europe the highest of all the gods, Odin (who as the Germanic Woden or Wotan gave his name to *Wednes*day), was himself the discoverer and lord of the Runes. Odin in fact provides the model for mastery of the runic system. In Norse myth, he descends the World Tree and undergoes a sacrifice to haul up the Runes from Mímir's Well. The Well of Mímir can be understood in several ways: as the psyche of the runecaster, the collective unconscious, and the world of energy forms underlying physical matter, for the story of Odin's quest is really a code for the process of looking within and attaining therein knowledge of all the worlds. The Runes are the physical tokens of his hard-won wisdom, offered to those "to whom they may avail."

How exactly do the Runes embody the wisdom of Odin? First, the runic signs carry many meanings. Each rune has a field of associations partially preserved for us in three ancient "Rune poems," which appear to be based on far older, oral traditions. In Norse myth, Odin was the god and patron of the oral tradition, so the wisdom of the Runes and the accumulated folk ways they represent can be seen as flowing from him and from various guises of the Goddess, from whose springs of knowledge Odin himself drew. For example, the image of the first rune, F *(fehu)*, is cattle. The primary correspondences are assets, wealth, and gain, for in ancient Norse culture you were worth as much as your herd of cattle. In a Rune reading, each rune is interpreted as an omen of personal significance—thus *fehu* signifies material luck and gain and is titled Abundance in this book. Obviously, we would be cheered by the appearance of *fehu* in a reading for the present or near future! Yet, as will be seen in part 2 of this book, "Runestaves," *fehu*'s association with wealth, good fortune, and greed evoke far deeper mythical and legendary themes in traditional runelore.

Runes can teach us self-mastery and gift us with its fruits. In the original sources, they are praised as a guide to action, a remedy for misfortune, and a magical tool for promoting empowerment, fulfillment, prosperity, and peace. This is the spirit in which the Runes function for us today.

RUNELORE

Nordic Runes is divided into three parts, much like the structure of a tree. The first part, "Runelore," follows the runic tradition back to its roots in pagan antiquity, introducing the reader to the history of the alphabet. Here you will encounter the world of runic mysteries encoded in old scripts and inscriptions, transmitted by the rune guilds, and echoed in the Rune poems. You will also learn the story of the Runes as told in the medieval Icelandic *Eddas,* those remarkable remnants of pagan Norse myth and literature. As well as being informative, these sources have great power and beauty. They bring us as close as the written word of a Christian age can to what was being said and recited in those times when the spoken word and whispered secret held sway.

Some readers may, of course, wish to proceed directly to the final part of the book, "Runecasting," and its practical divination work. Many runecasters, however, share a deep interest in the world of the ancient Norse and Germanic tribes, with the Runes acting as a bridge back to those founding cultures of European identity. As with Celtic culture, Norse heritage does not reside in the Romanesque remains of legal institutions and the written word; rather, it is found in the tribal, shamanic roots of a Europe once covered by forests and brimming with beasts both real and mythological, a world of mystery and magic.

Through Runes we can access this ancient pagan heritage, tapping a source that can continue to inspire us today. Devotees of the Northern Mysteries tend to regard Odin and the fertility goddess Freya (who lent her name to *Fri*day)* as guardian deities, profound guides to reclaiming the ancient ways. It is Odin who—like the magician-heroes of the Celtic world—drinks from a cup of divine mead and later imbibes the wisdom of the Runes. Yet Norse myth also

---

* Please note that the word *Friday* actually derives from Frigga, Odin's wife (in Old Norse it is *Frigga's daeg*). However, I believe, along with many scholars, that Frigga and Freya (respectively Odin's wife and mistress, after all) were at one time two aspects of the same goddess, as is suggested by the linguistic similarity of their names.

recognizes the power of the feminine and is inspirational for men and women alike. Indeed, several ancient tales relate how Odin was instructed by Freya in the arts of *seithr,* her own school of magic, and we can see that such ritual vessels as the well, cauldron, and cup, from which he drinks in his drafts of inspiration, are ultimately symbols of the "feminine" waters of the unconscious, which spring from the wisdom of the Goddess. Through the Runes, we too can draw on this deep well.

RUNESTAVES

The second part of this book, "Runestaves," is the "trunk" of the tree, the store of vital sap within which is distilled the waters of inspiration. Here you will find the twenty-four runestaves of the Elder Futhark presented along with their associations, meanings, and unique wisdom. While perfectly functional on the most superficial level for divination in the popular sense as a type of fortune-telling, the Runes are really a gateway, a set of potent teachings that can act as an initiation into a profound cultural tradition.

My commentary on each rune includes the rune's names, the Rune poem verses, a visualization, its divinatory meaning (with keywords provided), and the rune's unique background in myth and legend. In addition to the comments below, a section at the beginning of part 2 entitled "Guide to the Staves" will help guide you in using these commentaries. Remember that the art of divining with the Runes develops with practice and experience; once grasped, it is in reality a simple, elemental technique of accessing the wisdom that lies within.

What is in a rune name? First, different commentators use various titles for the staves, from Old Norse to Old English, and it is useful to know these variations. In many cases the names of the Runes are themselves meaningful, such as *fehu,* from which we derive our modern English word *fee* (as in "to charge a fee"). And in magical terms, the rune name itself is considered powerful and resonant, a vital part of the identity of that rune. Second, the names were traditionally accompanied by, and learned by virtue of, the Rune poem verses attached to each rune. These beautiful lines embody the traditional wisdom with which the staves are associated and greatly enhance our feel for them. For this book I have provided my own translations, removing the occasional, intrusive biblical references in order to repaganize the poems. In the full reproduction of the poems found in "Runelore," these changes have been noted with square brackets, and the bibliography directs the reader to further translations, for those interested. As we will see, such oracular poems are common to many divination systems, across cultures, and with patience they yield many insights. Next the reader will find a visualization for each rune that leads to the heart of its primary image. These images help take us beyond the written word to the intuitive and imaginative domain. They are there to be contemplated; traditionally they provided an aid to memorizing the stave's association. They also give a graphic picture of the rune's character to hold in the mind.

Following the visualization you will find the most crucial part of all: a section entitled "Meaning," which gives the oracle or key message of that rune. More than simply a prediction, it is a kind of lesson directly addressing you with guidance appropriate to the needs of the moment. Here is where the divination takes on a life of its own and acquires a personal bearing.

Finally, the myths and legends connected to each rune are given. Here you can explore the various themes underlying the meaning of the Runes and gain a more in-depth grounding in the pagan Norse system upon which the Rune lessons are founded. These themes also help explain the forking paths of association that each rune has in the vast body of Elder lore to be found in the Northern Mysteries (the term *Elder* being used in reference to all things connected with the pre-Christian Norse world, though sometimes it simply means "older"). You may wish to stop at the "Meaning" section, especially while still getting to know your Runes. In the longer term, however, it is most enriching to gain a deeper sense of the underlying unity of the runic cosmos and to grasp the ancient stories, beliefs, and rituals that created the great body of runic wisdom. This book draws to a greater extent than any other available on the fabulous treasure trove of Icelandic literature, whose storytelling tradition is the best preserved of the Northern peoples. In these materials, much of which has come down to us in a form known as wisdom poetry, one finds a treasure of archetypal guidance and insights, of myths, not in the modern sense of falsehoods and untruths, but myths to live by.

RUNECASTING

The third part of *Nordic Runes,* "Runecasting," is like the branches of the tree, extending into the infinite possibilities of the future. It has been said that "the myth is the symbol in motion," and divination could be described as setting the myth in motion; that is, it helps us observe how mythology and its archetypes play themselves out in our lives. Runes are best carved on small stones or some other natural material, though many people today own mass-produced sets made of clay. It is the "casting" or laying out of runestaves that sets the Runes in motion, as it were. Far from being a morbid, fate-bound exercise, runic divination is an empowering art that opens us to the myriad possibilities presented by life's branching paths.

In part 3 there is a brief account of the contemporary movement that is concerned with "Re-membering the Tradition" of runic divination, providing the reader with a sense of context of this magical and inspired art. Next comes a section titled "The Theory of Runic Divination," in which ancient Norse concepts such as *wyrd* and *ørlog* jostle with Jung's theory of synchronicity and quantum physics. This will be of particular interest to those curious as to how and why Runes should work. We then turn to the practical aspects of runework, such as traditional methods of casting runes and associated techniques such as "charging" a set of runestones and invoking good counsel.

Following this, a section entitled "Spreads and Castings" offers the reader five methods of casting runes that range from the simple to the more advanced. Also included here are case studies, which should help to establish some basic principles of rune reading. However, they are only starting points. Runic interpretation remains a highly individual practice relying on the intuition and inspiration of the reader. Innovation and evolution are possible because the system is a living, growing one. As Nigel Pennick says in his *Secrets of the Runes:* "If [runes] are to have any value at all, both meanings and the magical uses of the runes must relate to present conditions. Of course, while there are some meanings that will never be appropriate for certain runes, they must always be understood in terms of present conditions. This creative, non-dogmatic approach is a characteristic aspect of the Northern Tradition today, as it was in past times."[1]

This book may provide keys, but it is for the reader to choose which doors to open and how. The course traced in *Nordic Runes* is but one possible route through the "Woodland Path," to use Michael Howard's term for runework. Work creatively with the Norse and Germanic traditions, embroidering them with novel elements of your own. The meaning of runic signs is never taken to be totally fixed. Part of the vitality of the tradition lies in the fact that, as readers, you are encouraged to create your own correspondences from experience and intuition. Thus the ultimate aim is to personalize the rune meanings and for the external signs to become the tokens of an evolving inner cosmography. The true book of Runes, in this regard, is the one carried within: an internal book of associations built up through practice and experience.

I have found that there are great benefits to be derived from exploring the worlds of runic tradition. Many have found that the Runes become friends and guides, signposts in our progress through the labyrinth of life. No esoteric or divinatory system can answer all of life's quandaries, but Runes are richly suggestive of positive pathways that we can take, as well as agents of self-transformation, inner development, and empowerment in the world. They are tokens of a higher wisdom for those who learn the art of runic interpretation. May your own voyage through the fields of runework and runeplay be a fruitful and rewarding one!

Part 1

RUNELORE

I will sing from the sage's chair
by the Norn's sacred spring;
I watched and listened,   I looked and thought
about the words of the wise
when they talked of runes   and what they reveal
at the High One's hall,   in the High One's hall—
here is what I heard . . .

HÁVAMÁL (SAYINGS OF THE HIGH ONE),
POEMS OF THE "ELDER EDDA"

⊙DIN'S GIFT

Norse tradition attributes the discovery of the Runes to the "All Father," Odin, lord of inspiration, prophecy, secret communication, and wisdom and, on a more sinister note, god of crossroads, hanged men, and the dead. Odin's quest to Mímir's Well at the roots of the World Tree commences the tale. The well is a classic symbol of the collective unconscious, the pool of energies and forces that nourish the roots of all life and underpin knowledge and fate. It is also a feminine symbol, relating to the ancient mysteries of the Goddess. Odin's delving into the well's depths symbolizes a process of inner reflection, a quest for truth and meaning. It is a profound instructional and inspirational tale and an important gateway into the wisdom of the Runes for those who seek to draw from the waters of Mímir's Well.

The retelling of the story set out below is based on sources in medieval Icelandic literature that we will soon encounter more fully. In it you will also find illustrated the all-important nine-world model of Norse mythology (fig. 1.1, page 13).

> Here is the story of how Odin, the All Father, became the wisest of
> the gods. Yggdrasil, the great World Ash, stands at the center of the
> universe, overarching the nine worlds. The "uppermost" of these
> worlds are Ásgard, home of the high gods known as the Aesir,
> which stands at the apex; Ljossálfheim, land of the light elves; and
> Vanaheim, home of the fertility gods known as the Vanir. At the cen-
> ter stands Midgard, Middle Earth, "man's fair dwelling," which is
> connected to Ásgard by Bifrost, the rainbow bridge. To the north is

Niflheim, land of perpetual hail and ice; to the south is the realm of raging fire.

Some say that Jotunheim, domain of the hostile rock and frost giants, lies to the east of Midgard and Vanaheim to the west. Others hold that Vanaheim is above and that Niflheim is below the earth, in the realm of shades. The two worlds of the little people who work within the earth are as one: they are Nidavellir, land of the dwarfs, and Svartálfheim, home to the dark elves. Below all the worlds is mist-shrouded Hel, which some name as the citadel of Niflheim. Towering are its walls and forbidding its gates.

Three immense roots of the Holy Tree penetrate the worlds. The first of these roots dips into the Well of Urd in Ásgard, where the Norns weave the fates of gods and men. The second penetrates to Mímir's spring, beyond the citadel of the giants, where the waters of inspiration gush forth. The third root falls into Hvergelmir in Hel: here it is that the dragon Nidgehogg, a terrible devourer of corpses, dwells.

Yggdrasil is the axis linking all the worlds. Known as the Guardian Tree, it supports and sustains all life. It has no known beginning or end. Yggdrasil was and is and ever shall be. In the twilight of the gods, when the battle of Ragnaroc will be fought, even Odin is destined to die, along with many of the other holy gods. But Yggdrasil shall survive and from it new worlds shall arise. Yet even the great tree itself is protected by the three Norns: Urd (fate), Verdandi (necessity), and Skuld (being). It is they who tend and water the tree.

Odin set out, journeying from Ásgard down to the roots of Yggdrasil. Among its giant sinews he eventually found his way to Mímir's Well. Now, the waters of Mímir's Well carry a gift beyond compare, for they confer upon the drinker the elixir of wisdom. Alone, Odin approached Mímir and asked if he might drink from the well.

Mímir was the guardian of the well, and he knew its powers. He demanded from Odin one of the god's eyes in return for a draft of the water. Odin consented by plucking his eye from its socket;

without hesitation, he gave it in exchange for the precious liquid. He drank deeply from the well and received the wisdom he sought. But his ordeal was not yet over.

Immediately Odin saw what he must do and reached upward into the tree to break off a branch, which he then fashioned into a spear. Odin chose to wound himself with this spear as he hung upside down from the World Tree for nine agonizing days and nine nights. Half drowning in the well, he plumbed its depths for the Runes.

Finally, on the ninth day, Odin spied them, and groping downward with his tortured hand, he grasped and heaved them up with a shout of triumph. He had won the wisdom of the Runes. Knowledge of all things was his at last, for there he learned the mightiest of *galdr* (spells and incantations). So it was that Odin became known as the one-eyed god and god of the gallows, master of magic, mystery, and might who knows in an instant the entirety of the past, present, and future. That was Odin's sacrifice; this is Odin's gift: to offer the wisdom of the Runes to the inhabitants of Midgard or, at least, "to those to whom they may avail."[1]

Odin's quest is one of the great mythological themes of Norse literature, and his ordeal on the World Tree has parallels with the Crucifixion and other ancient Eurasian myths of symbolic death and rebirth. The great god's rite of initiation, like the Buddha's awakening beneath the bodhi tree, leads to enlightenment—in this case into the mysteries of Mímir's Well and the secrets of the Runes. As such, the lord of the Runes teaches by example rather than inviting worshipful obedience.

Odin's ritual threefold death (wounding, hanging, drowning) and sacrifice of an eye represent a symbolic transition from one mode of vision to another: from ordinary sight to prophetic insight, as we will see. This is the mystery path of the runic initiate. We are not, of course, counseled to blind ourselves in one eye! Like Odin, the runecaster sacrifices his or her everyday "sight" in order to visualize

Ásgard
Home of the Aesir

Ljossálfheim
Land of the light elves

Vanaheim
Home of the Vanir

Muspellheim
Realm of raging fire

Midgard
Middle Earth

Niflheim
Realm of snow, ice, and fog

Jotunheim
Land of frost and rock giants

Svartálfheim / Nidavellir
Land of the dwarfs and dark elves

Hel
Domain of the goddess Hella

Fig 1.1. The nine worlds. This system is described in contradictory ways in different accounts, and no one has been able to map it exactly. The diagram above formalizes the nine worlds into a Tree of Life symbol similar to that associated with the kabbalah.

a situation in a "higher," symbolic mode of awareness, through *intu*ition or *in*sight. This is the true meaning of the tale.

Odin is, therefore, the mythical prototype for many runecasters, the one who went before and established the pattern of gaining such knowledge. This function was almost certainly reflected in mystery cults associated with Odin in the ancient Norse and Germanic worlds, where the "Terrible One" stood as guardian of the oral and magical arts. Odin is also understood as being, in a sense, the channel through whom the wisdom of the Norns (goddesses of fate) flows into the human realm. As Edred Thorsson—a key figure in the Rune revival—puts it: "To communicate directly with a god, or the gods—that is what divination is all about. . . . Runes are a sort of traditional code, originally the gift of the god Odhinn (Woden), through which messages can be sent from one level of reality to another, from one world to another."[2]

As such, runecasting is a "mantic" art, a divination technique in which the runic signs and their significations become the active agents in an interactive process. They gainfully present themselves, so to speak, to the runecaster for contemplation. Thus casting runes is an attempt to peer into the looking glass of the Web of Wyrd itself. And Runes do more than starkly reflect the unfolding of fate's pathways. They help to develop and enhance intuition and psychic ability, making the user more receptive to the subtle flow of energy currents that underlie and create material reality, and empower us in the arts of its transformation.

THE WEB OF WYRD

The runic signs that Odin grasps are the tokens of his newly gained knowledge: magical glyphs embodying primal, archetypal forces. An archetype (in Jungian terms) is a basic, formative energy that creates patterns in the collective unconscious of humanity. Archetypal processes are also the underlying, generative elements of any situation, the "building blocks" of experience. Many people regard runestaves as an ancient attempt to capture in symbolic form primal archetypes of creation that gave rise not only to the material world surrounding us but also to the inner, experiential plane of our thoughts and emotions. We might say, in fact, that one is a reflection of the other.

The playing out of such forces is one aspect of the multifaceted concept of *wyrd*. The root of our modern English word *weird*, the Anglo-Saxon term *wyrd* derives from the Old Norse term *urd*, after which is named the eldest Norn, Urd, and the Well of Urd in Ásgard. *Wyrd* has no direct equivalent in modern English, and its meaning must be inferred from a variety of Norse and Old English sources. It means individual "fate," the web of all that happens, and ultimately, therefore, the forces of the universe itself. It is both an objective force and a shaping agent in the uniqueness of individual experience. Runecasters regard the process of reading runes as contacting the *wyrd,* thus opening the possibility of grasping the underlying threads of past and present and of glimpsing the seeds of the future, if one learns to "read staves rightly." Casting runes not only gives an indication of possible future fate paths; it tells the runecaster the tale of his or her own life and fate in the language of the signs, through the field of their meanings and associations, and thus ultimately retells our story to us through the themes of Norse mythology and thought. Such is the underlying philosophy of runic divination, the use of the Runes as an oracle.

Though Runes tend to hold a special place among initiates to the Northern Mysteries, the unique fragments of ancient pagan heritage embodied in its literature make the Norse tradition significant to all contemporary Pagans and, potentially, seekers of wisdom of whatever creed or label. Mímir's Well, from which Odin draws up the signs, symbolizes, after all, the infinite reaches of the unconscious and thus the fathomless depths of the self. The myths and legends, magic and lore, counsel and advice that runes evoke may connect us to the ancient past, but they also offer ways of living more fully in the now. In order for us to use the Runes as a divination system to complement personal intuition, it must be tailored to the needs of present generations. Indeed, it is in the very act of using them that we forge a continuity between past and present, the roots of tradition and the wellspring of the self.

It is to the remnants of that tradition—as preserved in echoes from ancient languages; inscriptions on sticks, metal, and stones; the wealth of ancient Norse literature; and the Rune poems—that we now turn.

DIVINE MYSTERIES

The very word *rune* conjures up magical associations in the word hoard of Old English and Germanic languages. The modern English word *rune* is derived from the Old English *run,* which has its equivalents in Germanic and Celtic and adopted into Latin.

The common Germanic root word *run* embodies the idea of mystery and secrecy: Gothic *runa* signifies "divine mysteries," and a related word, *garuni,* translates as "consultation" or "counsel." These terms both came into Old High German as *rūna* and *giruni,* with similar meanings. The Old Norse plural *rúnar* suggests "secret lore," or "mysteries," while Old English *runian,* Old Saxon *runon,* and Old High German *rūnen* mean "to whisper." Closely related are Old Irish *run* ("secret"), Middle Welsh *rhin* ("magic charm"), and Finnish *runo* ("song," perhaps "incantation").[3] Old English carries all these magical senses into our modern English word *rune.* Taken together, they suggest "spiritual mysteries" of a secret or whispered kind that embody the counsel of esoteric knowledge through secret scripts, symbols, or messages.

Also significant is the modern English *runestave,* which comes from the Old English *runstaef.* The German root *stabaz* means "stave" or "stick," and sticks carved with runes have been recovered from various parts of Europe. Some are everyday inscriptions, others more obscure. A few examples are almost certain to be magical formulas, while many remain unresolved. Carving runes upon wood is apparently the oldest method of inscribing them, and the difficulty of cutting a figure into grainy wood explains why the letters are so angular. The term *runstaef* originally referred to the pieces of wood on which runes were carved but later came to refer to the letters themselves. Such staves were generally colored with blood or ocher, known in Old Norse as *hlaut-teiner* (lot twig or blood twig) and *hlaut-vidhar* (lot wood).[4]

An account by the Roman historian Tacitus reveals that similar staves were used in the act of lot casting, a type of divination ritual practiced by the German tribes of around the first century of the Common Era.

> To divination and lot-casting they pay the greatest attention. Their method of casting lots is very simple. They lop a branch from a fruit bearing tree and cut it into slices, which they mark with distinguishing signs (Latin: *notae*) and scatter at random without order on a white cloth. Then the priest of the community . . . invokes the gods and, with eyes lifted to the sky, picks up three slices of wood, one at a time, and interprets them according to the signs previously marked upon them.[5]

We cannot be certain that this famous passage refers to the runic script, for Tacitus merely uses the Latin word *notae,* meaning signs. Writing around 98 C.E., he lived almost two centuries before the period of documented runic inscriptions, though the discovery of the Meldorf brooch (circa 50 C.E.), whose lettering may be runic, calls the earliest dates into question.

Another possibility is that Tacitus's "signs" were protorunes or even prerunic pictographs and that the same or similar ancient practices using runes were continued in the later period, placing them last in a long line of development. The rune scholar Ralph Elliot, who has provided a detailed survey of cultic and divinatory aspects of runelore, has this to say: "There is good reason why the word 'rune' should be so heavily charged with overtones: runes were never a purely utilitarian script; right from their adoption into Germanic usage they served for casting lots, divination, and other rites."[6]

In his hallmark work *Runes* (1959), Elliot goes on to suggest that the Futhark alphabet was created for the purposes of "lot-casting" by somebody already familiar with the use of prerunic pictographic symbols in divination. The idea has recently become unfashionable among mainstream rune scholars, and Elliot did modify the force of his argument in the 1989 edition of the same work. But we have strong evidence to suggest that Runes (probably Younger Futhark but perhaps the full complement of the Elder Futhark alphabet) had certainly come to be used as a divinatory system by the end of the first millennium, for a ninth-century account of contemporary Norse practices by a bishop named Hrabanus Maurus—which we will encounter below in the context of the Rune poems—states that the Norse used the runes to "signify their songs, incantations and divinations."

There are, as well, compound words in Old German and Old Norse dialects that, found together with the term *rune* or *stave,* are consistent with the signs for good or evil fortune that are a feature of divination systems worldwide. Good auguries (luck signs) include *líkn-stafir* (health staves), *gaman-rúnar* (joy runes), *audh-stafir* (health staves), and *sig-rúnar* (victory runes); *myrkir-stafir* (dark staves), *böl-stafir* (evil staves), *flaerdh-stafir* (deception staves), and Old English *beadu-run* (conflict rune) warn darkly of an inauspicious fortune.[7]

Old German, Norse, Icelandic, and English rune names are, moreover, preserved in lists that hint at the signification of the individual signs, and their meanings will occupy us in due course. However, it is the associated literary sources—especially the Rune poems—that provide the most concrete clues to their meanings. It is likely, as we will see, that these materials are fragmentary remains of a once vibrant tradition in which runes formed a system of mythological references with oracular meanings. First, however, let us look more closely at the uses of the ancient "rune rows" within which various types of runes took their individual places.

RUNES AND
RUNE GUILDS

he origin of the Runes is something of a mystery in itself. In the strict historical sense, runes are not a single alphabet but a collection of related scripts. The oldest is the Elder Futhark, a twenty-four-stave script widely believed to have arisen in the northern Italian alpine region, where the Germanic tribes of the day met with Roman influences, somewhere between 50 and 200 C.E. Each stave has a phonetic value similar to other Greco-Roman scripts, and the order of the Elder Futhark is probably based on its Italian model. The name Futhark is formed from the phonemes of the alphabet's first six runes: *fehu, urox, thurisaz, ansuz, raido,* and *kennaz* producing *f, u, th, a, r,* and *k.*

The Elder Futhark falls into three sets of eight known as *aettir.* Some of these names may reflect an "iconic" or visual interpretation of the letters: thus *urox* could have been named after the similarity between the stave shape and the horns of an ox. The following list includes the runes of the Elder Futhark, along with their phonetic (sound) values, original Germanic titles, and English meanings. *Note:* In part 2 of this book, "Runestaves," I present the Elder Futhark staves under their modern divinatory titles. On the right-hand side of the page, the reader will also find their original Germanic names along with a literal English translation. Please be aware, however, that many of these elements have variant forms (in terms of the stave shapes, original names, how they are translated and, especially, modern divinatory titles. The asterisks (*) indicate Germanic names whose meanings are lost or disputed.

The Elder Futhark and Its Associated Values

RUNE	SOUND	NAME	MEANING
ᚠ	f (as in *fee*)	*fehu*	cattle, wealth
ᚢ	u (as in *rune*)	*urox*	aurochs (wild ox)
ᚦ	th (unvoiced, as in *thorn*)	*thurisaz*	giant, ogre, demon
ᚨ	a (as in *art*)	*ansuz*	a god, Odin
ᚱ	r (as in *riding*)	*raido*	riding
ᚲ	k (as in *candle*)	*kenaz*	pine torch
ᚷ	g (as in *gift*)	*gebo*	gift
ᚹ	w (as in *win*)	*wunjo*	(clan) joy
ᚺ	h (as in *hail*)	*hagalaz*	hail
ᚾ	n (as in *need*)	*naudiz*	need
ᛁ	e (as in *sleet*)	*isa*	ice
ᛃ	y (as in *year*)	*jera*	year
ᛇ	i, e, or y (as in *tip, tree,* or *yew*)	*eihwaz*	yew tree
ᛈ	p (as in *play*)	*pertho*	*game piece
ᛉ	z (as in *zoo*)	*algiz*	*elk sedge
ᛋ	s (as in *sun*)	*sowulo*	sun
ᛏ	t (as in *Tuesday*)	*Tiwaz*	the god Tiwaz
ᛒ	b (as in *birch*)	*berkana*	birch tree
ᛖ	e (as in *equity*)	*ehwaz*	horse
ᛗ	m (as in *man*)	*mannaz*	man, humankind
ᛚ	l (as in *lake*)	*laguz*	water
ᛜ	ng (as in *sing*)	*Inguz*	the god Ing
ᛞ	d (as in *dawn*)	*dagaz*	daybreak
ᛟ	o (as in *home*)	*othila*	ancestral hall

A cursory glance at this list reveals that the Runes fall into several categories: mythological gods or other beings (Odin, Tiwaz, a "giant"), natural forces or objects (hail, ice, the yew, the birch, water, day, the sun, sedge), animals (the cow, the ox, horses, and perhaps the elk), human constructions (the torch, a hall, a game piece), and actions or concepts (riding, need, year, humanity). It seems unlikely that these runic letters arose in a vacuum: prehistoric sites from around northern Europe and objects found in them preserve traces of a much more ancient pictographic system of signs, similar to the primitive Swedish *hallristningar* designs found on standing stones throughout the Scandinavian peninsula. Ralph Elliot elaborates on his theory that the original, magical character of these pictographs was incorporated into the later Elder Futhark:

> This process may well have been facilitated by familiarity with earlier pre-runic symbols such as have been found carved into the rocks and stones of Teutonic lands. . . . Individual symbols of such 'embryo-writing'. . . have formal affinities with certain runes; others are reflected in the names given to some of the runes, for instance, man, horse, sun, type of tree. Possibly, pictures or symbols carved alongside some early runic inscriptions . . . represent a reinforcement of the runic legend, the two systems complementing each other.[8]

This "embryo-writing" of the Northern lands had several signs in its repertoire that resemble Runes, such as the sun-wheel pictograph known as the swastika, which is composed of two interlocking *sowulo* runes. The *sowulo* rune represents the sun. Can this be coincidence? Its seems unlikely, and so the possibility exists that the Elder Futhark Rune meanings may have roots very deep in prehistory. The Elder Futhark script is also the version that almost all contemporary runecasters use for divinatory purposes, though a few variants are also employed.

By far the majority of ancient runic inscriptions are to be found in

Scandinavia, where the script was adopted through the process of tribal migrations from more southern lands. There a sixteen-stave system known as the Younger Futhark developed around the year 800 C.E., replacing the Elder Futhark and flourishing until as late as the seventeenth century in Iceland. The Elder Futhark, which found its way into the British Isles and Frisia by way of Viking invaders around the beginning of the eighth century, actually expanded into Old English (Anglo-Saxon) and Frisian rune script variants of twenty-nine, thirty-one, and thirty-three letters. Typical objects with runes inscribed on them include swords, scabbards, brooches, neck rings and other pieces of jewelry, pottery, gold horns, funereal objects from grave hoards, and stones. Today this tradition continues, with a resurgence in talismanic objects, especially jewelry, carved with potent runes.

The True Erulians

Runes have left a perplexing legacy. They were never fully embraced as a literary script—the "savage tribes of the North" were largely "illiterate"—and were generally carved to convey short messages, as markers (for example, on tombstones), and for magical purposes. While a number of inscriptions on jewelry have been interpreted without any doubt as magical incantations, designed to consecrate objects as amulets or talismans, the presence of inscriptions on graves and associated relics also suggests that runes had a rather somber role in cults of the dead. Stephen Flowers, in his exhaustive study *Runes and Magic: Magical Formulaic Elements in the Older Runic Tradition*, argues that there must have been some sort of network of rune guilds or "cultic leagues" responsible for maintaining the art of rune carving and lore. He concludes that "'apprentices' were taught this system by 'masters' in some sort of traditional way, i.e. orally. This transmission of lore from teacher to pupil seems to be the social phenomenon at the root of the runic tradition."[9]

We know that there were "rune masters" who were carvers of runes and can imagine something in the order of rune guilds overlapping with initiatory cults linked to Odin. These cultic networks facil-

*Fig. 1.3. A runestone from the south of
Sweden (author's collection)*

itated the rapid, cohesive changes that occurred at various crossroads
in the script's history, as well as preserving the Elder lore—that is, the
original runic tradition. Some rune masters may have been involved
purely in carving secular inscriptions, but it would seem that the true
"Erulian"—the name for a rune-using tribe, which came to mean simply "rune master"—was a shamanic magician (male or female) versed
in runecraft. He or she was the keeper of the lore and the master of
rune magic.

As Flowers's research shows, runic practice was intimately connected with magic in the Elder age, and in the pages ahead I will argue
that rune wisdom formed a codex of mystical learning, a type of syl-
labus and book of spells carried by memory. Magic and divination
were the two main active techniques of utilizing this knowledge. In
this book we are concerned mostly with divination, though spellcraft
is also touched upon on more than one occasion.

Although the inscriptions on old stones, weapons, and votive and other objects are fascinating in themselves, they too are not generally helpful in the interpretation of the meanings of the Elder Futhark Runes as used in divination. Consequently, though one or two runes appear individually in ancient spells, they form a very small part of the wider picture.

Again, by far the most fertile historical source for uncovering the magical attributes of runes is to be found in the literary field, the popularity of which is presently undergoing a great revival. There are two bodies of texts that are crucially significant here. First, there are the Rune poems: cryptic verses preserved in medieval manuscripts that hint at the signification of individual runic signs. Second, we have the ancient Norse "lays," mythological and heroic. These magnificent writings provide a sense of the internal cosmology, the world paradigm in which the Norse lived, and contain the richest surviving traces of Northern pagan beliefs and cultic practices. In them we can hear echoes of the long-vanished *skald,* or tribal storyteller. The old poems and tales of the nine worlds, of gods and giants, of elves and dragons, of witches and heroes, also vividly evoke the magical pagan world of the Runes. These two sets of materials go hand in hand, for the clues given in the Rune poems provide threads that help us to navigate our way through the vast web of Norse mythology. In what follows we will enter the domain of the Rune poems and then go on to journey deep into the compelling world of Norse saga.

THE RUNE POEMS

This book presents the medieval verses connected to the Runes as oracular poems that teach and instruct with a type of lesson or message. This form of poetry has been well established in many cultures around the world and throughout history. The oldest layers of China's great divination book, the I Ching, are archaic "divinatory poems" associated with each hexagram. The Yoruba tribal culture of West Africa has an oracular system that may indicate how such verses evolved. Their Ise Ifa oracle consists of a vast body of traditional stories, in poetic form, that the diviner memorizes. The person who consults the oracle tosses cowry shells into a type of ritual bowl and from the "random" result activates a specific tale in the oracular tradition. This the diviner then recites to the listener for its message of personal significance. Only in the last several years has the Ise Ifa actually been published as a written document. Prior to this, it was inscribed only in the diviner's memory. Could things have been very similar with the Runes?

The Oxford scholar Marijane Osborn and her coauthor Stella Longland were the first modern authors to suggest a similar role for the Old English Rune poem, in their *Rune Games,* a book that is something of a forgotten classic. They write:

> The art of divination has many forms, but because we consider "The Rune Poem" to be a series of oracular utterances it is divination by oracles that concerns us here. . . .
>
> In a creative way oracles, by their use of analogy and symbol,

paradox and ambiguity, stimulate the individual's imagination in new directions so that he can, if he is able, perceive his relationship with the outside world in a different way and so change his future. . . . The contribution the oracle makes is to provide an enigmatic utterance which can trigger unused creative potentials. . . .

The possibility of change through self-analysis is the real "magical" quality of fortune-telling systems, which could more aptly be called "fortune-making" systems.[10]

The value of such an approach is that it provides us with interpretive material that is historically verifiable and yet whose symbols are open to interpretation and intuitive work on many levels. Moreover, the evidence presented in the remainder of this part of the book, "Runelore," supports Osborn and Longland's claim that the Rune poems have a divinatory and oracular kernel.

There are three Rune poems in all: the Old English Rune poem, the Norwegian Rune poem, and the Icelandic Rune poem. Exact dating for these is elusive: the Old English Rune poem, also known as the Anglo-Saxon Rune poem, is thought to have been composed sometime in the eighth, ninth, or tenth century, probably late in the ninth. The Norwegian Rune poem was probably set down no later than the thirteenth century, and the earliest manuscript for the Icelandic Rune poem dates to the fifteenth century. The authorship and probable monastic "scriptoria"—manuscript production centers—are unknown for all three poems. However, their original sources(s) seem likely to have been far older than the poems themselves. We must bear in mind that the Iceland of the fifteenth century still retained deep pagan undercurrents; the use of runes there was widespread enough for the Church to ban and condemn it as "witchcraft" as late as 1639.

Basically, the Rune poems give a verse for each rune, naming each stave and giving some indication of its mysterious signification. The Old English Rune poem provides stanzas for the twenty-nine-stave Anglo-Saxon Futhark that developed in England after the Viking invasions, while the other two poems are composed around the sixteen staves of the Younger Futhark alphabet. Thus, they do not elaborate the meanings of all twenty-four of the original Elder Futhark Runes. There is no doubt, however, that these poems share a similar function, which was first to act as mnemonics (memory aids) for the memorization of the arcane Rune names. But is there a deeper significance to the poems than that which some scholars have perceived—were they originally devices for memorizing more than a mere miscellany of terms?

Indeed, there is startling evidence that the Rune poems are remnants of a far more elaborate system of mnemonics used for the memorizing of ancient myth, legends, and esoteric material. In his *De inventione linguarum* (The Invention of Writing), the ninth-century scribe and archbishop of Fulds, Hrabanus Maurus, discusses five alphabets: Hebrew, Latin, Greek, an alchemical script, and a runic script. Of these runes, which were used among the "Marcomanni," or "Northmanni," a term that denotes certain tribes north of the Danube (Norsemen), he writes: "These forms of letters [runes] are said to have been invented among the people of the Northmanni [Norse]; it is said that they still use them to commit their songs and incantations to memory. They gave the name *runstabas* to these letters, I believe, because by writing them they used to bring to light secret things."[11]

What is divination if not the bringing to light of "secret things"? Moreover, a second version of the manuscript reads: *"with these [letters] they signify their songs, incantations and divinations, [for] they are still given to pagan practices"* (italics mine).[12] Here we are at the heart of the matter: Runes, we are being told, signify and embody an inventory of pagan Norse myth, spellcraft, and divinatory lore and were memorized as verse. Understood in this light, the Rune poems would appear to be late but vital survivals echoing this venerable tradition, their original function being to aid in the preservation of sacred lore connected with the runestaves.

INTERPRETING THE RUNE POEMS

At first the Rune poems appear to be a set of obscure old verses, but set against the backdrop of the Norse themes we will explore, they are quickly revealed to be an immense store of practical and esoteric wisdom. The Old English Rune poem, though the oldest of the three, is also more Christianized in its treatment than the other two, owing to the early success of Christian incursions into the British Isles. As will be seen, it consists of a series of three- and four-line verses—one verse per rune. Let us use the example of the verse corresponding to the *ansuz* rune:

> *The mouth is the source of the word,*
> *bringing wisdom and counsel to the wise,*
> *hope, inspiration, and a blessing to all.*

This style is technically described as "gnomic wisdom verse" and has parallels across Old English poetry. It employs a number of kennings (puns, riddles) that come from the traditional stock of poetic phrases used to describe objects, forces, and other "natural" (often supernatural) phenomena. In this case, the poem apparently alludes to, yet disguises, the god Odin, who traditionally ruled over the sacred word, if we read it in conjunction with the other Rune poems.

Compare this with the Norwegian Rune poem, which offers two-line stanzas for each rune that are "contrastive," or seemingly unrelated. To use the example of *ansuz* again:

> *Rivermouth opens most journeys;*
> *but the sword belongs in its sheath.*

The term *rivermouth* may be a kenning for Odin's command of oral lore, a subtle masking of the rune's original signification. His esoteric function (the one from whom the word flows, like water from a river's mouth) is contrasted with the god's role as patron of battle, symbolized by the sword, for Odin is, of course, also the lord of

Valhalla and often given to warmongering. This riddling literary technique corresponds to a skaldic model (the *skalds* were the official poets of the Norse world) known as *drottkvaet,* which is designed to "jolt its audience into an awareness" of whatever is being referred to.[13]

Finally, the Icelandic Rune poem is the most recent, yet, in terms of pagan material, by far the richest of the three poems. It gives three lines for each rune, as we see in the following verse on the *ansuz* rune:

> *Odin is the ancient creator,*
> *and Ásgard's king*
> *and lord of Valhalla.*

The first line provides the rune name followed by a crystallized definition, while the next two lines are kennings that offer a wider field of traditional associations to help fix the meaning of the rune. In this case the poem leaves us in no doubt as to the rune's true nature: the High One himself.

The Rune poems are indeed riddling and cryptic: they are extremely compact statements that invite the listener to muse over their significations. They do, however, clearly help identify each runic sign with its corresponding god, object, or force of nature. We can compare them tangentially to the Zen *koan,* the riddling "poem" that is designed to induce *satori* (enlightenment), and, once again, to the divinatory verses of the I Ching, ancient China's grand oracle of changes. Divinatory verses or oracular poems always contain images upon which the questioner meditates until their meanings and personal applications are revealed. With a little practice, we can easily revive this profound and enlightening art.

Let us now turn to look more closely in this light at the first twenty-four verses of the most complete of the poems, the Old English Rune poem. (The texts to the Norwegian and Icelandic Rune poems can be found as verses attached to the runes they match in part 2 of this book, "Runestaves.") *Note:* Where I have replaced the few direct Christian glosses with pagan ones, I have enclosed them in square brackets.

OLD ENGLISH RUNE POEM

Wealth provides comfort,
but you must share it who hope to cast lots
for judgment before [the gods].

The wild ox has great high horns
with which it gores; a fierce fighter
who boldly stamps the moors.

Thorn is wickedly sharp and causes pain
to those who grasp it, hurt
to you who rest among them.

The mouth is the source of the word,
bringing wisdom and counsel to the wise,
hope, inspiration, and a blessing to all.

Riding is easy for heroes
inside a hall; it's much harder astride a strong horse
pounding the great mile paths.

The torch we know by its flame,
which brings illumination and light
wherever noble souls congregate.

A gift returns to adorn the giver
with greatness and honor; it helps
and heartens those who have nothing.

Joy comes to you who know no sorrow,
blessed with gain and plenty,
content in a strong community.

Hail, whitest of grains, whirls down from heaven,
is tossed by the wind, and turns to water.

Need constricts the heart but can bring
help and healing, if heeded in time.

Ice is cold and slippery;
jewel-like and glistening,
fair to behold, the frozen field.

Harvest time brings joy
when the [goddess] Earth
gifts us her bright fruits.

Yew has rough bark without
but holds the flame within;
deeply rooted, it graces the land.

Gaming means play and laughter
among the high-spirited who sit
merrily together in the mead hall.

Elk sedge grows in the fen,
waxing in the water, grimly wounding;
it burns the blood of those
who would lay hands upon it.

The sun guides seafarers
who ferry across the fishes' bath
until the seahorse brings them to land.

Tiw is a sign that spells
confidence to the noble; unfailing,
it holds true through the night clouds.

The birch though fruitless
sends out countless shoots;
leafy branches, high crowned,
reach to the sky.

The horse brings joy;
proud on its hooves,
by heroes praised, it is
a solace to the restless.

We are each other's mirth
yet must one day take leave,
for [the gods] will allot
our frail bodies to the Earth.

Water to land folk seems never-ending
when they set sail on a heaving ship;
the huge waves overwhelm them
and the seahorse won't heed the bridle.

Ing, first seen by the east Danes,
later rode his wagon away
eastward over the waves;
thus was the great [god] named.

Day is [the gods'] messenger;
the light of [the gods] grants ecstasy,
good hope, and a boon to all.

Home is loved by all
who prosper there in peace
and enjoy a frequent harvest.

It is hard to escape the impression that there is more to the poem than immediately meets the eye, and the existence of the three Rune poems has led to speculation that they might be the remnants of either a single common and preexisting source or may echo widespread ancient oral traditions of memorization of runic correspondences. This hypothetical preexisting poem is entitled the *Ur Rune Poem*, but there may, of course, have been differing versions of a basic set of ur-meanings that changed and evolved over time and place. Whether the Rune poems are branches that have sprung from one tree or simply separate independent survivors of a once diverse field of runic poetry relating rune names and meanings is thus an open question.

Many academics view the Rune poems in a purely naturalistic light, as nothing more than amplifications on a list of names, passively reflecting the common cultural vocabulary of the times. It pays, however, to remember that pagan philosophy never separated the natural world from the supernatural: Plants, animals, and "natural phenomena" were an integral part of the sacred. Signs representing such entities, beings, and forces could not help but be supernaturally charged with meaning and power and were underpinned by a wealth of mythological correspondences. As Thomas DuBois writes in *Nordic Religions of the Viking Age:*

> Nordic people in the Viking Age had a vast array of equals—human, near-human, and nonhuman, mobile and immobile, visible and invisible—with which they shared and competed on a daily basis. These included other people (alive or dead), elements of the landscape and nature, flora and fauna, and unseen spirits, all of which . . . required or expected communication and negotiation from the human community.[14]

Many of the runic signs representing pagan gods, animals, trees, and a variety of other entities, forces, or objects clearly fall into this category of magical luminosity.

Of course, in many cases use of the Runes for divination in early times probably encompassed very pragmatic ends, such as predicting the weather and advising when to set sail, go to war, plant crops, marry, or conduct other rites. But the literal meanings can carry more symbolic, metaphorical correspondences. The *jera* rune, ◇, for instance, literally means "year" or "harvest"—in the agricultural sense—but its wider meaning could easily be read in more philosophical terms to refer to a cycle of events, annual or otherwise, and our reaping what we have sown, for better or worse. *Hagalaz*, ᚻ, refers to the primal force of hail, yet can be related more generally to a delay or disruption caused by circumstances beyond our control. *Tiwaz*, ↑, symbolizes the god Týr, who, as one of the bravest of the Aesir gods, represents justice, honor, and the correct application of the warrior energy. Thus, through the Rune names and poems, we are led directly into the wider domain of Norse cosmology.

In divinatory terms, each rune is multifaceted and can refer to a number of different states or conditions of being. The outward, visible aspect of the symbol has many hidden facets of meaning contained within its core. If it were not so, the twenty-four runestaves could never serve the purpose of embodying and describing so many varying situations in the range of human experience. And these symbolic aspects of the staves are also the vehicle within which is contained their inner mystery and profound wisdom. For awareness of the archetypal planes of reality elevates us above the chain of causality and into the realms of higher consciousness. Runes are therefore both a wonderfully versatile divinatory system and an instrument of spiritual enlightenment. Let us now turn to the celebrated mythology in which they figure so prominently and whose themes they evoke.

RUNES AND SAGAS

The portrait of the Vikings that people carry today is typically composed of fierce warriors and ruthless marauders, the scourge of Dark Age Europe. This is partly true, yet the majority of Norse generally lived relatively quiet, settled lives. There were three main social classes. At the bottom were the serfs, who were manual laborers and virtually slaves, often lumped together with the slightly better-off peasant class. They venerated fertility gods and goddesses or local deities, and theirs was the "popular religion." The "middle classes" consisted of smallholders and freemen whose patron god was Thór, god of thunder and war. These people's lives, though modest, at least boasted certain rights and freedoms. At the top of this tripartite social structure were the earls and warriors, an aristocratic class whose patron was Odin. It was they who organized the seasonal expeditions of loot, plunder, and settlement. The backdrop to this somewhat raw life, close to animals, the seasons, and the elements, is the vast Northern mythological canvas that the Icelandic and Norwegian poets spun with such skill.

Icelandic sources are the chief key to what the Runes meant to the peoples who used them. Yet the very presence of written texts (which indicates the presence of monasteries) informs us that the rich, pre-Christian oral culture was under siege by the time the myths and legends were being put to parchment. This raises the complex and currently insoluble question of just how much of the recorded data reflects genuinely ancient material.

It must be acknowledged that mainstream scholars have become increasingly pessimistic about the possibility of proving the survival of genuinely archaic, pagan content in the early literary sources, preferring instead to scrutinize their immediate (courtly and Christian) social settings. This has certainly produced a sharper sense of historical context and challenged some of the more simpleminded assumptions to which some esoteric commentators have been drawn. However, this approach can be dangerously one-sided. Competent medievalists have been able to show how the scholars of the early Icelandic and Norwegian monasteries drew on Greek and Roman mythological models and the influence of the Christian, Continental literature of the times. Yet they are seldom able (and increasingly unwilling) to place the recorded myths in the broader domain of Indo-European mythologies, with which Norse myth has profound and doubtless ancient links. Of the role in the Norse creation account of a primordial Cow Goddess and androgynous Frost Giant, by contrast, Kevin Crossley-Holland writes:

> These parallels are such that it is certain that these two elements . . .
> were oriental in origin. What is not so certain is when they were
> incorporated with the Norse tradition. They may have resulted from
> contact along trade routes in the first few centuries after the birth of
> Christ. But a more exciting theory dates the contact to between one
> and two thousand years before Christ. Teutonic tribesmen moving
> west into Europe from the Russian steppes in the Age of Migrations,
> and then north into Scandinavia, may have brought with them the
> fundamentals of the Norse creation myth (just as other Indo-
> Europeans carried the same elements east into India, China, and
> Japan and south to Iran and the Near East).[15]

Some mainstream scholars have, in recent times, scoffed at such apparently ancient underpinnings, suggesting that in the absence of conclusive evidence of contact and continuity, interesting parallels remain just that. But we should, at the same time, be equally skeptical of the tendency to try to locate these literary materials in a pre-dominantly Christian milieu. In the ninth and tenth centuries, to which the earliest literary compositions are dated, the Northern world was still deeply pagan, with conversion proceeding piecemeal and often more in name than in substance. And it is hardly to be believed that the vast accumulated structure of belief that had developed there over the ages simply fell over like a house of twigs in the face of a new dogma emanating from courtly circles and a few scattered monasteries, however influential they may have been.

The Norse pagan world was, after all, one in which the skald was a central figure: a weaver and preserver of sacred lore. The generous respect accorded to poets reflects the archaic notion of the poet as a type of traveler in the otherworlds who meets and communicates with otherworldly beings, then returns with freshly won insights to the human community. Charles W. Dunn writes: "The role of the pre-Christian Norse poet was that of a shaman, a tribal seer. . . . He was expected, through his control of the magical process of poetry, to discover and reveal wisdom."[16] The creation of poetry was a vital part of the process of maintaining links with the realms of the sacred, with gods and other mythological beings, and preserving the cosmography of the nine worlds and the networks of relationships among them. The background against which this poetry must be understood, maintains Ursula Dronke, one of the foremost scholars of Norse myth, literature, and religion, is one "of cult, involving close associations with mythological themes, meticulous preservation of tradition, and a heightened, obscured, periphrastic [long-winded] language. . . . It is ancient and rooted in ancient, pagan religious practice."[17] And however problematic the scholarly issues they raise, nowhere is this sense of ancient underpinnings more pervasive than in the Icelandic *Eddas.*

THE EDDAS

There are two main branches of written texts from the Norse world that concern us here. First and foremost is Snorri Sturluson's *Prose*

Edda. Set down in 1220 by this extraordinary Icelandic statesman, historian, and mythographer, the work purported to summarize the pre-Christian Norse lore of its author's native land. How seriously should we take the self-confessed Christian Snorri's claim? It is true that he drew on Greco-Roman models and his own creative powers in his depiction of a "pantheon" of Norse gods. Coming two centuries after the arrival of Christianity, Snorri's status as an eyewitness to archaic pagan lore is obviously questionable. Nonetheless, the work remains the primary written record of Norse mythology, including several scattered references to the uses and functions of runes. Snorri was clearly concerned to ensure that upcoming generations did not lose the poetic vocabulary of their forebears, and although he was working within a Christian context, the *Prose Edda* seems designed to preserve the exploits of the elder gods and goddesses, whose worship

Fig. 1.4. Thór wrestling with the World Serpent, from a late-medieval, illuminated version of the Prose Edda

was rapidly fading. The degree to which he held sympathy with this older zeitgeist is open to interpretation, but he seems to have felt that the world would have been a poorer place without some record of past beliefs. Whatever its limitations, without Snorri's effort our understanding of Norse myth today would be infinitely diminished.

In 1643 Bishop Brynjólfur Sveinsson acquired a vellum manuscript of forty-five leaves, which he wrongly took to be a compilation by an Icelandic magician named Saemundr-the-Wise (1056–1133). Actually composed around 1270, it is, together with a work by Haukr Erlendsson of the same period named *Hauksbók*, the chief source of the second major branch of Icelandic materials: the so-called *Poetic Edda*. Also known, rather confusingly, as the *Elder Edda*, it is a collection of poems couched in verses of various meters. Many of its pieces also occur in the *Prose Edda*, which frequently bursts into verse, and its compilation may have been a continuation of the project of recording the tales and sagas that Snorri began. Like the *Prose Edda*, the *Poetic Edda* can be roughly divided into "mythological" and "heroic" traditions; the family or "tragic" sagas telling of clan warfare, for instance, are heroic, while the creation stories and tales primarily concerned with the exploits of the gods are labeled mythological. However, in reality there is some overlap, with themes from the great myths appearing in the heroic sagas, in which divine characters often intervene. Heroes may meet high gods on the mile paths they travel!

Alongside the prose tales by Snorri, there are several Eddic poems that figure in part 2 of this book. They include the great tenth- to eleventh-century prophetic poem *Völuspá* (The Song of the Sibyl), the verses attributed to Odin contained in *Hávamál* (Sayings of the High One), and the question-and-answer "dialogues," full of wisdom verse, found in several other Eddic poems. This format was used in the recitation of pagan lore in both the Norse and Celtic worlds, so it probably reflects an ancient stratum of material. The chief pieces of this kind include the tenth-century *Vafþrúðnismál* (The Lay of Vathrúdnir), where Odin bandies charged words with a giant, and *Alvíssmál* (The Lay of Alvíss), where Thór gets the better end of a riddling contest with a dwarf. Although there are elements of outside influence (both classical and Christian), the scribes generally seemed concerned with recording with considerable care what they knew, innovating from the new traditions along the preestablished lines of their own Norse heritage. Some magical repositories of pagan matter that explicitly involve the Runes include *Grímnismál* (The Lay of Grímnir) and *Sigdrífomál* (The Lay of Sigdrífa), encountered below. You may wish to explore these sources for yourself, in one of the translations of the Eddas listed in the bibliography.

In *Nordic Runes* we work mainly with the mythological materials from both the *Prose Edda* and the *Poetic Edda,* especially stories concerning the high gods and goddesses. Thus each rune becomes a powerful divinatory token, evoking a tale or theme from the mythological tradition. This, as I have argued, was one of the original functions of Runes: to signify the "songs, incantations, and divinations" of a people who by the turn of the first millennium were "still given to pagan practices," in the words of Hrabanus Maurus. While the recording of these sources dates to the Christian era, the presence of compositions from as early as the ninth century suggest that they may indeed have be tapping into what Charles W. Dunn describes as a "massive, old rooted poetic tradition"[18] with thousands of years behind it. Much, perhaps even the greater part, is probably lost to us, and thus what remains must be reckoned a treasure of incalculable worth. However piecemeal the process of preservation, to many today the myths, legends, and sagas preserved in these manuscripts are the sacred texts of the Northern Mysteries, and re-membering them is an act both enlightening and devotional.

Let us now look a little more closely at some of the central themes related to the Runes in Norse mythology, such as the World Tree, the three Norns, the faces of the Goddess, Odin's quest, and runes in ancient magic and divination. This will not only inspire a better understanding of their important role within the framework of traditional Norse pagan religion, but also help set the scene for the wisdom lore associated with individual runes in part 2. What is more, these materials are filled with power and beauty of a kind found nowhere else.

THE WORLD TREE

One of the foremost symbols of ancient Norse religion that shines forth from the Eddic literature is that of the World Tree, called Yggdrasil. The World Tree is a recognizable emblem or archetype in world mythology that is widespread across Eurasia. It stands as a center point, or *axis mundi,* of the globe, a life-sustaining force that supports and ties together the very fabric of reality. In Norse myth Yggdrasil is a lofty ash tree that overarches and yet somehow underpins and pervades all the nine worlds. Its trunk marking the center of the worlds, Yggdrasil figures as a friend and protector to humankind. Even today in Iceland the yards of many solitary farmhouses are graced by their own "guardian trees," and many contemporary pagans across the world venerate personal holy trees as embodiments of the life force.

A beautiful description of Yggdrasil is to be found in *Völuspá* (The Song of the Sibyl), a poem in which a *volva,* or prophetess, sings about the beginning and ending of the world. The language of these verses helps us visualize the power and mystery of Yggdrasil:

> *There is an ash tree—   its name Yggdrasil—*
> *a tall tree watered   from a cloudy well.*
> *Dew falls from its boughs   down to the valleys;*
> *ever green it stands   beside the Norns' spring.*[19]

Yggdrasil carries many levels of meaning: It is the source of nature's regenerative power and the fount of nourishment on which all life feeds; the tree is said to groan continually because of this terrible burden. Yggdrasil is also the link between the worlds and is the thread of continuity that ties into coherence the ages of the world. It is a profound ecological symbol for our times.

The World Tree is another of those elements found in Norse myth that have a common Indo-European underpinning, for the Vedas of the Indian world contain similar depictions. Compare the uniquely Norse elements celebrated above with this poem from the Bhagavad Gita, where a great tree is also linked to knowledge of sacred themes.

> *There is a fig tree*
> *In ancient story,*
> *The giant Aswattha,*
> *Rooted in heaven,*
> *Its branches earthward:*
> *Each of its leaves*
> *Is a song of the Vedas,*
> *And he who knows it*
> *Knows all the Vedas.*[20]

In fact, both these holy trees correspond to the archetypal features that the great comparative mythologist Mircea Eliade has found in descriptions of the World Tree worldwide. He writes:

On the one hand it represents the universe in continual regeneration, the inexhaustible spring of cosmic life, the paramount reservoir of the sacred (because it is the 'Centre' for the reception of the celestial sacred, etc.); on the other hand, it symbolizes the sky or heavens. . . . In a number of traditions, the Cosmic Tree, expressing the sacrality of the world, its fertility and its perenniality, is related to the ideas of creation, fecundity and initiation, and finally to the idea of absolute reality and immortality. Thus the World Tree becomes the Tree of Life and Immortality as well. Enriched with numerous mythical doublets and complementary symbols (Woman, the Wellspring, Milk, Animals, Fruits, etc.), the Cosmic Tree always presents itself as the very reservoir of life and the master of destinies.[21]

According to *Vǫluspá*, after Ragnaroc, the final battle where Midgard (Middle Earth, the human realm) is consumed in fire and even Odin dies, the World Tree Yggdrasil "remains visible, like a flaming torch against the sky, after the earth and stars have been destroyed,"[22] an enduring symbol of timelessness and eternity.

THE ΠORΠS AΠD
THE WELL ⊖F URD

Beneath one of the roots of Yggdrasil lies the Well of Urd, where the three Norns dwell. The proximity of these "fate maidens" to the Well of Urd is no accident. This well and the eldest Norn, Urd, share the same name and together the three of them clearly relate to the old European triple-goddess figure.

> *Much wisdom   have the three maidens*
> *who come from the waters   close to that tree;*
> *they established laws,   decided the lives*
> *men were to lead,   marked out their fate.*[23]

Mistresses of destiny, the Norns parallel (and, according to some scholars, may borrow from) the Three Fates in Greek mythology: the maiden, mother, and crone aspects of the "Weaving Sisters" who spin, measure, and cut the threads of life and fate.

The nature of the Norns is revealed by their names: Urd (fate), Verdandi (necessity), and Skuld (being), for the Norns are said to pronounce their fate over the newly born, and in the sagas this fate is said to be fixed. Indeed, one of the Norns is described as a "scorer of fate" in *Völuspá*—literally, "one who incises on slips of wood." Could these slips be runestaves? The Norns can appear as either great allies or hateful hags, depending on your fortunes. In the *Volsunga Saga* (Lay of the Volsungs) from the *Poetic Edda*, we hear that when the hero Helgi was born in the middle of a storm with eagles shrieking outside, the Norns came to fix his fate:

> *The Norns came   to the house that night,*
> *those who would fashion   the prince's fate;*
> *great fame, they said   would mark his future,*
> *he would be called   the best of kings.*
>
> *Then they wound   the threads of fire,*
> *in Bralund's castle   where the hero was born,*

gathered the strands   into a golden rope,
and made it fast   in the moon's high hall.[24]

Others were not so lucky. But while the Norns' decrees were regarded with fatalism, it was considered that understanding their ways could nonetheless bestow knowledge and wisdom on the recipient. In modern-day Rune consultation, it is the Norns to whom questions are addressed, and in the three-stave spread (where the stones or staves are laid out according to what is past, is passing, and is to come) we see a direct reflection of the Norns' prescience over past, present, and future. They are the weavers at the center of the Web of Wyrd.

ODIN—THE HOODED ONE

Odin is the Merlin of Norse literature, a mighty god and magician who is quite clearly echoed in J. R. R. Tolkien's character Gandalf. Odin is often pictured as traveling the highways and byways under various guises but most commonly in a blue cloak, supported by his staff, his felt hat drawn low over his face. The *Eddas* leave us in little doubt that Odin is the highest and wisest of the gods of Ásgard: the All Father and Lord of Valhalla, the Hooded One who is lord of hanged men, the crossroads, wisdom, and the Runes. In the *Loddfáfnismál* (The Lay of Loddfáfnir) we read:

I will sing   from the sage's chair
by the Norns' sacred spring;
I watched and listened, I looked and thought
about the words of the wise
when they talked of runes   and what they reveal
at the High One's hall,   in the High One's hall.[25]

The poet is celebrating Odin's discovery of the Runes, his reference to the "sage's chair / by the Norns' sacred spring" referring to the widespread theme of the ritual office of the poet (or seer) as a keeper of tradition. And, of course, in his quest for wisdom, Odin descended the World Ash to a root of Yggdrasil and, as we have seen, drank from the waters of inspiration at Mímir's Well.

The episode of Odin gaining the Runes is perhaps the greatest epic event in ancient Norse poetry. You can read about this in one of the most famous poems of the *Poetic Edda, Loddfáfnismál,* which is part of *Hávamál* (Sayings of the High One), a celebrated set of verses composed of advice by a poet who speaks as Odin. Here Odin recounts some of his greatest exploits, such as stealing the mead of inspiration from the giantess Gunnlod, his questing and sacrificing an eye for the Runes, and his learning the great *galdr* (spells, incantations). In a lore-laden section of the poem, known as the "Runatal" (Song of the Runes), Odin sings of his sacrifice, his discovery, and how that discovery can aid humankind:

> *I know that I hung   on a high windy tree*
> *for nine long nights;*
> *pierced by a spear—Odin's pledge—*
> *given myself to myself.*
> *No one can tell   about that tree,*
> *from what deep roots it rises.*
>
> *They brought me no bread,   no horn to drink from,*
> *I gazed toward the ground.*
> *Crying aloud,   I caught up runes;*
> *finally I fell.*
>
> *Nine mighty songs   I learned from the son*
> *of Bolthorn, Bestla's father,*
> *and I came to drink of that costly mead*
> *the holy vessel held.*
>
> *Thus I learned   the secret lore,*
> *prospered and waxed in wisdom;*

I won words   from the words I sought,
verses multiplied   where I sought verse.

You will find runes   and read staves rightly,
the strong magic,
the mighty spells
that the sage set down,
that the great gods made,
wisdom of Odin.[26]

Bolthorn the Giant is Odin's grandfather, and the "nine mighty songs" he learned are *galdr,* as we will see. But the chief wisdom won by Odin is that of prophecy, the power to see from the beginning to the end of time. Indeed, like the Greek Tiresias, Odin is the patron of prophecy, and when the *volva* (seeress) of *Völuspá* prophesies, she states that it is "by Odin's will" that she speaks the ancient lore. In this guise Odin is truly a magician, shapeshifter, and chief shaman.

THE SHAMAN'S QUEST

In shamanism, perhaps the first and founding religion of humankind, the theme of the shaman's descent or ascent of the World Tree is a deeply embedded one. In fact, this is one of the primary metaphors used for the acquisition of shamanic knowledge, and it is still active among the Inuit (Eskimo) tribes to this day. Joseph Campbell has this to say:

The vision of the tree is a characteristic feature of the shamanism of Siberia. Like the tree of Woden [Odin], Yggdrasil, it is the world axis, reaching to the zenith. The shaman has been nurtured in this tree, and his drum, fashioned of its wood, bears him back to it in his trance of ecstasy. . . . The magic of his drum carries him away on the wings of its rhythm, the wings of spiritual transport. The drums and the dance simultaneously elevate his spirits and conjure to him his familiars—the beasts and the birds, invisible to others, that have supplied him with the power to assist him in his flight.[27]

Although Odin descends before ascending, and wounds himself with a spear stripped from Yggdrasil rather than taking up a drum fashioned from its wood, the parallels are obvious. The High God representing the powers of higher consciousness descends to the realms of the underworld with its feminine waters to drink of that deep wisdom. He then returns, imbued with the secrets of the well. Odin is, in fact, the archetype of the ecstatic shaman who rides the World Tree. At some point he became connected with the "alphabetic magic" of the Runes, giving a novel twist to an old story, perhaps partly in imitation of myths of alphabet gods among the alphabet-using cultures in the north Italic region from which the Norse borrowed (or rather, adapted) the runic script. Contemporary shamans of the Northern Mysteries seek to follow a similar path to Odin when questing for the secrets of the Runes, by similarly daring to ride between the worlds.

Odin, like the shamans of old, also comes with a host of animal familiars. These include two eagles (sometimes ravens) that perch on his shoulders and whisper knowledge into his ears; his two wolves, Freki and Geri; and the horse Sleipnir, whom he rides into the otherworld. Here he corresponds to a truly ancient figure known as the Master of the Animals or Beasts, a character of hoary antiquity who teaches us about our relationship to the animal and spirit worlds.

FREYA AND THE FACES OF THE GODDESS

The heavily "masculine" character of Norse myth is not as pronounced as it first appears. Although Odin is chief of the Aesir, for example, the power of the Norns and the Valkyries also points to the pivotal role of the Ásynja (goddesses) in Norse religion. Snorri assures us in the *Prose Edda* that the sixteen great goddesses (really twelve if we compress their various titles) were "no less holy and have no less power" than the twelve gods, and we are elsewhere told that the goddess Freya, mistress of *seiðr* (*seithr:* fertility and earth magic), taught her arts to Odin.

Freya is the most prominent of the goddesses. Handed over by the Vanir (fertility gods) to the Aesir (sky gods) to conclude a truce in the distant, mythical past, Freya became queen of Ásgard *and* of Vanaheim. Pictured as a gorgeous Norse Aphrodite in later treatments, such as Wagner's *Der Ring des Nibelungen,* she is really an extremely complex figure. Often depicted in a chariot drawn by two cats, Freya is reminiscent of Egypt's Isis: queen of Heaven and Hell. Sometimes she behaved like a Valkyrie, choosing the battle-slain, and she also ruled over a hall in Ásgard named Fólkvangr, to which she conducted the souls of the dead. She is Odin's match and, not surprisingly, also sometimes his lover. Indeed, the close similarity between her name and that of Odin's rather less glamorous wife, Frigga, suggests that the two may be twin forms of the same goddess.

Freya's chief possession is a golden girdle named Brísingamen. In order to win this treasure, she descended to Svartálfheim (land of the dark elves) and slept with four dwarfs, deeming this trade of flesh for gleaming metal to be an equal exchange. She then ascends, Venus-like, to the upperworlds. This story has parallels with the Greek myth of Persephone, representative of the fruits and flowers of the earth, who must spend half the year in the dismal underworld with Pluto. Clearly, one of Freya's aspects is that of the earth goddess who forms a compact with the gnomish fertility powers of the underworld and embodies the fruitfulness of the land. Her belt, Brísingamen, may symbolize a golden field of wheat or the like, sprouting anew at harvesttime after the dark months when the life force of the land was locked away in the icy grip of the powers of winter.

Equally compelling figures of myth are the ominous yet captivating Valkyries, female warrior women who accompany the Germanic Woden (Odin) in his aspect as god of the dead as he rides the night sky in the ghostly Wild Hunt or "Furious Horde." The Valkyries singled out the battle-slain, who would accompany the dread lord back to the world of the dead. There, those fortunate enough to die in battle had the honor of feasting and sparring with Odin's chosen elite, until Ragnaroc (the Norse apocalypse) in Valhalla, the hall with spears for rafters and shields for thatch. Valkyries are, if you like, practical administrators of the Norns' decrees. Originally fierce and blood-thirsty, they later became romanticized—in *Volundarqviða* (The Lay of Volund), we see the Valkyrie as a beautiful swan maiden. In *Sigdrífomál* (The Lay of Sigdrífa), the Valkyrie Sigdrífa instructs the hero of the tale in the art of rune magic, as we will see—an indication that Valkyries could be skilled in runelore, and establishing for us a mythic prototype of the transmission of runelore, in this case through oral instruction, from woman to man.

Although there are many other important goddess figures in Norse myth, such as Idunna, who guards the apples of immortality, and Frigga, wife of Odin, it is Freya who has captured the most devotion in recorded times. In contemporary Norse Paganism, she tends to function as the Great Goddess, parallel to the Wiccan goddess of witches known variously as Diana, Aradia, Ceridwen, Astarte, Ishtah, and Anu. For in the Northern Mysteries, as in contemporary Paganism in general, there are many faces of the Goddess but only one Goddess.

SPELLCRAFT AND CHARM RUNES

Odin's descent of the World Tree and discovery of the Runes is deeply imbued with shamanistic lore, as we have seen. What, then, is the nature of the knowledge and spellcraft that he gains through their discovery? How, in other words, are the Runes revealed as being magical and potent in the lays and sagas?

We have learned from *Hávamál* how, after acquiring the Runes, Odin is gifted with various magical skills. These are set out as benefits for which we are enjoined to strive. Before reciting them, Odin challenges us:

Do you know how to write? Do you know how to read?
Do you know how to paint? Do you know how to prove?
Do you know how to wish? Do you know how to worship?
Do you know how to summon? Do you know how to sacrifice?[28]

"Write" here refers to the act of magical inscription, and "read" refers to the interpretation of omens. Similarly, the "paint" referred to in the third refrain relates to what we have read earlier in the *Hávamál* about

. . . the sacred runes
given by the gods
that Odin set down
and the sage stained with colour . . . [29]

Runes were traditionally inscribed or "painted" in red, usually ocher or blood. The "prove" of the fourth refrain is the practice of divination, a time-honored technique of proving the nature of a situation, for Runes are connected to the term *rede* or *rad* (counsel, advice), and terms related to the word *rune* itself, as we have seen, mean "to counsel" and "to advise." The "wish" of the fifth refrain, coupled as it is with "worship" and "summon," suggests invocation, the use of magic to achieve specific magical and practical ends. Finally, the "sacrifice" of the final refrain harks back to Odin's own sacrifice to gain the Runes and appears to be prompting the listener to maintain the act of sacrifice to the gods. This passage is a closely and beautifully interwoven ritual formula.

The connection of the Runes with spellcasting is certainly beyond doubt: In the next section of *Hávamál,* Odin goes on to describe the eighteen magical *galdr* and associated abilities he has gained. These include raising the dead! He tells us:

I know a twelfth [spell]:   if up in a tree
I see a corpse hanging high,

the mighty runes   I write and colour
make the man come down
to talk with me.[30]

Other magical skills of which Odin boasts include healing (including helping the sick and careworn, relieving them of their sorrows);
blunting the edge of an enemy's sword; breaking fetters that are used
to bind a man; stopping a speeding spear in midair; redirecting an
enemy's harm runes (written on a tree root) back at the enemy; putting
out a fire; soothing the hatred that waxes among warriors; saving a
ship in a storm by calming the sea; overcoming witches; blessing
friends with good fortune in battle; keeping a friend from fight;
bestowing knowledge of the gods and Aesir; bestowing power, triumph, and understanding; seducing a girl; keeping her; seducing
another's wife.

Elsewhere we learn in greater detail the procedures for activating
runes for magical purposes. In *Sigdrífomál* the hero Sigurd is, as
mentioned, instructed by the Valkyrie Sigdrífa, whom he awakens
from an enchanted sleep, into which she has been thrown by Odin. In
a prose version of the tale, we read: "Sigurd asked her to teach him
wisdom if she had knowledge of all the words. Then she took a horn
full of mead and gave him a drink which would make him remember." She tells him:

First I will bring   beer to the warrior—
might brewed it,   mingled it with fame—
full of spells   and potent songs,
rich in charms   and runes of joy.[31]

The horn, like the well, cauldron, and cup, is a sacred vessel con-
taining the wisdom of the otherworlds. The "beer" it contains reminds
us of the mead of inspiration that Odin tastes, a divine draft linked to
the ecstasies promised by the Greek god Dionysus or the sacred soma
that the gods of India drink. Sigurd (the Norse equivalent of the
Germanic hero Siegfried) is being initiated into the path of the *vitki*, or

runic initiate. His "remembering" involves a transformational rebirth, for Sigurd is remembered as a more empowered and primal being.

Essentially, the use of rune charms taught by Sigdrífa involves inscribing the relevant stave upon an associated object to achieve its effect. Her first example involves "charging" a sword.

> *I shall teach you   runes of triumph*
> *to have on the hilt of your sword—*
> *some on the blade,   some on the guard;*
> *then call twice on Týr.*[32]

As noted earlier, Týr is the old war god of Norse religion, known in his Germanic form as Tiw or Tiwaz, and one of the Elder Futhark runes is named after him (*Tiwaz* is the Germanic stave name, which becomes Týr in Norse and Old English). The charm rune is inscribed upon the blade and hilt of a sword and Týr is invoked to empower the weapon for battle. Here we receive a direct insight into the old magical practice of runic spellcraft through inscription and the recitation of *galdr*.

This account demonstrates an important principle: Runes invoke certain archetypal energies. Among these we find such examples in *Sigdrífomál* as ale runes scratched on a drinking horn and the "need" rune *(naudiz)* upon your fingernail to prevent another man's wife from betraying your trust or your drink from being poisoned; runes written on the palm to help a woman in labor; runes cut on the prow and rudder to save a ship; runes written on the bark of a tree to heal the sick; speech runes to "wind," "weave," and "twist" so that none harms you out of hatred; and mind runes to surpass all men's wits. These archaic examples are only some of the many possible applications of the ongoing art of rune magic. Today many people employ runes in spells and affirmations to great effect. This aspect of runelore is not the main focus of *Nordic Runes*, which is primarily concerned with divination, but my commentaries on the identities of the Runes in part 2 provide some suggestions as to how the Runes may be employed in certain situations for the purposes of magic. For in runic tradition, divination was often used in tandem with magic, with divining as a diagnostic tool and magic as the cure.

The model of a female—if superhuman—figure teaching runic arts reinforces the sense that elements of runelore are derived from the wisdom of the goddess. Women were also particularly strongly associated with divination, a widespread feature across Europe but a direct influence on the Norse through contact with the Sami and Balto-Finnish peoples to the north. In *Eiríks saga rauða* (Erik the Red's Saga), for example, a powerful shamaness named Thórbjorg, working in the *seithr* tradition, arrives at a family homestead and performs a circle-casting of sorts and a divinatory ritual there. Though runes themselves are not mentioned, there are many correspondences with features of runelore that we are profiling. For example, this *finna ein fiolkunnig* (woman skilled in magic) has nine sisters and is described as occupying a "High Seat" similar to that of Odin in *Hávamál*. The description of her garb also leaves a rich impression:

> This is how she was attired: she was wearing a blue cloak with straps which was set with stones right down to the hem; she had glass beads about her neck, and on her head a black lambskin hood lined inside with white catskin. She has a staff in her hand, with a knob on it; it was ornamented with brass and set around with stones just below the knob. Round her middle she wore a belt of touchwood, and on it was a big skin pouch in which she kept those charms of hers which she needed for her magic. On her feet she had calf-skin shoes with long thongs, and on the thong-ends big knobs of lateen. She had on her hands catskin gloves which were white inside and hairy.[33]

It is tempting to imagine, as some runic commentators have, women of this kind traveling the countryside and plying the art of runecasting among their wares, no less patronesses of occult arts than the Valkyrie Sigdrífa with all her runelore.

RUNIC DIVINATION

The profound magic potency of runes and their use as charms is illustrated throughout the Eddic literature, as we have seen. Clear references to divination are more scarce; one has to read between the lines. One of the few direct descriptions of a divination ritual by the gods is found in the *Hymisqviða* (The Lay of Hymir), where the Aesir use lot twigs to locate ale for feasting.

> *The gods were happy—   they'd had a good hunt*
> *and felt like feasting;   they found out,*
> *   by shaking small branches   steeped in blood,*
> *   that Aegir had everything   for brewing ale.*[34]

The poem does not specifically name runes, but small branches "steeped" in blood reminds us of the inscribing of runes in red ocher or blood and Snorri's *hlaut-teiner* (blood twigs). In any case, runes are so often spoken of in the same breath as other matters obviously linked to foreknowledge of the future and prophecy that their role in the mantic (divinatory) arts is unquestionable. The wisdom that Odin sought from Mímir's Well, after all, was foreknowledge as well as magical proficiency.

This theme is reinforced in the great prophetic poem *Vǫluspá*, where the volva, or seeress, describes Odin's coming to her in a way that parallels the classical tradition of the priestesses of the oracle, known as *pythia*, being possessed by divine inspiration of the god Apollo. Here the volva identifies herself and her cultic relationship to Odin:

> *Heidi men call me when their homes I visit,*
> *A far-seeing witch, wise in talismans,*
> *Caster of spells, cunning in magic,*
> *To wicked women welcome always.*
>
> *Arm rings and necklaces, Odin, you gave me*
> *to learn my lore, to learn my magic:*
> *Wider and wider through all the worlds I see.*

Outside I sat by myself when you came,
Terror of the gods, and gazed in my eyes.
What do you ask of me? Why tempt me?
Odin, I know where your eye is concealed,
Hidden away in the well of Mímir;
Mímir each morning his mead drinks
From Valfather's Pledge. Well, would you know more?[35]

The context here, it pays to recall, is that of the volva relating the history (and future) of the world to gods and men, and Odin's dipping in Mímir's Well is central to her prophetic ability. Indeed, the words "outside I sat by myself" are not a description of physical space but a clairvoyant state of being: the Old Norse *"Ein sat hon uti"* has been better translated as "Alone she held seance out in the night," words that "traditionally implied 'to sit out of doors to listen for, contact, spirits,' an occupation of wizards and witches."[36] Here we are deep in the domain of the spirit world.

Runes are an integral part of higher knowledge of history's coils and cycles. We later read in *Völuspá* that after Ragnaroc, the fiery Norse apocalypse, the Aesir gods regroup and meet on a plain named Idavoll to

> consider all   that came to pass
> the ancient runes   offered to Odin.[37]

Here the whole cycle of the world's progress—from creation to destruction—is contained within the wisdom of the Runes that Odin gained at Mímir's Well amid the roots of Yggdrasil. We see runes functioning prophetically and on a grand scale.

Taken together, these threads form a backdrop, a sort of mosaic of myths, beliefs, and practices that have come down to us in a fragmentary form. Any reference to divination ritual with runes seems to consist of the barest hints. However, given the associations of secrecy and "whispering" that are attached to the word *rune*, this may be no coincidence. The *Eddas* clearly establish the Runes as a magical set of letters in Viking thought—glyphs with power to invoke the energies they represent: to bless, to curse, to consecrate. Archetypal symbols are the stuff of divination, which is a sort of turning around of the active workings of magical signs into the passive reading of them in order to understand fate "by the Norns' decree."

Perhaps this area of cultic practice has left few traces because it was shrouded in secrecy from the beginning. As *Hávamál* says:

> *He who would read   the sacred runes*
> *given by the gods,*
> *that Odin set down*
> *and the sage stained with colour*
> *is well advised   to waste no words.*[38]

THE NORTHERN
TRADITION

Our exploration of the field of runelore has revealed that while the sources available are patchy and in some cases open to interpretation, there is no doubt about some core facts. The origins of runes remain somewhat obscure, but there is no question that on one level they embody magical and divinatory meanings—this, along with their role as common or garden-variety letters, may even have been the purpose of their invention. Use of runes for divination is not strictly confirmed until late in the Viking age, but such use is itself grounded in the more ancient magical and shamanic heritage of northern Europe.

In terms of recovering this system, part 1 of this book has shown that we are not totally reliant on conjecture in reconstructing the Rune meanings. While intuition plays a profound role in an actual reading, the Rune names and associated Rune poems point to concrete mythological references within the great body of Norse mythological lore. Indeed, they provide a powerful key to this lore, one that, moreover, takes on a personal bearing through the processes of divination. With *Nordic Runes,* the reader can access the authentic tradition of using the Runes as tokens that invoke the themes and story lines of the old myths and legends. Turning to the commentaries set forth in "Rune-staves," we can restore the purpose of the "runes of good help" and the ancient wisdom they evoke. By applying their meanings to the actual contours of our present-day lives, we ensure that not only the Runes but also these attendant tales take on a powerful, contemporary relevance.

In the form of the Runes, we have perhaps the most precious inheritance of Northern paganism: a set of divinatory tokens with esoteric and practical significations, a veritable spell book of magical operations, a system of spiritual teachings and pointers to higher pathways on a par with kabbalism or the I Ching. The Northern Mysteries branch of contemporary Paganism draws on these great wells of knowledge and learning, keeping alive and innovating a unique magical tradition. Indeed, the Runes provide a bridge for us between our age and the vanished world of pagan Norse culture. They lead the questing initiate down the World Tree to the sacred well of that collective wisdom, a domain where the word is sacred, potent, and ever living. For many people in the modern West today, these old teachings provide an indigenous wisdom that can complement and lead us into rapport with the native traditions of societies that we have too often suppressed and spurned.

In part 3 you will find a section called "Re-membering the Tradition," which explores in somewhat more depth the relationships among the Runes, their contemporary revival, and Paganism today. It is enough to note for the moment that the appeal of the Northern Mysteries is in their primal, elemental power. Here is a system in which at the center of the universe lies not a male, anthropomorphic god but a mighty tree from whose branches worlds hang like ripe fruit. This connects us powerfully and directly to the greenworld, to the regenerative and fecund energies of Earth herself. The primal elements of nature underpin and pervade all of Norse thought. Our world, Midgard (Middle Earth), is a fortuitous point of equilibrium between the clashing forces of fire and ice. The female aspect of this fabric is the Goddess, who takes many forms; the male face is the God, likewise multifarious. Together they contain many aspects that have been ignored or suppressed in our culture through both monotheism and the godless ideology of material science. Odin and Freya embody many themes from which we can learn profound truths: those of the mystic quest; the mastery of magic; the wisdom of plants, trees, and animals; the power of the elements; legends of love, crisis, and rebirth.

In Norse myth, human beings are shown to be woven out of the same fabric of creation as the natural world, elemental beings, and gods. The Icelandic creation account describes how the first human beings, Ask and Embla (ash and probably elm), were themselves derived from "two feeble trees" into which Odin breathed life. Moreover, another emblematic pair of human beings escape the final destruction of Ragnaroc by sheltering on the trunk of the World Tree, Yggdrasil, returning at the time of peril to that living nature from which they arose, and from which they will emerge again, to a regenerated world. We are thus seen as being of the same stuff as Yggdrasil itself, living embodiments of the Cosmic Tree, with our ancestral and evolutionary roots deep in the soil of prehistory, our bodies trunks that stand and face all weathers, our arms branches reaching out into infinity. Having breathed life into us, the gods and goddesses then go on to gift us with many more boons, including, ultimately, the Runes, which are there to be used as tools of an expanded consciousness.

No esoteric system alone provides the answer to all life's mysteries, of course, and we should be careful not to totalize the significance even of runes. It has been commented that the ultimate value of a system lies in our ultimately dispensing with it. Its worth, in other words, stems from what we have learned along the way: It is not a final destination in itself. Similarly, however much we identify with a particular cultural tradition, we must never lose sight of the fact that each is merely a thread in the larger whole of human spiritual growth and inquiry. Modern-day seekers live in very different conditions from the Norse of times past, who passed much of their lives in isolated dwellings lit by tallow (animal or whale fat) lamps in dense woods and lonely fjords, by turns hunting, farming, fishing, and raiding. Our ancestors were as liable to be fallible as we are—but their wisdom can still flow from the past into the present and future. Runes embody their outlook and their attempts at higher understanding. The magical and divinatory system attached to these fascinating signs was itself, in my opinion, created in an act (or perhaps series of acts) of divine inspiration. Their universality is attested by the fact that they can still speak to us today after almost two thousand years.

The Runes can be thought of as the true sacred text of the Northern Tradition and they embody its great mysteries. As an esoteric system, they encapsulate the mysterious powers and processes of the cosmos, because the inner and outer worlds are connected and the same archetypal themes that are found in ancient myths are reflected in our personal lives. The Runes, therefore, connect us *through and beyond* our personal situations with the great rhythms and forces that animate everything. In so doing they initiate us into the greater mystery of which we are a part. Runes empower, even as they instruct and transform with their "whispered secrets." This book is specifically about the Runes, but in divining with them, you will come to know and understand more of the Northern Mysteries. Wisely used, they will promote the flow of wisdom, happiness, and abundance into your life.

Part 2

RUNESTAVES

You will find runes   and read staves rightly
the strong magic,
the mighty spells
that the sage set down,
that the great gods made,
wisdom of Odin.

HÁVAMÁL (SAYINGS OF THE HIGH ONE),
POEMS OF THE "ELDER EDDA"

GUIDE TO ⊙
THE STAVES

n this part of the book, "Runestaves," you will find each individual rune of the Elder Futhark listed in original order under a modern name. Next to each rune you will see its original Germanic name followed by an English translation of this name's literal meaning (see below for more information about these rune names). Included after this are the corresponding Rune poem verses and their associations, which were discussed at some length in part 1, "Runelore." You will note that the twenty-four staves are grouped in three ancient divisions: Frey's Aett (sacred to the fertility god Frey), Hagal's Aett (sacred to the elemental force of hail), and Týr's Aett (sacred to the old Norse god of the sword, Týr—known to the Germanic peoples as Tiw or Tiwaz). These divisions, of course, won't concern you much when you divine with the Runes.

Names of the Runestaves

As you will see first in the details for each rune provided, each stave has various names in different languages. For example, in Germanic, ᛒ (birch) is *berkana;* in Norse, *bjarkan.* When cast, these runestaves should be looked at as visual images, graven signs that have a great power and potency as magical charms, with resonant names that roll off the tongue wonderfully when chanted. Freya Asswyn, for instance, has produced a haunting invocation based on singing the old Germanic names of each of the runes in sequence.

While the runestaves and their various names as given here will in time become familiar to you and easily recognizable, other commentators often choose to use the runes' Norse or Old English titles, which can lead to some confusion. Consequently, I have also provided a list of the most commonly used alternative titles for each rune, including, sometimes, *variant* Germanic names, as well as the names employed in Old English, Gothic, and Scandinavian languages (the latter as found in the Norwegian and Icelandic Rune poems). Learning these alternative names will help you to identify the rune names in other commentaries you may read. The following key serves as a guide to understanding the source of each rune's names and each rune's correspondence given in the pages to come.

Key to the Rune Names

Gmc	Germanic	The proto-language spoken by the Germanic people before the emergence of regional dialects. It contains the earliest titles for the Elder Futhark Runes, although there are often variant Germanic forms of their names, which I have included in the section below.
OE and OERP	Old English	The English language of the period 450–1110 c.e. Sometimes there are Old English variants of the names found in the Old English Rune poem.
Gothic		The Goths were originally from Scandinavia but later migrated southward into mainland Europe. The first Gothic name provided is in Old Gothic, which contains very early forms of the Rune names. The second name comes from a new, standardized form of Gothic developed by the fourth-century Christian bishop Ulfila and influenced by various other scripts. Most of the Gothic meanings match the Germanic ones.
NRP	from the Norwegian Rune poem	These names are generally derived from Old Norse, which was spoken in Norway, Iceland, and parts of Britain 800–1100 c.e. Thus the Rune names from the Norwegian Rune poem are generally the same as those from the Icelandic Rune poem (see IRP, below).
IRP	from the Icelandic Rune poem	Generally derived from Old Norse (see NRP above).

Along with the names for each stave, its *sound* and its *correspondence* are given. With regard to the *sound* associated with each rune, I have provided as much as possible the earliest phonetic value. In the case of one or two runes, there is some argument about these, and in fact the sounds several of them represented did shift periodically to reflect linguistic changes in the speech communities of the Rune cultures.

The *correspondences* given come from a set of so-called marginalia: one-word elaborations, generally of a classical, astrological, or (occasionally) indigenous nature, attached to the margins of the Icelandic Rune poem. They are interesting in that they either confirm the suspected identity of a stave or provide correspondences that some runecasters consider to have esoteric value, especially when they relate to the classical gods/planets.

THE RUNE POEMS

Following the information on each stave's name, you will meet the Rune poem verses connected to each rune. As noted in part 1 of this book, my versions show the Rune poems restored to what I believe to be the original, pagan character. Treat them as riddles to ponder. Once you have learned to crack their "kennings," they become quite profound oracles of wisdom in their own right. It is through the Rune poems that the old traditions find their voice. We should remember that poetry in the ancient pagan world was not the book-bound phenomenon we now know, but a vital, living form—entertaining and instructive—linked to the magic spell and magician's charm. We have seen in part 1 how the "oracular poem" is a cross-cultural tradition of great antiquity and venerability; through the Runes we have the opportunity to reclaim the art of its interpretation.

VISUALIZATION

The image attached to each rune in this book is derived from its primary identity (evident in each rune's name) and from the picture painted by the Rune poems. These are combined and presented after each Rune poem in a set of visualizations to aid you in your understanding of each rune. In oracular traditions, the image always has primacy over the word, bypassing language and leading straight to intuitive wisdom. Contemplate these images as gateways into the identity of the rune concerned. As a basis for creative visualization, these images are fine vessels and take us into the heartland of runic wisdom: the ancestral forms that lie in Mímir's Well. Of course, you may ultimately choose to picture them in a different way from that set forth in these pages, but these visualizations are a good place to begin.

MEANING

Last in the information on each runestave comes the most personally relevant part: the "Meaning" section, which contains the oracle or message of the rune as it applies to your situation. Because the Runes are multifaceted and a very compressed body of signs, we must sometimes fish around in their well of associations before grasping their exact message. Try to decide which area of life they specifically relate to, so as to activate the particular aspect of the rune that is relevant to your question. This is not so much a logical process as it is an intuitive one in which one waits for the "click" that signals that the correct interpretation has been found. The use of the Runes is a process of establishing a dialogue and can take some time and practice. You can turn to part 3 of this book, "Runecasting," for more details.

Most of the staves have reversed meanings; that is, if the rune in question appears upside down in a reading, it takes on a contrary meaning. If you draw one of these *murkstaves,* read the main commentary anyway, so as to understand the essential nature of the rune.

Then look at the reversed meaning at the end of the commentary and ponder what it means that this rune is reversed. A murkstave literally shows the omen of the rune in question turned around, the shadow side of the event or energy current being represented. Here you may like to work on trying to bring the energy of this rune back into alignment—that is, to get it into the upright position. This could include using the rune image in a positive creative visualization or carving it magically on a talisman or performing some similar ritual of personal significance. *Note:* Poetically enough, in light of the Norse obsession with the number 9, there are nine "nonreversible" runes that look the same upside down as right-side up. Some esoteric commentators accord them a special status and regard them as signifying more profound or intrinsic qualities than the other runes. But for our purposes, it is enough to note that they do not have a reversed meaning.

MYTHS AND LEGENDS

The final section of information for each stave, entitled "Myths and Legends," introduces you to the mythological background of each rune and its meaning. Here you can explore the different themes from traditional Norse belief, practice, and literature that underpin the wisdom of the oracle.

You may not wish to read all the themes connected to each rune the first time but, rather, choose what seems of most interest and assimilate the wider background over time. Through doing so, a quite comprehensive map of the Norse nine-world system will come into focus, deepening your appreciation of the overall runic system. Remember, however, that runelore is not just a thing of the past: it is an evolving system of ancient understanding.

The art of runecasting is a profound tool that can empower and enlighten, a vital and living system that can avail us in our lives today. Although the traditions surrounding the Runes have lain dormant for many centuries, contemporary Paganism has revived them so that their inner import shines through unblemished and ever adaptable to the unfolding dance of reality. For as the Valkyrie Sigdrífa instructs the hero Sigurd regarding the "runes of good help":

> *Whosoever holds them   unbroken, unchanged*
> *will have good luck*
> *and be glad of his lore*
> *until the day of doom.*[1]

FREY'S AETT

Abundance: *fehu* (Cattle)

Names: Gmc *fuhu* (cattle, goods); Gothic *faihu/fe;*
OE *feh;* NRP and IRP *fe* (wealth)

Sound: *f* (as in *fee*)

Correspondence: gold

OLD ENGLISH RUNE POEM

Wealth provides comfort,
But you must share it who hope to cast lots
for judgment before the gods.

NORWEGIAN RUNE POEM

Money causes strife among kin;
the wolf grows up in the woods.

ICELANDIC RUNE POEM

Money causes strife among kin,
and the fire of the flood tide
and the path of the serpent.

VISUALIZATION

A cow with curved horns stands in a fertile field. To the left a wolf lurks in a dark wood and in the foreground a snake lies coiled like a ring in the grass.

MEANING

Fehu is an omen of abundance. As the foremost runic symbol for wealth, it indicates gain in terms of riches and possessions, and luck in general. This could relate to a one-time windfall or an improvement in your financial circumstances or indicate that you are enjoying an overall state of abundance. Wealth and plenty are in the offing, and with some strong warnings against the excesses of materialism in mind, this rune is highly positive when upright.

The original meaning of *fehu* in early divination was "cattle" or "livestock," so it has long been a sign of gain and plenty. In nomadic times cattle were the foremost source of wealth for the Norse, and this association is preserved in modern English with the word *chattel*. Materially, cattle provided the owner with milk, butter, cheese, meat, leather, and status in tribal times. We still speak, rather crudely, about something with great earning potential as being a cash cow. *Fehu,* therefore, relates not just to gain and goods but also to those investments or possessions that you can use to generate further wealth.

It is, however, the image of the cow goddess as provider that underpins and deepens the signification of the *fehu* rune. In Norse paganism cattle were sacred to the earth goddess Nerthus, signaling that all abundance stems from the earth, the great provider. After all, everything we own, eat, drink, or enjoy has sprung from the land or sea. Here, fruits from her cornucopia—literally, "horn of plenty"—are being poured upon you.

This rune also corresponds to gold, and thus coins and money. It affirms that you can make money at this time. Yet *fehu* provides a clear distinction between positive and negative aspects of accumulating cash. As Odin once said: "Money makes monkeys of men"! Gold lust leads to endless strife, so do not sacrifice the interests of the wider community to individual gain. Otherwise the social and environmental fabric begins to fray, impoverishing everybody. And as the Norse well knew, a treasure hoard wrongly gotten draws down a curse.

We are entitled, however, to invoke a fair measure of abundance in our lives. In Norse belief the guardians of the earth, gods and goddesses of plenty and fertility known as the Vanir, are venerated for their gifts of wealth and plenty. Embodying the fruitfulness of the natural world, they were called upon in ancient times for fertile harvests and luck in hunting and sea expeditions. *Fehu* is still used as a lucky charm for generating abundance in modern-day rune magic. You can engrave it on an amulet or meditate upon *fehu* while visualizing the horns of Nerthus.

Reversed, *fehu* can signify a blockage to the flow of abundance in your life, leading to poverty and lack. Take action, magical and practical, to break through this condition. As a murkstave, *fehu* can also signal spiritual poverty despite material prosperity. This is "the path of the serpent" and the wolf. Though not necessarily evil, the snake was often used in the oral tradition to illustrate the principle of venomous greed. The wolf was also a dangerous opportunist who symbolized the outcast, haunting the fringes of society, always ready to carry off what is unguarded. The lesson of this stave, therefore, is that wealth is a blessing, but beware the paths of the serpent and the wolf!

Keywords: Abundance, riches, investments, possessions, prosperity, luck, windfall, gain, plenty, bounty, fruitfulness, cornucopia. *Murkstave:* Impoverishment, material loss, greed, miserliness, excessive materialism.

MYTHS AND LEGENDS

In the *Prose Edda* creation account, the primordial cow Audumla nurtures the frost giant Ymir with her milk and licks away at the primeval ice to reveal the form of Búri, Odin's grandfather. Audumla symbolizes the life-giving fire that melts the hostile ice associated with the next stave, *urox,* and thereby creates a fertile and habitable world. This could, incidentally, recall the period at the end of the last ice age, when herdsmen reemerged to reclaim the land for cattle grazing. In any case, the cow goddess Audumla clearly conforms to the archetype of the Earth Mother, and therefore the Great Goddess herself, as the ultimate source of bounty and fertility.

Fehu also happens to be the first rune in Frey's Aett, dedicated to the god Frey. Frey and his sister Freya are king and queen of the Vanir (fertility gods), who are associated with the richness and fecundity of the earth, as well as with hoofed animals. Their reign was preceded by that of their father, the sea god Njórd, whose consort was the early Germanic earth goddess Nerthus. In some versions of the mythology, Frey himself was said to be the lover of Nerthus, who was at the center of a cult of cattle worship. And there are links here to the worship of cattle in other parts of the ancient world: in Egypt, for example, the cow goddess Hathor was a symbol of plenty and fertility, and cattle are, of course, sacred to this day in India.

Golden Game Boards

In the Old English Rune poem, wealth is said to provide comfort— with the proviso that it is shared. Its distribution through the clan, tribe, or community, the virtue of generosity, and the tradition of gift giving were of paramount importance to the pagan Germanic and Norse long before the coming of Christianity, as the *gebo* (Exchange) rune illustrates. The divisive impact of money when hoarded is evident in the Norwegian and Icelandic verses, in which it evokes "strife among kinsmen."

The fact is that gold, however desirable, was always known for the terrible cost it could exact. A traditional kenning for this glittering metal was *rogmálmr*—"strife metal." This had a fateful precedent. In the great mythological poem *Völuspá* it is partly greed—"want of gold"—that destroyed the innocence of the gods, provoked the first war in the world, and began the slide toward Ragnaroc, the Norse apocalypse:

> *Sitting in meadows,   smiling over gameboards,*
> *[the gods] never knew   any need of gold,*
> *but there came three maidens   monstrous to look at,*
> *giant daughters   of Jotunheim.*[2]

These three giant maidens represent the forces of materialism and its destructive effects. Though not necessarily evil, the character of giants in the Norse myths is, generally speaking, greedy, possessive, and usurping. They are, by and large, creatures of gross appetites. But gods, men, and dwarfs, too, fall victim to gold lust and the acts of treachery it breeds.

Fenris, Jormungand, and Ragnaroc

Against the friendly image of the cow, the Icelandic and Norwegian Rune poems present the malevolent totems of the wolf and snake to represent the temptations of wealth. Both these animals are traditional emblems of greed and are commonly used as such in the *Eddas*. The most infamous examples of the wolf and snake in Norse myth are Fenris and Jormungand, both offspring of the trickster god Loki and a frost giantess. The wolf who "grows up in the woods" in the Norwegian Rune poem corresponds to the great and terrible Fenris wolf, who, in the end days of Ragnaroc, escapes from his chain and runs free, wreaking complete destruction. Loki's other menacing offspring, the serpent Jormungand, plays a part in the catastrophic events of Ragnaroc, when, in the words of *Vǫluspá:*

> *the world-girding serpent*
> *rises from the water,*
> *lashing at the waves.*[3]

Here we have a vision of planetary catastrophe involving rising seas, and these poems, based on earlier, oral traditions, issue both a personal and a collective warning. Greed is not good; it can become a source of strife, conflict, and ultimately apocalyptic destruction.

The Ring of the Nibelungs

The proverbial role of the wolf and snake is perfectly illustrated by the famous *Volsunga Saga*, with its cursed Niflunga treasure hoard. Here family members turn murderously upon each other over its fabulous treasures, the centerpiece of which is a ring of great power named Andvari. Forged by the dwarf of the same name, it had been cursed and labeled as *wergild* (blood money paid to the family of a slain man). For the thieving Fafnir's part in the murder of his father, we read in the *Prose Edda*, he is turned into that king of serpents, the dragon, while in *Atlakviða* (The Lay of Atli) Gunnar utters this curse over the hexed treasure hoard of the Niflunga: "The wolf shall rule the inheritance of the Niflunga!" This cautionary tale, which formed the basis of Wagner's *Der Ring des Nibelungen* and, of course, Tolkien's *Lord of the Rings*, was the source of another traditional kenning for gold: *rog Niflunga*, "strife of the Niflunga." Thus, although *fehu* signals gain, the warning that a person can very easily become possessed by his or her possessions is all too clear.

Challenge: *urox* (Wild Ox)

Names: Gmc *uruz* or *urox* (aurochs), whence modern English "ox"; Gothic *urus/uraz;* OE *uur;* NRP *ur* (slag); IRP *ur* (drizzle)

Sound: *u* (as in *rune*) and sometimes *v*

Correspondence: shower

OLD ENGLISH RUNE POEM

The wild ox has great high horns
with which it gores; a fierce fighter
who boldly stamps the moors.

NORWEGIAN RUNE POEM

Slag is cast from bad iron;
reindeer cross the hard snow.

ICELANDIC RUNE POEM

Drizzle is the weeping of clouds,
and blights the harvest
and is hated by the herdsman.

VISUALIZATION

A wild ox, taller than a man, rears up against an icy landscape. A hunter with a spear stands to one side.

MEANING

Urox represents a challenge, archetypal trial, or rite of initiation. It warns of a contest of strength in which you will be pitted against some hostile foe, adversity, or other unwelcome experience. You face a formidable challenge and will be tested, perhaps to the limits of your strength. However painful, this process is a necessary one for personal growth.

The aurochs was a wild ox, the hoary ancestor of domestic cattle, that used to roam the forests of prehistoric Europe. Fought by young men in trials of initiation, it was "an enormous, black beast standing six feet at the shoulder and with great spreading, forward-curving horns."[4] Clearly then, the wild ox was no mean adversary and was respected as a fierce fighter. You can translates this in personal terms as a testing element that you must face and master in order for growth and progress to occur.

The notion of a trial or rite of passage encompasses the equivalent tests and obstacles that we face in our daily lives. In a society such as ours, which lacks elaborate rituals of initiation, it could correspond to many events of a difficult nature. The crisis could be psychological, romantic, spiritual, or ethical. The area of life concerned will be indicated by surrounding runes, but whatever it is, there are major issues to wrestle.

The enormous black ox with its lacerating horns is a fearsome symbol of all you must overcome on the path to mastery. Yet you are not alone or helpless in your quest. The strength of your ancestors, who faced many such menaces, flows in your veins. Meet the challenge with courage, for this is actually an initiation into a higher state of being. You will be stronger and wiser for it.

Reversed, this rune signifies difficulty in accepting the challenge. You may fear being torn apart. This is a sore trial, but by confronting the beast—which translates, in Jungian terms, into facing the shadow—you will be led to a far greater degree of personal empowerment. Thus the very thing that terrifies you may ultimately become a source of strength and wisdom. As a parallel, there are many stories in tribal traditions of slain animals becoming the totems of heroes, actually acting as protectors and guides from their realm in the spirit world. Similarly, your greatest fear may become your teacher and ally.

Keywords: A challenge, trial, contest, or meeting with adversity; initiation, testing times, trial by ordeal, facing adversity. *Murkstave:* Failing to meet life's trials; suffering conquest; being gored in the game of life.

MYTHS AND LEGENDS

The signification of *urox* is partly found in the tension that exists between it and the first rune, *fehu:* the primal and creative opposition of bull and cow, untamed and tamed, ice and fire. This last pair (ice and fire) helps explain the Scandinavian Rune poem references to drizzle, snow, and "the rim of ice" by linking *urox* with the primordial ice—literally, the "ur-matter," the elemental material—of Norse creation. The previous rune, *fehu,* by contrast, suggests the cow Audumla, who, in the creation accounts, licks the primal ice and melts it, thus representing life-giving, maternal warmth. So while *fehu* is warm, nurturing, and benevolent, the icy *ur* is a challenging or hostile force in nature. From this stems the meaning of *urox* in original divination: It is a challenge, danger, and trial to be confronted.

Furthermore, although at first glance the three Rune poem verses given for *urox* seem quite different, they all emphasize challenge and hardship. The *ur* (slag) referred to in the Norwegian Rune poem is from "bad iron," the offcast of the metal, the unusable, and, in a way, the untamed. In the Icelandic Rune poem we have *ur* (drizzle) as a hostile element that "blights the harvest" and is understandably "hated by the herdsman." Once again, it is a raw element that challenges the settled life.

The Gilded Drinking Horn

Although *urox* has a threatening aura, the lore connected with the wild ox suggests its deeper significance as an instigator of an important trial, test of strength, or rite of passage. For in ancient Norse culture, the aurochs was an adversary that young men combated in order to claim their manhood. Caesar, writing of the Germanii (ancient German tribespeople), tells us that the killing of such a beast was a test of manly strength, a trophy in the coming of age of a young man:

In size these are somewhat smaller than elephants; in appearance, colour and shape they are as bulls. Great is their strength and great their speed, and they spare neither man nor beast once sighted. These the Germans slay zealously, by taking them in pits; by such work the young men harden themselves and by this kind of hunting train themselves, and those who have slain most of them bring the horns with them to a public place for a testimony thereof, and win great renown. But even if they are caught very young, the animals cannot be tamed or accustomed to human beings.[5]

He goes on to record how the wild ox's horns were collected, lined with silver, and converted into drinking cups, trophies of initiation. Because of its original role in presenting young men with an opportunity to test themselves, *urox* also came to symbolize strength, valor, achievement, and renown, and the aurochs functioned as a cult animal, a type of tribal totem.

Hunting peoples in general show great respect for their prey; as Joseph Campbell put it: "The hunt itself . . . is a rite of sacrifice, sacred, and not a rawly secular affair."[6] The trial of strength against such a creature is simultaneously an attempt to match its vigor and courage. The victor then takes on the kudos of the conquered. Consequently, the *urox* rune is also identified with strength itself and the associated qualities of valor and courage.

Thór and the Giant's Herd

In Norse mythology, there are many contests of strength wherein the gods set out to prove (or simply enjoy) themselves by wrestling with primal forces throughout the nine worlds. A favorite theme is the visit to Jotunheim, the land of the giants. In *Hymisqviðá* (The Lay of Hymir) the giant Hymir challenges the god Thór to a trial of strength, provoked by Thór's consumption of two of Hymir's precious oxen in Hymir's own hall! The god consents to row far out to sea with Hymir in a fishing contest in order to prove his prowess to the uncouth churl. Before they can begin, Hymir rudely tells Thór he must find his own bait. We hear how Thór fells a wild ox named Himinhrjot (Heaven Bellower) from the giant's herd:

> *Thór went quickly   into the wood,*
> *and soon a black ox   stood in his way;*
> *the giant-killer   caught the horns,*
> *broke the beast's head   right off his body.*[7]

Thór then joins Hymir onboard a boat. Angling with this bait, Thór goes on to fish up the greatest challenge of his career (and perhaps more than he bargained for): the World Serpent, Jormungand, in whose mouth the bait lodges.

Such accounts in the oral tradition once provided the heroic models for human conduct. We can readily imagine young men listening in the mead hall to the skald's tales of divine bravery, these stories fortifying them for the challenges that lay ahead, their own battles with an aurochs from "the giant's herd."

Misfortune: *thurisaz* (Giant)

Names: Gmc *thurisaz* (giant) or *thurnuz* (thorn); Gothic *thairis*/*thyth*; OE *thorn*; NRP *thurs*; IRP *thurs* (giant)

Sound: *th* (unvoiced, as in *thorn*)

Correspondence: Saturn

OLD ENGLISH RUNE POEM

Thorn is wickedly sharp and causes pain
to those who grasp it, hurt
to you who rest among them.

NORWEGIAN RUNE POEM

Giant causes the sickness of women;
bad luck pleases nobody.

ICELANDIC RUNE POEM

Giant is the torment of women,
and the dweller of rocky vales
and husband of Varthrun the giantess.

VISUALIZATION

In a rocky domain, flecked with ice, mighty frost giants battle each other. A tangle of thorns stands at the entrance to their valley. Above, in the sky, is Thór's hammer, Mjollnir.

MEANING

Thurisaz represents a disruptive, threatening, or painful upset to the order of human life. It relates to a misfortune that undermines your security and creates disorder. It could, in some cases, be a challenging personal issue, a "thorny" problem in the area of health, romance, or finances. Or you may be struggling with hostile, outside forces that seem chaotic and far beyond your control.

The early title for this rune was "giant," later Christianized to "thorn." The Norse term includes the associations of "ogre" and even "demon." Giants are ill-natured, meddlesome creatures in Norse myth, and a person drawing the *thurisaz* stave may experience great difficulties or powerful opposition. You may suffer torment and even feel as if you were being persecuted.

Often *thurisaz* signals that you are being blocked at home or work, perhaps by one or more individuals working against you or because of a generally hostile environment. The problem may involve large, thoughtless entities such as public institutions and big corporations.

Giants are traditionally agents of chaos, of blind, malignant, and unconscious forces, so the misfortune is generally of the undeserved or unfair kind. You may be caught up in a struggle larger than yourself and hit by the fallout. The difficulty usually has to be borne, although in some circumstances you can take effective action.

Thurs has also long been associated with Thór—the giant-slayer. Much like a giant himself, Thór nonetheless defended the gods and men from these marauding and rebellious titans. This brings in the theme of counterdefense against attack from without, symbolized by Thór's hammer, a protective amulet that resembles the shape of the *thurisaz* rune. In magical practice, Thór is sometimes invoked as a force to combat overwhelming opposition. You too can draw on the strength of higher powers to assist you, for such energies are real and willing to help. Take heart! Whatever your "giant" may be, you will find that help in defeating it is at hand.

Reversed, *thurisaz* signals a terrifying brush with hostile forces. You may feel overwhelmed and a victim of dark energies. *Thurisaz* was in early times a stave of black magic used to bring ill luck on the victim. This does not mean you are the victim of a hex, but it does suggest knotty difficulties, especially for women, as it is sometimes linked, in matters of health, to those problems that women specifically encounter. The prickly thorn *may* sometimes translate as a menstrual or (for both men and women) sexual or fertility health issue, for which medical advice should be sought.

Keywords: A threat or disruption, pain through unfortunate and unpredictable events, the need to counter attacks from without, misfortune, an upset, pain or discomfort, a threat to the established order. *Murkstave:* An intensification of the above; women's health problems.

MYTHS AND LEGENDS

In the Norse creation account, the mighty frost giants—or *rime thurses*—existed long before humans and even before the gods. Odin and his two brothers had to kill the father of the frost giants, Ymir, before they could create the safe haven of Midgard. The frost and rock giants were so hostile to men and gods that they had to be herded into one place, Jotunheim, where they settled and remain. Occasionally, however, the giants reemerge to upset both the upperworlds and Midgard, and the three terrible children of Loki and a giantess menace the world to the very end.

In order to fully appreciate the significance of the sign "giant," we have to recall the deep structure of the nine worlds of Norse myth. The Aesir dwell in Ásgard at the apex of the three upperworlds, humans in Midgard (Middle Earth, the human realm), with the giants finally penned in by the walls of their domain, Jotunheim, which lies to the east of Midgard. The Aesir are effectively the rulers of the nine worlds, the upholders of the cosmic order. The giants, by contrast, just like the Titans of Greek mythology, stand in belligerent defiance of that order. As Kevin Crossley-Holland comments: "There is little to choose between one giant and another. The giants largely represent the forces of chaos, attempting through physical force, trickery, and magic to upset the cosmic order."[8]

Giants are not necessarily evil, but they do act as harbingers of disorder and destruction and are often identified in esoteric runology with unconscious forces. As agents of chaos, the connection with the world of giants predicted by this rune tends to spell an interlude of difficulty and misfortune for the person who draws *thurisaz*. It is as if one were suffering an incursion from the primal chaos of the giant's realm.

Thór and the Frost Giants

The word *thurs* and the name Thór are close and may be linguistically related. Indeed, our *Thurs*day was originally "Thór's day." The *thurses* and Thór are like forces. The distinction is that Thór wields his might in defense of order rather than for purposes of ill. It is "far-famed" Thór, as strongman of the gods and scourge of the giants, who, with his great hammer Mjollnir, seeks to put the usurpers in place. He staunchly defends the worlds of Ásgard and Midgard. Yet paradoxically Thór in his brute strength most strongly resembles the giants, and it is not always clear that he can prevail against them. In one tale, Thór's hammer, Mjollnir, is stolen by the giant Thrym, an act deeply worrying to the gods. In the previous rune, you can read about Thór's struggle with the menacing giant Hymir, who challenges him to a titanic trial of strength.

Some commentators have noted the resemblance this stave has to the shape of Thór's hammer. Is this significant? The *Prose Edda* provides us with a cryptic clue. A line from Snorri's *Skáldskaparmál* (Poetic Diction) states that the heart of Hrungnir, chief of the frost giants, is "sharp and three-sided," hence "the carven rune that is called 'Hrungnir's heart.'" The story in which these facts are found tells how the troublemaking Hrungnir has challenged the Aesir gods in Ásgard itself, and when Thór returns, enraged, he takes him on. The god launches his mighty hammer, Mjollnir, at Hrungnir, who throws his own "three-cornered stone" at the giant-slayer. The weapons meet in the air, and though Thór's hammer shatters Hrungnir's and crushes the giant's skull, some of the stone fragments from the exploding implement lodge in Thór's head. While Mjollnir prevails, Thór is destined to carry shards from Hrungnir's weapon. The giant's heart, after which this rune is said to be named, and his weapon are both described as three-sided and may indeed be the same object. Furthermore, Thór's weapon meets Hrungnir's in a motif that seems to profoundly connect the god and the giant at some level. Thór even walks the rest of his days with shards of the giant's stone in his head.

For such reasons, this stave may be linked to Mjollnir, and thus the theme of magically protecting ourselves from attack from without. Thór's hammer has long been worn as a protective talisman, and some traditional pieces of jewelry work the *thurisaz* motif into their design.

The Sickness of Women

In the Scandinavian Rune poems, *thurs* is described as harmful to women. There is a parallel in the Eddic poem *Skírnismál* (Skirnir's Journey). Frey's servant Skirnir has been sent to win a beautiful girl,

Gerthr, for the amorous god who is in love with her. When the girl plays hard to get, Skirnir threatens her with a number of curses, among them *thurs,* which is used as a negative "bind rune" (a binding magical spell involving more than one rune). He utters these words:

> [Thurs] *I carve for you   three characters*
> *"Lust" and "Burning"   and "Unbearable Need."* [9]

Reversed, *Thurisaz* can relate to the problems—especially of a sexual or menstrual nature—that women may encounter, and can sometimes indicate reproductive problems. Because of its raw nature, the stave is also sometimes linked to erotic matters that may be intense but thorny in their outcome.

A Bed of Thorns

As we saw, the Old English Rune poem names this stave "thorn" rather than "giant." Why, when in Scandinavian tradition this rune is certainly associated with giants? *Thurisaz* does, of course, resemble the shape of a thorn, though, as we saw above, the link with the heart of the giant Hrungnir is more likely. What probably happened is that the poet chose to identify this rune as *thorn* because of its unintended resemblance, creating at the same time a verbal pun with the similar-sounding Old English word *thurs* (giant). This plays on the traditional associations of the rune. Both giant and thorn are, after all, disruptive or painful: giants were a constant thorn in the side of the gods in Norse mythology, and there is even a giant in *Skáldskaparmál* named Thorn.

Moreover, in Celtic magic the thorn is linked with ill luck, hexing, and black magic. In the medieval Welsh *Mabinogion* tale *Kilhwch and Olwen,* the king of the giants who confronts the hero Gwainn is actually named Yspadden Penkawr, meaning "giant hawthorn"—another instance, then, of a giant named Thorn. Viking invasions of England and Irish settlers in Scandinavia ensured that ideas like this could easily travel across the seas, so the interpolation by the poet of the Old English Rune poem may not be entirely arbitrary.

In *Volsunga Saga,* moreover, Odin uses a sleep thorn to cast the

Valkyrie Bryndhild (Brunhild) into a kind of magically induced coma. This episode is the original Sleeping Beauty myth, in which a maiden lies in an enchanted sleep, surrounded by thorns, until a hero comes to rescue her, providing another potential link with the theme of *thurisaz* being harmful to women. In poetry, thorns are emblems of problems in one's love life ("Roses have thorns, silver fountains mud," as Shakespeare put it), and the ninth- or tenth-century Old English Rune poem poet may also have been thinking of the crown of thorns. In divinatory terms, all these later associations underline the stave's original augury of a painful misfortune that comes partly as a result of our own unwariness or from our grasping or clinging to the thing that causes pain. This carries with it the challenge of pulling away from the agent of ill luck, whatever it may be.

Breath: *ansuz* **(Odin)**

Names: Gmc *ansuz* (god); Gothic *ansuz/aza;* OE *oss* (mouth); NWP *oss* (rivermouth); IRP *oss* (god, specifically Odin)

Sound: *a* **(as in** *art***)**

Correspondence: Jupiter

OLD ENGLISH RUNE POEM

The mouth is the source of the word,
bringing wisdom and counsel to the wise,
hope, inspiration, and a blessing to all.

NORWEGIAN RUNE POEM

Rivermouth opens most journeys;
but the sword belongs in its sheath.

ICELANDIC RUNE POEM

Odin is the ancient creator,
and Ásgard's king
and lord of Valhalla.

VISUALIZATION

The god Odin faces you, his eye of wisdom burning. Two ravens perch on his shoulders, and two wolves sit at his feet. Runes are carved on his drinking horn.

MEANING

Ansuz refers to Odin, the high god who embodies—among other things—breath, senses, and the sacred word. As custodian of esoteric traditions and prophecy, Odin represents "the word" as it flows from the gateway of the mouth into the wider world. This rune, therefore, rules over not only the word but the spell, the chant, the prayer, and breath as well.

On a mundane level, *ansuz* relates to how we express ourselves, especially our central message in life. You may have much to say, but breathe deeply and compose yourself before speaking. Odin has parallels with the Roman Mercury, god of communication, so *ansuz* can signify matters regarding correspondence, speech, letters, communiqués, and even legal matters. Try to ensure that all the possible channels of communication are clear and that information is flowing as it should. Being alert and well informed is crucial.

In Norse myth Odin presides over many mysteries. As the one who breathed life into the first human being, he is the creator god who gifts breath as the very source of existence. Odin's connection with the mead of inspiration and the Well of Runelore also reveals him as guardian of the spoken word and whispered secret. His presence in this reading suggests that there are sources of wisdom and inspiration around you, if only you are attentive to their counsel. Watch and listen carefully, for a mentor may appear in an unexpected guise.

Odin has more than one face and is the archetypal shapeshifter. In Norse myth he goes by many names, and he also has many parallels outside it. He is the Merlin of Arthurian romance, the master magician Gwyddyon of Welsh lore, Gandalf in *The Lord of the Rings:* omnipresent, sublime, and terrible all at once. In magical terms, Odin is the master of wizardry and incantations and the archgod of divination. The appearance of this rune in a reading may signal that you are ready to move deeper into these mysteries in order to enlighten and empower yourself, or it may represent another person in your life who embodies these qualities.

Reversed, this rune can signify miscommunication, misinformation, or even trickery, so pay attention to details and listen as much as you talk. In personal communication there may be wordy discussions; in business, negotiations. Words are important now and should be chosen with care. Breathing exercises may be employed to help clear the mind and refresh body and spirit. Sacred sounds and chants are powerful consciousness-altering tools and may be used to aid in meditation or creative visualization.

Keywords: The god Odin, the mouth, breath, issues connected with speech and writing, the spoken word, communication, the sacred oral tradition. *Murkstave:* Misinformation, lies, falsity, and deceit; beguiling words bereft of truth or sentiment.

MYTHS AND LEGENDS

Odin is the unrivaled chief of the gods of Norse mythology and religion. At the dawn of creation Búri was licked out of the primal ice by the cow Audumla, and his son Borr coupled with Bestla to give birth to Odin and his two brothers, Hoenir and Lodur (also known as Vili and Vé). It was these three who slew the frost giant Ymir and from his body parts made the lakes, sea, earth, and sky. Odin and his brothers also fashioned the first human beings out of two trees, Ask and Embla—(ash and probably elm); it was Odin who breathed life into them, hence my translation of this rune name as "Breath." Odin went on to set up day and night and, with his brothers, the sun and moon in their orbits. Odin is, therefore, indeed the "ancient creator."

As ruler of heaven and chief war god, he has parallels with the Indian Indra, Greek Zeus, Roman Jupiter (see the Icelandic Rune poem correspondence above), and Hebrew Jehovah: storm and thunder gods, mighty rulers, warrior chiefs. The All Father is, after all, the king of Ásgard, the abode of the Aesir, and thus the ruler of all the worlds. It pays to recall here, however, that in Norse mythology the rulership of creation was contested between the Aesir (sky gods) and the Vanir (earth gods), with the Aesir ultimately gaining the upper hand through a truce and Odin succeeding as their chief and king. This legendary account of the old gods of fertility and magic giving way to their rivals parallels the general shift in Indo-European mythologies from fertility-centered religion to worship of the sky gods. But a measure of the Vanir's earlier supremacy is preserved in the account of how after Freya, Vanaheim's queen, goes as a hostage to live among the Aesir, she becomes their high priestess and teaches them (including Odin) skill in magic. Indeed, some devotees of the Northern Mysteries today identify more closely with Freya than with Odin, and the school of magic she founded and taught to Odin *(seithr)* has seen a considerable revival in recent times.

Odin the Magus

Odin is a complex character. Named the All Knowing, High One, and Ravengod, he is a trickster to be regarded with as much dread as respect. He is known to walk abroad in Midgard under false names, such as Grímnir (the Hooded One), Gandalf-like with his felt hat pulled low over one eye and his robes wrapped about him. The Terrible One is, after all, the god of hanged men and the dead, for it is to his hall, Valhalla, that brave warriors are conducted by the Valkyries after their death. Odin's hall, with its shields for thatch and spears for rafters, is not, however, a bad place; there you may find eternal feasting, fighting, and merriment.

It is in his role as a god of divine knowledge, spellcraft, and prophecy that Odin interests us. To runecasters he is the god of magical arts who gains the mead of poetry and wins the wisdom of the Runes. From the shaman throne of Hlidskjálf in his personal hall, Valaskjálf, he can see throughout the nine worlds, and two ravens, Huginn (thought) and Munnin (memory), perch on his shoulders, continually whispering secrets into his ears. These birds point to both the gift of seership—the raven flight of the soul into regions of knowledge and inspiration—and the sacred art of memorization so important for the preservation of lore in an oral culture.

Odin stems from a very ancient indigenous shamanic tradition, yet as the master of Runes and magic he also parallels such deities as the Egyptian Thoth, the Greek Hermes, the Celtic Ogmios—gods of wisdom and the word, of communication, of writing, of scripts and sacred alphabets. As such, Odin is the master of the "word runes" praised in *Sigdrífomál* (The Lay of Sigdrífa):

> *Word Runes learn ye well   if thou wilt no man pay back*
> *Grief for the grief gavest;*
> *Wind thou these,   cast thou these*
> *All about thee*
> *At the Thing where folk throng*
> *Until the doom faring.*

The Cup of Inspiration

The winning of wisdom is set forward in several myths surrounding Odin. In the *Hávamál* and other Eddic sources, we learn the tale of his quest for the mead of poetry, with the god tricking Gunnlod, a giant's daughter, into letting him drink "a cup of costly mead," which brings instant illumination. This mead was originally made from the blood of the Vanir god Kvasir mixed with honey. While still alive, Kvasir was regarded as the wisest and most understanding of the gods, as Kevin Crossley-Holland elaborates from the *Prose Edda:*

> He was so steeped in matters and mysteries of the nine worlds since fire and ice first met at Ginnungagap that no god nor man nor giant nor dwarf ever regretted putting him a question or asking his opinion. And wherever Kvasir went, news of his coming went before him. . . .
>
> Sitting back in his ill-fitting clothes, as often as not with his eyes closed, he would listen to recitals of problems and sorrows with a kind of grave, blank face. He never intruded or insisted; rather, he suggested.[10]

It is obvious from such descriptions that Kvasir is a seer, a god of revelation, of divination. Odin, through sipping the mead mingled with Kvasir's blood, acquires the prophetic and oracular powers embodied in Kvasir. This theme of drinking a magical elixir from a cup is linked to Celtic tales of the cauldron of inspiration, which helped inspire the later legends of the Holy Grail.

The Well of Runelore

But Odin's greatest quest is undertaken to gain the Runes—his initiatory journey to and from Mímir's Well at the roots of Yggdrasil, the Cosmic Ash. As described in the introduction to this book, Odin sacrifices an eye to Mímir, the guardian of the well, wounds himself with a spear, and hangs himself from the branches of the great tree while groping in the waters of the well. This motif of the threefold death (hanging, immolation, and drowning) also has parallels in the Celtic domain, most notably involving the magician-druid-poet figures of Merlin and Taliesin.* The wider theme is the archetypal shaman's

---

* The threefold death, of course, has its minor variants. In the tale of *Lailokin and Kentigern* (Lailokin is a guise of Merlin), Lailokin dies from blows by sticks and stones, being pierced by a wooden skewer, and drowning all at once! Jean Markale, *Merlin: Priest of Nature,* trans. by Belle N. Burke (Rochester, Vt.: Inner Traditions, 1995), 65. See also end note 14 for chapter 3, 199.

ascent and descent of the World Tree and gaining of the wisdom of the otherworld. After nine days and nights (nine, of course, is the number of worlds in Norse myth), Odin grasps the Runes and heaves them up with a cry. Then, in a kind of trance, he recites the *galdr* (incantations, spells) he has learned. Odin's initiation thus forms the symbolic model for the winning of wisdom and runelore.

In another intimately related myth, the wise Mímir is beheaded by the Vanir, a terrible loss to the Aesir. But Odin takes Mímir's head, smears it with herbs, and then sings charms over it, so that the head begins to sing. Mímir's wisdom thus becomes All Father's—"many truths unknown to any other being."[11] These interrelated tales give a good idea of the value put upon the spoken, poetic, and oracular word in the oral society of the ancient Norse and Germanic peoples.

The (River) Mouth

In England this rune was Christianized to *oss,* meaning "mouth." Although the change disguises the heathen associations, it still preserves some of the essential elements associated with Odin in paganism. The poet of the Old English Rune poem praises the mouth as the "source of the word," which "brings wisdom and counsel" to the wise and benefit to all. While not mentioning Odin, this leaves obvious clues as to the original signification of the stave: It is hard to imagine the mouth being given quite such a positive function outside the context of sacred oral traditions. Norse and Anglo-Saxon cultures were well enough acquainted with the tongue's less desirable qualities; as we are told in *Hávamál,* "the tongue is the bane of the head."[12]

The rivermouth meeting the sea, mentioned in the Norwegian Rune poem, may in fact be making a pun on the image of the spoken word leaving the body in liquid form. After all, Odin is clearly linked to an elixir of inspiration and in one tale even carries the mead stolen from a giantess, Gunnlod, back to Ásgard in his mouth, finally spewing it forth in a torrent so the liquid can be imbibed by the other gods. We can easily see, then, how the apparently unrelated identities of Odin, mouth, and rivermouth conceal unexpected connections.

Rhythm: *raido* (Riding)

Names: Gmc *raitho* (riding); **Gothic** *raida/reda;* **OE** *rat;*
NRP *raeith* (riding); **IRP** *reith* (riding)

Sound: *r* (as in *riding*)

Correspondence: journey

OLD ENGLISH RUNE POEM

*Riding is easy for heroes
inside a hall; it's much harder astride a strong horse
pounding the great mile paths.*

NORWEGIAN RUNE POEM

*Riding is said to be the worst for horses;
Reginn forged the best sword.*

ICELANDIC RUNE POEM

*Riding is a sweet sitting,
and a swift journey
and the toil of the horse.*

VISUALIZATION

A swift black horse with hooded rider pounds the woodland mile
paths, sparks flying as its hooves strike the flagstones.

ΓΠ EΛΠIΠG

Raido is an omen of movement and momentum. It literally refers to the act of riding—especially a horse—which gives us practical associations of journeying and adventure, accompanied by pleasure and a measure of toil. It can also signify a journey, such as travel by land or overseas, and what may happen along the way.

The rune embodies rhythm and motion, the roots of all movement. It signifies the power that keeps us going forward, firmly seated on the saddle. That is why *raido* on a deeper level symbolizes the journey of life itself, the paths taken and the courses followed. Move outward, taking the initiative and staying in charge of situations. Extend yourself into the world of action, even if this takes you outside your sphere of comfort.

The Northern Tradition places a great emphasis on venturing out and exploring the world. Voyaging was a virtue to hard-bitten Vikings, and as Odin put it: "A man must go to many places, travel widely in the world."[13] For men and women alike, by taking risks and striking out we expand the field of possibilities that lie before us.

This rune also encourages us to take stock of our progress in the journey of life, including the manner in which we are making progress. Take the horse and rider as the model for action. The horse is the "vehicle" we use to carry ideas and plans to fruition. It is our mount, that which carries and lifts us aloft. Are you firmly in the saddle, yet not applying too much pressure? Have you established a working rhythm with your steed?

Raido can be further linked to rhythm and dance, fluid and graceful movement rather than plodding steps forward. It can correspond to the inner dance of ecstatic experience, for the symbolism attached to the act of riding in Norse mythology includes magical quest. Odin's horse leads him down to the roots of the World Tree, Yggdrasil, in the classic shaman's journey into the otherworld. Physical movement can take us to new places, but inner movement leads to equally novel territories. Thus, this is also a rune of trance states and vision questing.

Reversed, *raido* suggests that you may be having a rocky ride and are finding it difficult to stay in the saddle. Perhaps you feel you are getting nowhere. Try to adapt to the rhythm of events and not get stuck in fear and other negative responses to what is occurring. Holding the reins too tightly and exercising too much control may, alternatively, also break your rhythm. Try to move in sympathy with the flow of energies to skillfully surmount life's many hurdles.

Keywords: Travel by land, going places, rhythm, movement, momentum, shamanic journeying, vision questing. *Murkstave:* A lack of rhythm and momentum, a failed or fruitless voyage, going astray.

MYTHS AND LEGENDS

On the most literal level, *raido* is linked to the role of the horse in everyday life in the Northern world. The horse was the prime means of land transport in agrarian Europe, the vehicle by which people could travel great distances. As such this beautiful beast became one of the most highly valued domestic animals. Horse-worshiping cults were a feature of the ancient world. The Celts venerated the goddess Epona, the Romans worshiped her as Equis, and Norse myth is stacked with sacred horses that hold significant roles in the functioning of the cosmos.

Two horses were, for instance, responsible for drawing the sun and moon in their orbits: the horse of day, Skinfaxi (Shiny Mane), and the horse of night, Hrímfaxi (Frost Mane). The compound *ehwar* (meaning horse: see the *ehwaz* rune) seems to have been regarded as a magical word, for it commonly appears on protective amulets.[14] Horses were, incidentally, also employed in divination rituals for determining, among other things, the correct path to be taken.

The Great Mile Paths

Whereas the *ehwaz* rune refers to the horse itself, *raido* means specifically "the act of riding." Riding implies themes of journeying, movement, and, crucially for traditional Norse and Germanic cultures, the importance of striking out rather than remaining in too much safety and comfort. The Norwegian and Icelandic Rune poems underline this, focusing on the act of riding and the sense of movement this conveys.

In fact, in the Old English Rune poem the contrast between riding a horse "inside a hall" and while "pounding the great mile paths" stresses a common theme of wry humor in Norse thinking: Thoughts, talk, and boasts are easy and often cheap, while deeds of adventure, courage, and valor in the outside world are hard-won. Similar sentiments are found scattered throughout the lays and sagas. As Odin says in *Hávamál* (Saying of the High One): "It takes sharp wits to travel in the world—they're not so hard on you at home."[15]

The Hero's Horse

The Reginn who "forged the best sword" referred to in the Norwegian Rune poem is an important figure in the heroic lays, the foster father and instructor of the hero Sigurd. In the *Volsunga Saga* and *Reginsmál* (The Lay of Reginn), he teaches the boy runelore, arms him with a sword, and prompts him to claim a horse from the king, Gray Beard (a thinly veiled guise of Odin).

> Now Sigurd's foster father was hight [named] Regin, the son of Hreidmar; he taught him all manner of arts, the chess play, and the lore of runes, and the talking of many tongues, even as the wont was with king's sons in those days. . . [One] time came Regin to talk to Sigurd, and said—
>
> "A marvellous thing truly that thou must needs be a horse-boy to the kings, and go about like a running knave."
>
> "Nay," said Sigurd, "it is not so, for in all things I have my will, and whatso thing I desire is granted me with good will."
>
> "Well, then," said Regin, "ask for a horse of them."
>
> "Yea," quoth Sigurd, "and that I shall have, whenso I have need thereof."

Sigurd then goes to the king and is granted his request:

So the next day went Sigurd to the wood, and met on the way an old man, long-bearded, that he knew not, who asked him whither away.

Sigurd said, "I am minded to choose me a horse; come thou, and counsel me thereon."

"Well then," said he, "go we to drive them to the river that is called Busil-tarn."

They did so and drove the horses into the deeps of the river, and swam back to land but one horse; and that horse Sigurd chose for himself; grey he was of hue, and young of years, great of growth, and fair to look on, nor had any man yet crossed his back.

Then spake the grey-beard, "From Sleipnir's kin is this horse come, and he must be nourished heedfully, for it will be the best of horses"; and therewith vanished away.[16]

This mythical subplot demonstrates this rune's link with our gaining of a vehicle that will enable us to move outward into life. The horse is the totemic animal ally that may be enlisted to assist in this process. We might add that this theme was drawn into service by Tolkien in full Northern style in his depiction of the relationship between Gandalf and his steed, Shadowfax.

Riding between the Worlds

On an esoteric level, there are profound shamanistic associations attached to the concept of *riding* that lead us into the domain of the traditional Norse and Germanic spirit world. The shamanistic runologist Kenneth Meadows has this to say of *raido:* "The power of REID [rad] can be felt in the measured rhythm and monotonous beat of the shaman's drum, which 'moves' the awareness on its visionary journey through 'inner' space. This is why REID is associated with the horse, for the drum was often referred to as 'the shaman's horse,' conveying him or her to an awareness of other realities."[17]

Finally, in his quest for the Runes, Odin journeys down the World Tree, Yggdrasil, to its roots. Yggdrasil literally means "Odin's horse"

(*Ygg* being "terrible one" and *drasill* being "horse"). From this arises the theme of Odin "riding" the World Ash, an image that is widely recognized as the shamanic journey to the otherworld. Here "the god of hanged men" rides the ash, or "gallows tree," and thus passes through the gateway into the realm of the dead. The ancestral knowledge of the underworld (including the Runes) thus becomes Odin's, and in these actions, he becomes a symbolic prototype and guide for the runic initiate, who also seeks the knowledge of the nether realms.

Flame: *kenaz* (Torch)

**Names: Gmc *kenaz* (pine torch) or *kaunaz* (ulcer);
Gothic *kusma/chosma* (illumination); OE *cen* (torch);
NRP and IRP *kaun* (ulcer)**

Sound: *k* (as in *candle*)

Correspondence: ulcer

OLD ENGLISH RUNE POEM

*The torch we know by its flame,
which brings illumination and light
wherever noble souls congregate.*

NORWEGIAN RUNE POEM

*Ulcer is the curse of children;
grief turns us pale.*

ICELANDIC RUNE POEM

Ulcer is the bane of children,
and a grievous blight
and the house of rotting flesh.

VISUALIZATION

A pine torch flames in the dark. It illuminates a sacred woodland enclosure beyond.

MEANING

Kenaz, meaning "pine torch," refers to the instrument used to light a hall or outdoor place. It is therefore a symbol of light and illumination. On a personal level, it stands for warmth, friendship, and love. The wisdom of the heart is crucial to happiness, and emotional fulfillment is the omen of this stave in an upright position.

Romantically, *kenaz* can augur being in love—holding a torch for someone. Its flickering flame embodies the dance of feeling in all its finesse and the raw heat of erotic expression. Signifying intensity rather than partnership, it may also relate to more than involvement with another person. *Kenaz* can stand for your creativity or a burning dedication to an outside cause.

Spiritually, the torch represents enlightenment, the brightness of spirit that resides within. It is the inner light that you must tend as you walk through the often dark wastes of the world. Bearing such a torch, you have the power to keep at bay any evils that may assail you. Nor are you alone, for *kenaz* symbolizes unity, the gathering of people in a spirit of harmony. Just think of a circle of friends gathered around a bonfire.

Because of the torch's ancient connection with initiation rituals, it is proverbially linked to learning. We still talk about the torch of learning, the light of knowledge and wisdom that is passed from one generation to another. Such a gift is perhaps being offered to you. All in all, therefore, *kenaz* has a highly positive meaning. It is truly a "brightstave."

Reversed, however, *kenaz* reveals the destructive, biting side of fire. Fire is bright but can burn — in love, in friendship, in war. Sometimes *kenaz* reversed alludes to health issues, the burning inflammation, fever, or ulcer of the Scandinavian Rune poems. A change of diet and lifestyle may be in order if you feel yourself cankered by the world. Seek another source of flame. Nurturing the new light where you find it will bring illumination back into your life.

Keywords: That which is lit, flame itself, the element of fire, heat, warmth, erotic love, illumination, learning, knowledge, gathering, togetherness. *Murkstave:* Blockage of the vital light; the burning, biting aspect of flame; inflammation, fever, ulcer.

MYTHS AND LEGENDS

Norse mythology furnishes us with the cosmic context of fire, which is one of the two primal elements of creation. "Burning ice, biting flame; that is how life began," the Eddic account opens: "In the south is a realm called Muspellheim. It seethes and it shines. No one can endure it except those born into it. Black Surt is there; he sits on the farthest reach of that land, brandishing a flaming sword; he is already waiting for the end when he will rise and savage the gods and whelm the whole world with fire."[18]

Although seething Muspellheim may be reckoned as one of the nine worlds of Norse mythology, and therefore an actual location, it represents a force or principle as much as a physical place. Midgard (Middle Earth, the human realm) was believed to owe its temperate and life-sustaining character to a delicate balance between the primal forces of fire and ice. Thus fire, while inherently dangerous, is, in its positive aspect, life sustaining and promoting.

The Flaming Torch

The torch represents a sort of triumph for humanity because it embodies a measure of control and regulation over the anarchic force of fire, which is temporarily bound and made of service to humankind. Humanity's initial mastery of fire, as myths from around the world show, was a milestone in evolution, a symbolic seizure of power from the realms of the gods. With fire, many possibilities are suddenly open. Food can be cooked on demand, space reclaimed from darkness for practical and creative ends, warmth generated, wild animals kept at arm's length. Before fires could be kindled on demand, they were kept continually burning and were preserved with great care and considerable ritual. Preserving the flame must have taken on sacred associations at an early time, and accrued far-reaching religious symbolism. Ancient Rome maintained its vestal fires, and as Joseph Campbell writes: "Perpetual flames and votive lights are known practically everywhere in developed religious cults."[19] The *kenaz* rune resonates with these associations, for as the Old English Rune poem states: "The torch we know by its flame . . ."

The Faces of Fire

Fire, however, has more than one face in Norse thought. It can be both radiant and baleful, depending on where you sit. In *Alvíssmál* (The Lay of Alvíss), Thór asks the "all-wise" dwarf Alvíss: "What is fire called whose flames men see / in every one of the worlds?" Alvíss replies:

> *Men call it Fire   the Aesir Flame,*
> *for the wise Vanir   it's Warmth*
> *giants say The Ravenous,   dwarves call it Ravager*
> *Hasty it's called   in Hel.*[20]

The "Flame" and "Warmth" of the Aesir and Vanir imply fire civilized and put to service, while the dwarfs, giants, and dead in Hel see the other, devouring face of fire. The terms *ravenous* and *ravager* have also been translated as "Hungry Biter" and "Burner," which corresponds to the *kaun,* or "ulcer," referred to in the Scandinavian Rune poems as a type of inflammation.

This negative, deathly association also flows naturally from the phenomenon of the Viking funeral ship, with its burning pyre, so vividly described by the Arabic traveler and diplomat kidnapped by Viking raiders, Ibn Fa'dlan, in his *Risalah of Ibn Fa'dlan:* "The people then came forward with sticks of firewood. Each one of them had with him a piece of wood, the end of which he had set on fire, and which he now threw upon the wood packed beneath the ship. This spread to the firewood, then to the ship. . . . There then began to blow a mighty and frightful wind, and the fire was intensified, and its blaze flared up."[21]

To Hold a Torch . . .

Yet again, as far as the living are concerned, fire's benefits outweigh the risks. Odin observes in the *Hávamál* (Sayings of the High One):

> *For human beings   the best things are fire,*
> *the sight of the sun,*
> *and to be granted   good health*
> *and to live a blameless life.*[22]

Elsewhere in *Hávamál* he states: "Hotter than fire friendship flames."[23] And apart from the literal functions of warmth, cooking, light, and protection, *kenaz* has corresponding associations in divination of emotional warmth, love, and also erotic experience—which is, after all, to hold a torch for someone.

The esoteric meaning of *kenaz* almost universally accepted in contemporary divination is "the light of illumination." Light has, of course, long functioned as a symbol for divine energy and spiritual vision. These associations are preserved in the modern English words *can*dle and in*can*descence, whose hypothetical common Indo-European root *(kand)* signifies something "white, bright, shining,[24] an obvious symbol for divine consciousness. So it is with *kenaz,* which, overall, embodies a benevolent, enlightening power that shows the way and guides us.

The Torch of Learning

Some runologists have argued that the torch may have figured as a symbol of recognition among the initiated. Thus the Old English Rune poem's reasonably concrete image of "noble souls" (OE *aethlingas, athlings,* or "princes") gathered together becomes a coded reference to the existence of initiatory societies in pagan times and into the so-called Christian era. In modern terms, this image extends to encompass the notion of any kind of spiritual community, a gathering of bright souls in the light of mutual support.

The "light within," then, is linked to the notion of the "torch of learning" of proverbial lore. This association of learning with the torch may be extremely ancient, as it seems likely that the sacred images in the labyrinthine Neolithic cave complexes were revealed to the tribal initiates of prehistoric cults by torchlight; similar practices recur in the classical mystery religions. While there is no evidence for a direct parallel, for this is Norse myth, Odin does link fire to mental agility in the *Hávamál:*

> *Flames from one log   leap to another,*
> *fire kindles fire;*
> *a man's wit   shows in his words,*
> *stupidity is silent.*[25]

Exchange: *gebo* (Gift)

Names: Gmc *gebo* (gift); Gothic *giba/giwa;* OE *gebo/gefu* (gift); common root of modern English "gift." (*Note:* There is no *gebo* stave in the Younger Futhark and therefore no accompanying Norwegian or Icelandic Rune poem.)

Sound: *g* (as in *gift*)

OLD ENGLISH RUNE POEM

*A gift returns to adorn the giver
with greatness and honor; it helps
and heartens those who have nothing.*

VISUALIZATION

Two arms bearing gifts cross each other in a gesture of pledging.

MEANING

Gebo signifies a gift, gifts, or the act of exchange, whether of your goods, time, energy, or love. It counsels you to give generously and without too much expectation, for if by giving we regard the receiver as thereby obligated, then what have we actually parted with?

This does not mean that *gebo* counsels allowing yourself to be taken for granted. As the marvelous wisdom poetry below illustrates, in friendship the exchange should always be equal. The runes do not encourage martyrdom; the hand that takes should be matched by that which bestows. Size or value is not the most important thing, but the impetus behind it. Learn also to receive, for gifts can be great teachers.

Sometimes *gebo* also relates to a sexual and romantic relationship, which, in a mature form, involves a continuous flow of giving and receiving between partners. You can even see in the shape of the rune a union of two staves, joined at the hip, as it were, in a kind of model of sharing and exchange. Similarly, love and friendship are types of ongoing exchange in which each person cultivates his or her own gifts in order to be able to share more fully with the other.

In wider spiritual terms, *gebo* expresses the bond between the parts and the whole that characterizes the divine gift of life itself. It hearkens to the web of interconnection and sacrifice that binds creation into its immeasurable and immaterial fabric. In ancient times, this vision led to the need to sacrifice to the gods—in one way or another—in recognition of their gifts to humanity. Perhaps you are being called upon to make such a votive offering.

Gebo is not a reversible rune, but ill placed in a reading it may signify a blockage in the area of giving and receiving in your life. Who is at fault, you or the other party? Visualize the principle of exchange, on a material or an emotional level, as a constant stream of energy that flows to and from you unceasingly. Tend the flow unstintingly.

Keywords: Giving or receiving a gift, exchange, receiving the gifts of Odin, the need to make an offering, sacrificing. (*Note: Gebo* is not reversible.)

mYTHS AND LEGENDS

This rune reflects the all-important custom of gift giving held by the ancient Germanic and Norse cultures. In early divination, *gebo* doubtless augured the receiving of a gift or the need to bestow gifts upon others. A custom central to the pagan Northern world, gift giving cemented the bonds of friendship and community and was rooted in the paramount significance that was given to the tribe or group to which one belonged. As such, generosity was one of the noblest of virtues, a reflection of the status of the giver and essential to esteem in the eyes of others.

Gift giving also undoubtedly had a cultic significance. In lands where the worlds of the gods interpenetrate the middle world of men and women, the notion of reciprocal gift giving extended beyond that between people to encompass sacrifices to (and gifts received from) the divine realms. Apart from animal and sometimes human sacrifice, votive offerings and the dedication of one's service were the principle forms of gifting to the gods. As in the Celtic world, one of the main sources of artifacts from the ancient Germanic and Norse world comes from votive offerings left in shrines, graves, rivers, bogs, and lakes.

The Aesir and Vanir gods and goddesses are notable in Norse

religion for their gifts to humankind. Although the gods could be capricious, ultimately all blessings flowed from their realms. Odin and his "brothers" (really aspects of the one All Father) give humankind "breath, blood, and senses," and it is Odin who makes the supreme sacrifice in order to win the wisdom of the Runes, which he then offers as a gift to those who choose to draw upon them. Thór defends Midgard against giants; the god Heimdall offers the gift of fertility. Vanir deities such as Frey, Freya, and Njórd bestow the boon of wealth in the form of the fruits of the land and sea. The World Tree Yggdrasil ultimately feeds all beings. So a wider reading of *gebo* incorporates the principle of giving and sacrifice as an eternal cycle that binds together the fabric of the nine worlds.

Gift for Gift

The great and fundamental significance of gift giving is celebrated in many sources, literary and historical. In *Hávamál* (Sayings of the High One), whose "wisdom verses" doubtless reflect much older oral traditions, Odin advises the listener:

> *I've never met   a man so generous*
> *you couldn't give him a gift. . . .*

> *Give your friends gifts—   they're as glad as you are*
> *to wear new clothes and weapons;*
> *frequent giving   makes friendships last,*
> *if the exchange is equal.*

> *A man should keep faith   with his friends always,*
> *returning gift for gift;*
> *Laughter should be   the reward of laughter,*
> *lying of lies.*[26]

The last verse makes obvious that underlying the act of giving is the principle of like for like: Just as a gift demanded a gift, an insult demanded recompense. To question the hospitality of a host was one of the greatest slights that could be offered, tantamount to a battle challenge.

In *Vafþrúðnismál* (The Lay of Vathrúdnir), Odin implies that the giant Vathrúdnir is "a cold hearted host." The giant replies by asking the god if he'd rather try his luck "with both feet on the floor"—that is, in a trial of strength.[27]

The Lifted Goblet

The second half of the Old English Rune poem for this rune asserts that *gebo* "helps and heartens" (literally "aids and assists") those who have nothing. In Germanic, Norse, and Anglo-Saxon cultures, a chief or person of rank could demonstrate his status by the giving of gifts to the poor or vagrant. The rune scholar Ralph Elliot comments that *gebo* may have related to "gifts presented by a chief to trusty and loyal followers."[28] In fact, there was a measure of social responsibility (fueled by self-interest in one's chiefly status) to do this. These pagan notions were later overlaid by the Christian duty of almsgiving, but in both cases it provides a model of generosity from the haves to the have-nots in society, roles today filled by redistributive taxation, welfare agencies, and charities.

We should always repay service offered to us, the wisdom tradition states, but the gift need not be overly grand. As Odin says in *Hávamál:*

> *You don't have to give   large gifts always*
> *small things often suffice;*
> *half a loaf   and a lifted goblet*
> *have found me friends.*[29]

This is a wonderful affirmation of friendship and exchange and takes on added significance for many contemporary Pagans, for whom a chalice and ritual loaf are shared within the ceremonial circle. As a general augury, *gebo* suggests that the gifts you give and receive, on all realms, will prove sufficient to the occasion.

Bliss: *wunjo* (Joy)

Names: Gmc *uunio* (joy); **Gothic** *winja/winne;* **OE** *huun.* (*Note:* There is no *wunjo* stave in the Younger Futhark and therefore no accompanying Norwegian or Icelandic Rune poem.)

Sound: *w* (as in *win*)

OLD ENGLISH RUNE POEM

Joy comes to you who know no sorrow,

blessed with gain and plenty,

content in a strong community.

VISUALIZATION

A village on a hilltop surrounded by fields rich with grain is framed by the rising summer sun.

MEANING

Wunjo represents joy, the unalloyed state of pleasure and bliss. It is both the simple, unbidden moment of happiness and the more lasting condition of fulfillment. Joy would seem to need little explanation, except to say that in Norse culture it was specifically linked to a sense of community. As the saying goes, pleasure shared is pleasure doubled.

At this time, your projects and undertakings grow and prosper. Happiness flows from favorable involvements, both personal and professional. Although joy cannot be pinned down, conditions are ripe for deepening and extending your relationship with the things in life that bring you joy. This is a sign of blessings and plenty.

Wunjo is also a "wishing rune" used in rune magic to manifest wishes in conjunction with other runes, depending on the particulars of what is being sought. It is also used to invoke happiness in general. Spellcraft and other white magic can be wonderful aids to promoting your affairs, when approached in the right spirit. You can inscribe *wunjo* onto an object connected with some desire to be fulfilled, though it helps to link it to another rune that covers the specific area concerned, so as to create a bind rune.

Reversed, *wunjo* suggests a blockage in the flow of joy in your life. What attitudes, opinions, preconceptions, or negative programming may be interfering with your ability to experience joy? Reach out to others, remembering that a positive attitude actually attracts good fortune. It is imperative not to become bowed by negativity. Last, avoid a joyless situation or occupation that provides superficial security. Without happiness, any other benefit is hollow and useless. In Joseph Campbell's words, follow your bliss!

Keywords: The unalloyed state of joy, happiness, bliss, fulfillment, especially as these relate to a group or community; a happy, joyful time. *Murkstave:* Unhappiness, misery, blighted experience, loneliness.

MYTHS AND LEGENDS

It seems obvious that this rune functioned as a good omen in early divination rituals, as it does today. "Gain and plenty" are highly favorable auguries. "Gain" implies increase and relates especially to the image of things growing. The term *plenty* is linked to peace and prosperity. The fact that you are "blessed" with these things suggests favor from the gods.

Joy is set in direct contrast to sorrow in the Old English Rune poem, which, apart from the obvious, reflects the fact that a buoyant, carefree state of mind was held to be a virtue by the Anglo-Saxon and Norse cultures. It also serves as a warning against becoming too mired in negativity, for a buoyant outlook clearly encourages bracing yourself and wading through the trials of existence rather than succumbing to self-pity or psychological paralysis.

The only proviso for the concept of joy is that the original Viking, Germanic, and later Anglo-Saxon derivative from *wunjo*, *wyn* (which has a common root with the modern English *win* and *venerable*), has some quite specific associations. *Wunjo* is sometimes translated as "clan joy," reflecting the notion that joy is to be had not in isolation but, so to speak, in the bosom of one's peers—or in a "strong community," in the words of the Rune poem.

Wishing Runes

When the opening line of the Rune poem states that "joy comes to you who know no sorrow," it implies that through positivity we actually attract good fortune to ourselves, an ancient affirmation of the value of positive thinking. Moreover, it is suggestive of *wunjo*'s role as a charm rune, evidence of which survived into Old English, for the linguistic roots of OE *wyn* link it to terms meaning "to wish," "to desire," and, crucially, "to obtain."[30]

Just as "victory runes" could be used as an aid in war, so benevolent runes can be used to promote success and happiness. As the Valkyrie maiden instructs Sigurd in *Sigdrífomál* (The Lay of Sigdrífa) regarding the "runes of joy":

> *Whoever holds them   unbroken, unchanged,*
> *Will have good luck*
> *And be glad of his lore*
> *Until the day of doom.*[31]

Joy and Wisdom

Like madness and sanity, there is a fine line and, perhaps, potential conflict between wisdom and joy. How should we balance celebration with seriousness? In this case Odin has the last word on the subject, for as he says in *Hávamál* (Sayings of the High One):

> *Moderately wise   a man should be—*
> *don't wish for too much wisdom;*
> *a man's heart   is seldom happy*
> *if he is truly wise.*

> *Moderately wise   a man should be—*
> *don't wish for too much wisdom;*
> *if you can't see far   into the future,*
> *you can live free from care.*[32]

HAGAL'S AETT

Disruption: *hagalaz* (Hail)

Names: Gmc *hagalas* (hail, sleet); **Gothic** *hagl/haal;*
OE *hagal;* **NRP and IRP** *hagall* (hail); common root
of modern English "hail"

Sound: *h* (as in *hail*)

Correspondence: hail

OLD ENGLISH RUNE POEM

Hail, whitest of grains, whirls down from heaven,
is tossed by the wind, and turns to water.

NORWEGIAN RUNE POEM

Hail is the coldest of grains;
All Father shaped the world in ancient times.

ICELANDIC RUNE POEM

Hail is a cold grain
and a shower of sleet,
and the bane of snakes.

VISUALIZATION

Hail falls, blighting a landscape of farms and fields; a haglike face forms in the sky.

MEANING

Hagalaz, meaning "hail," is a rune of disruption and delay. It suggests a potentially frustrating time, when your plans are hit by unforeseen difficulties. If we picture our progress in life as being like passing through a landscape, this is the point where you have to stop and take shelter until conditions improve. Only a fool would fail to heed the warning of the elements.

Hail stands as a hoary, hostile force in Norse thought and experience. In the daily life of peasants, small farmers, and warriors alike, the cold white grain falling from the sky was a bane in winter and an ever present threat in all seasons. Hail has the power to blight crops, render a familiar landscape unpassable, and stymie seagoing voyages. Archetypally, it is a manifestation of the dark, haglike aspect of Mother Earth, betokening dangerous or damaging forces in nature and the sudden, undeserved misfortune they bring.

These unfavorable conditions could take form in any area of your life, personal, interpersonal, or professional, but *hagalaz* especially relates to difficulties with present projects. You may have to rethink some plan or could already be wrapped up in frustrations.

Things are not all bad, however. Although *hagalaz* is widely regarded as an omen of sudden change, disruption, or delay (just as hail may cause merchants or travelers to postpone or even abandon their plans), it does have a more buoyant outcome than seems possible. In the last line of the Old English Rune poem we read that hail ultimately "turns to water." This is literally true, of course, but the implications extend further.

Hail turns to water with the rise of the life-giving sun, and water is itself a flowing, fertilizing aspect of the life force. Similarly, emotional blockages are often resolved by tears, which dissolve like rain in the light of a new day. Indeed, we can note here that the final rune in Hagal's Aett is *sowulo,* the sun. So however challenging, *hagalaz* provides a lesson in the cyclical nature of fortune and misfortune: how a baneful event may later become a source of luck or even — in the light of understanding — growth.

Keywords: Hail, a hostile element; disruption, change, delay, and even cancellation of plans, though the difficulty may be temporary. (*Note: Hagalaz* is not reversible.)

MYTHS AND LEGENDS

Living in such a harsh, uncompromising landscape, the Norse knew the extremes of the elements only too well. In the Eddic creation account from Iceland, there are two primal powers in existence "in the beginning." Muspellheim, land of fire, lay to the south; Niflheim, land of ice, lay to the north. Between them was Ginnungagap, "a gaping emptiness . . . nowhere green," in the words of the great mythological poem *Völuspá.*[33] The creator who "shaped the world in ancient times" out of this void is named in the unrepaganized Norwegian Rune poem as Christ, which is absurd because he does not even create the world in Christian mythology. This is surely a transparent gloss on Odin, for it was he who vanquished the frost giant Ymir and, with his body parts, set about constructing a more habitable world.

But before the emergence of life, this void, Ginnungagap, was sluiced by eleven terrible rivers whose "yeasty venom" created slag, ice, and hail. As Kevin Crossley-Holland elaborates from the *Prose Edda:* "That venom . . . spat out drizzle — an unending hagger [hail] that, as soon as it settled, turned to rime. So it went on until all the northern part of Ginnungagap was heavy with layers of ice and hoar frost, a desolate place haunted by gusts and skuthers of wind."[34]

Out of this rime Midgard—Middle Earth—sprang into being. Thus hail, like ice, is linked to the creation of the world and was seen as a type of sacred ur-matter, or cosmic substance, a building block of creation. The Rune poems reflect its pristine beauty, but in practical, human terms, the *hagalaz* rune makes us mindful of the extreme forces of the elemental void that predate human life.

Urd and the Norns

This and the next two staves, *naudiz* (need) and *isa* (ice), form a triad of menacing runes that embody forces indifferent, dangerous, or hostile to humanity. As the Rune poems reflect, each has associations with the cold, harsh elements of winter. Hail, then, is kept good company by frost and ice. In contemporary divination, these staves are often associated with the three Norns, the triple goddesses of fate known as Urd (fate), Verdandi (necessity), and Skuld (being). Their somewhat somber role as Norse harbingers of fate is thus reflected in these runes.

In the case of *hagalaz*, the white grain that falls from the heavens, like the will of the sovereign goddesses of fate, is a capricious element that can strike at any time. We must accept its portents or run the risk of having to contend with worse conditions. *Hagalaz* can be identified with Urd, the Norn of fate itself, for this is a stave of fateful difficulties. Urd, oldest of the Norns, recalls the archetype of the crone, the hag, the dark sorceress. As Freya Asswyn points out, the word *hagalaz* is linked with the High German *hatchel* (witch) and the Anglo-Saxon *haegtessa* (hag). This connects the stave with the realm of Hel and its ruler, the goddess Hella, the embodiment of "dark feminine power . . . negative witchcraft, [and] destructive female magic."[35] This does not, however, mean that hail or Urd or the crone archetype is evil. Without the challenges they place in our path, growth would never occur. Moreover, as the powers of winter loosen their grip with the coming of spring, the trials of the dark season ultimately resolve themselves into a fruitful result.

Weather Runes

On the surface, the first four runes of Hagal's Aett all seem to be concerned with weather: The connection of *hagalaz* and *isa* (ice) is unambiguous, while the Norwegian Rune poem links the next stave, *naudiz,* to frost. The forth rune in this row, *jera,* represents a year or annual cycle, but more specifically harvesttime—summer or late summer. If you think of the rather bleak nature of the agricultural year in northern Europe, with its long desolate winters and poignantly brief summers, the proportions match those of this set of four runes rather well. The rune scholar Ralph Elliot saw weather prediction as a function of the runes in divination, with several esoteric runologists following suit. It certainly seems logical that in a society as subject to intense elemental forces as that of the Norse, this would be both a practical use of runes and a priority in the survival stakes.

My own experience has shown me that runes certainly do resonate with weather conditions. Once I was reading runes on a strip of grass in a marketplace framed by a charming quadrangle of Gothic facades. It had been a beautiful sunny day until shortly before, but then gray clouds began to form overhead and I came to the decision that it was time to pack up. As I was leaving, I decided on impulse to pull a single rune from its leather pouch—something I seldom do. I was a little displeased to see *hagalaz* appear in my hand and began to wonder what sort of irritation or delay I could expect. Running through a list of possibilities in my mind, I was suddenly distracted by a kind of din in the distance. Looking around, I could see no immediate cause for this faint but growing tumult. At that moment I entered a courtyard and could now see what appeared to be a gray curtain drawing itself across the sky. Suddenly the tumult became an uproar as the violent hailstorm—as I quickly realized it to be—hit the roofs of the row of houses across the street. Then it was upon me and I had to run for shelter as huge hailstones began to hit the pavement. It struck me—as I was in turn struck on the head—that here was the answer to my question as to the signification of the *hagalaz* stave I'd pulled a few minutes before. I always look back on the incident as a lesson in not being too abstract or esoteric in interpreting the runes. Sometimes they can be surprisingly literal.

Constraint: *naudiz* (Need)

Names: Gmc *nauthiz* (need); Gothic *nauths/noics;*
OE *nod/nyd;* NRP *nauthr* (need); IRP *nauth* (need);
common root of modern English "need"

Sound: *n* (as in *need*)

Correspondence: service

OLD ENGLISH RUNE POEM

Need constricts the heart but can bring help
and healing, if heeded in time.

NORWEGIAN RUNE POEM

Need leaves one little choice;
the naked freeze in the frost.

ICELANDIC RUNE POEM

Need is the bondmaid's grief,
and a hard condition to suffer,
and toilsome work.

VISUALIZATION

A bondmaid toils in service at the task of washing linen in a cold, running stream.

MEANING

Naudiz warns of hardship and constraint. Lying between the oppressive staves of *hagalaz* (hail) and *isa* (ice), it pairs two unpleasant aspects: suffering and the inability to act. You are in a difficult, restrictive situation with little room to move. Even with hard work and toil, conditions seem difficult to improve. Struggle may just tighten the bonds, so act with caution.

Naudiz represents what is sometimes described as a "karmic challenge." The Norse parallel is *wyrd,* the force that dictates our individual fate path. The shadow side of *wyrd* appears when difficult events cluster in a tangled web, sometimes of our own making, within which we are held fast. This is extremely uncomfortable but may prompt us to question easy assumptions and finally face issues we attempt to ignore.

Present conditions may, of course, seem outside your control, but in psychological terms, *naudiz* is linked to the way in which our own neuroses generate negative experiences. Thus "external" events may in fact spring in part from your own restrictive internal programming. Belief systems, often unconscious, based on life's disappointments, biases inherited from parents and society, and our own fears and limitations, can condition us to expect (and therefore attract) crisis after crisis.

In relationships, *naudiz* spells compulsion or obsession. Grief may result. At work or in business, everything is an uphill struggle. You may be under severe stress, to the point that coping becomes difficult. Perhaps it is time to bow to the inevitable—for *naudiz* also means "necessity"—and take a new tack in life.

In health, this is a warning. Take heed of any signs your body may give. *Naudiz* is described as constricting the heart (literally, "narrow on the breast") in the Old English Rune poem. This can sometimes relate to heart disease, high blood pressure, or some other accumulative or stress-related illness. Yet the heart here functions not just as a physical organ but also as a symbol of the inner being. Its "constriction" suggests that you are concerned, careworn, or pinched of soul.

Help may, however, be at hand. The Old English Rune poem tells us that, like a venom that can sometimes be used as an antidote, need can "bring healing" (OE *haele*—literally, "to heal," "to make whole") if heeded in time. This implies that the emotional state of need, brought about by life's constraints, can ultimately be overcome. Acknowledge your bonds. Meditate on their roots. Recognize the pattern. Do not strain against the knots; simply unpick them with painstaking care. Believe that you are capable of self-transformation; nothing less will suffice.

Keywords: Hardship, constraint, constriction, necessity, being bound, inability to act, karmic challenge, negative events, discomfort, spiritual inoculation, healing, untying the knots, acceptance, transformation of perception. (*Note: Naudiz is not reversible.*)

mYTHS AnD LEGEnDS

This rune embodies an abstract concept rather than an object, animal, or deity. Need was experienced in Norse and Anglo-Saxon cultures as a severe and challenging condition. In one early Saxon literary source we read *"Ned bith wyrda heardost"* (Need is the worst lot—or fate—one can obtain in life). *Nyd (*an Old English term for *naudiz)* is elsewhere referred to as an *enge rune* (constraining rune) associated with the experience of *nearusorg* (oppressive grief).[36] This rune therefore embodies the idea of a fate in life that constrains the receiver within the condition of hardship and need.

As mentioned above, the Old English Rune poem describes *nyd* as constricting the heart, while in the Norwegian Rune poem we read that need "leaves one little choice." Together, these paint a picture of a person in difficulty with few options, laboring under restrictions, having to bow to a hostile fate or to the sovereign force of necessity itself. "The naked freeze in the frost" is a naturalistic enough observation, which also implies that the heart and human happiness freeze under the restraints of *naudiz*. The harsh-sounding Icelandic Rune poem offers the figure of the bondmaid (basically a slave girl with no say whatsoever in her fate) as the symbol of need. As we will see below, this is in all likelihood a reference to a scene from the celebrated *Volsunga Saga* in which a king's daughter is forced to disguise herself as a bondmaid in the midst of many griefs. Yet the reference in the Old English Rune poem to *nyd* as a help "if heeded in time" also conveys the sense of hope and challenge embodied in this rune. Even the description of *naudiz* as a "hard condition" and "toilsome work" can be read more positively as the burden of transforming our perspective toward outer circumstances, where these cannot be altered.

Because of the abstract, conceptual nature of this rune, there are a number of mythological and legendary themes that we can relate to it, rather than a single episode, and these are explored below in some detail.

Fetters and Slings

We can begin by contrasting several types of bondage in Norse myth: those concerning the All Father, Odin; those having to do with the malignant Fenris wolf; and those related to the guileful trickster Loki. In the *Runatal* Odin descends the World Ash, Yggdrasil, and comes to Mímir's Well. Here he must undergo a kind of triple-death ritual of hanging, wounding, and drowning. Much is made of Odin's sacrifice of an eye, self-mutilation with a spear, and tortured delving into the depths, but little of his binding himself to a branch of Yggdrasil. Odin, presumably, ties one of his legs to a bough, presenting for us an archetypal image of a man bound in a drama of self-sacrifice. Thus, although this binding is an oppressive lot, it has a positive function as part of the High One's path of initiation and may have formed one piece of a ritual complex undergone by runic initiates.

This can be contrasted with two less ennobling episodes. The first is the binding of the Fenris wolf by the gods. The *Prose Edda* tells of how they must employ trickery in order to bind Fenris, whose blood cannot be spilled in the holy realm of Ásgard. The gods resolve to trick him in the following manner: Fenris has already broken through two mighty chains named Laeding and Dromi. The situation is becoming desperate, and the gods press the dwarfs of Svartálfheim into service. They use all their skill and magic to create a noose called Gleipnir, made of such rare ingredients as the footfall of cats, beard of a woman, roots of a mountain, sinews of a bear, breath of a fish, and spittle of a bird. This deception is eventually successful (though at the expense of the god Týr; see the *Tiwaz* stave) and the evil wolf is kept in check until Ragnaroc. Odin, king of the gods, undergoes a voluntary binding, whereas the gruesome Fenris wolf must be bound through trickery.

Finally, Loki illustrates a more ribald form of the binding theme when he attaches one end of a sling to a he-goat and the other to his testicles in order to amuse the giantess Skadi. Given Loki's overtly sexualized nature, this capering about might best be described as an act of primordial fetishism!

The Grief of the Bondmaid

The "bondmaid's grief" referred to in the Icelandic Rune poem is understandable enough, given that the lot of the menial serfs and slaves in Viking times, which the poem harks back to, was hardly to be envied. Women, in particular, who were caught in the violent raids for which the Vikings were infamous could expect a harsh lot of physical servitude, in more than one sense of the term. Yet the term *bondmaid* could also refer to the ladies surrounding and servile to a queen or other important personage. Even so, their own needs would be totally sublimated to their ruler's.

There may, however, be a more specific allusion here to the *Volsunga Saga,* as is often the case in the Scandinavian Rune poems. There we meet the princess Hjordas, daughter of King Eylimi, whose hand is sought by both King Lyngi and Sigmund of the Volsungs. Triangular love was a dangerous thing for all concerned in the Viking age. Sigmund wins his suit in the end, but Lyngi, slighted and smarting from his rejection, gathers an army that slays both Hjordas's new-found husband, Sigmund, and her father, Eylimi. Bound to this terrible fate, she laments over her father's body as he utters his dying words—"I go to see our kin that have gone before me"—at the break of day. Then, seeing a fleet of longships sailing in to land and fearing another invasion force, she turns to her bondmaid and says, "Let us now change raiment, and be thou called by my name, and say that thou art the king's daughter."[37] In other words, they exchange clothes and switch identities. This deception helps her to find safety (and ultimately marriage) at the hands of King Alf, but her grief became proverbial for this sort of misfortune and may well be the "bondmaid's grief" referred to in the poem above.

Verdandi and the Norns

Finally, like *hagalaz* and *isa, naudiz* points to the often restrictive force of fate. In Norse mythology, the goddesses of fate are the Norns, who directly parallel the Greek Fates (the sisters who spin, measure, and cut the threads of life). They find a later echo in Shakespeare's "weird sisters"—the three witches of *Macbeth*. The oldest of the Norns, Urd (fate, the force of *wyrd*), presides over the past, that which "had to be"; the second, Verdandi (necessity), rules over what is "coming to be"; and the third, Skuld (being), dictates the future, that which "has to be."

Naudiz corresponds, in my estimation, to Verdandi, for she is the queen of necessity and rules over our coming into being in the world and the unfolding of our unique *wyrd* (or fate path), including its necessities and constraints. This can be translated as the particular psychological complexes (needs, compulsions, neuroses) from which individuals struggle to free themselves. We could call them "nornic" challenges, with the term *nornic* taken to mean something like "karmic."

A particularly common theme in the lays and sagas, also found in Celtic mythology, is the "doom" (or magical taboo) under which the hero lives, a set of constraints, prohibitions, and obligations peculiar to that individual. Such taboos—such as not being allowed to eat a particular animal or shirk from a battle—set certain boundaries on one's actions that, if respected, preserved one from danger and destruction. When broken, however, they spelled disaster. This teaches us that constraint or restriction may in some cases be a limiting condition from which we rightfully seek to break free. At the same time, there are certain restraints we should observe, for they are present to preserve our well-being.

Danger: *isa* (Ice)

Names: Gmc *isa* (ice); Gothic *eis/iiz;* OE *iss;* NRP *is* (ice); IRP *iss* (ice); common root of modern English "ice"

Sound: *e* (as in *sleet*)

Correspondence: ice

OLD EnGLISH RUnE POEM

Ice is cold and slippery;
jewel-like and glistening,
fair to behold, the frozen field.

NORWEGIAN RUnE POEM

Ice we call the broad bridge;
the blind need to be led across.

ICELAnDIC RUnE POEM

Ice is the rind of the river
and roof of the waves,
and a mortal danger.

VISUALIZATION

An ice maiden enshrined in a frigid landscape stares out with pale, cold eyes; behind her Bifrost, the rainbow bridge, arcs skyward.

MEANING

Isa means "ice," the most hostile of all elements in Norse thought. It is a symbol of stasis, emotional frigidity, and generally "icy" conditions. You are in risky territory, feeling the cold, frozen in your tracks, or perhaps skating wildly out of control. There is danger in the situation, so be attentive to the *isa* rune's counsel.

In the frozen North, ice was a seasonal affliction that intruded with painful regularity to rob the community of fertile land, warmth, and comfort. Coinciding with the darkness of the long Northern winter, it was a terrible force to contend with, constantly threatening to catch the unwary off guard. Think of Norse mythology, where the warlike frost giants inhabit icy Niflheim, land of perpetual ice and snow.

In contemporary divination, *isa* implies that a person is locked in a kind of stasis. Emotionally, the deep freeze is on, whether you are the victim or perpetrator of unyielding coldness. Sexually, frustration and even frigidity are augured. Financially, poverty may be the creeping ice that robs you of contentment.

In spiritual terms, you have reached a deadlock, bound in the coils of a crisis of the soul. Try to remain open to change and movement; beware of dogmatic perspectives that shut you out from the warmth of living truth. Psychologically, you may be suffering from a seemingly intractable complex, an incarcerating fixation that appears almost impossible to shake.

Further examples of *isa*'s implacable grip include unrequited love, separation, imprisonment, drug addiction, and even psychosis—in fact, any hostile state that is utterly rigid and unyielding. Whatever the condition, you are held in its thrall. Ice has an insidious, even entrapping, beauty, and similarly, you may be blind to danger, fascinated by the very thing that immobilizes and robs you of life. You must beware of false appearances that seduce your senses.

However, in the seasonal cycle, even ice eventually melts with the coming of spring, and so *isa* can indicate that after a long cycle of stasis and standstill a thaw will ultimately come, and with it new life. To achieve this, it is essential to draw away from any entrapments. The warmth of light and love are needed to break the icy grip. Thus the very conditions that torment you can ultimately become the bridge to renewal.

Keywords: Stasis, contraction, danger, frigidity, coldness, deadlock, entrapment, seductive beauty, conditions thawing, new life, renewal. (*Note: Isa* is not reversible.)

MYTHS AND LEGENDS

In the Eddic creation account, there are three primordial realms: Muspellhcim, land of fire, in the south; Ginnungagap, the void or middle ground, and Niflheim—literally, "ice world"—in the north. Although icy Niflheim has a definite aura of foreboding about it in Norse myth, it was nonetheless out of the extremes of ice and heat that life emerged. The ice of Niflheim formed a kind of rime that proved fertile when it met with the warmth from the south:

> Just as the Northern part was frozen, the southern was molten and glowing, but the middle part of Ginnungagap was mild as hanging air on a summer evening. There, the warm breath from the south met the rime from Niflheim; it touched it and played over it, and the ice began to thaw and drip. Life quickened in those drops, and they took the form of a giant. His name was Ymir.[38]

The birth of the *rime-thurs* (frost giants) represents the entry of the first, crude consciousness from out of the primeval ur-realms. The frost giants' domination of the world represents an archaic era of hostile, if pristine, powers. Next emerged the primal cow, Audumla, from the melting ice, and she liberated the form of Búri, Odin's grandfather, from a block of ice by licking it. Thus a fertile tension between the two poles of creation (ice and fire) is reached.

From these facts, a picture of a Norse belief in "ice as the cosmic ur-matter,"[39] the originating substance of all life, has also been built up—unsurprising in a creation account that stems from Iceland. This motif might also reflect some distant racial memory of the return of pastoralists to the fertile fields that blossomed after the close of the last ice age some ten thousand years ago. Furthermore, the seasonal emergence of vegetation from ice every summer must have under-lined the perception of ice as a harsh element out of which new life could nonetheless arise as the sun made the land fruitful again. And, too, melted ice (water) is the primordial element from which life emerged; scientists now believe that this happened near a volcanic vent, where jets of warm water from Muspellheim's realm may have fostered primitive microorganisms.

Skadi—Frost Giantess

Skadi is a frost giantess who traverses the frosty wastes on snowshoes and embodies their primal hostility. In the *Prose Edda*, it is told how Skadi is married to the sea and fertility god Njórd, after mistakenly choosing him over Balder in a lineup of gods in which only their feet were visible. Although she stands by her decision, Skadi ultimately comes to despise Njórd's fertile and fruitful realm, just as he cannot abide her windswept haunts. This trying relationship, which is paral-leled in the frustrated union between the god Frey and a giantess, Gerthr, represents the conflict between the fertile powers of land and sea and the death-dealing dominions of ice. Frey must wait nine months (representing the interminable Nordic winter) before he can consum-mate his love for the frosty Gerthr, while Skadi eventually disbands her alliance with Njórd and returns to her own icy domain. The dark and light aspects of the year remain implacable opposites, it seems.

Skadi's name literally means "destruction," which reminds us of the Icelandic Rune poem when it notes that ice is a "mortal danger," elsewhere translated as the "destruction of doomed men."[40] Though she was once an object of worship, hers was by all accounts a chilly cult. She warns: "From my shrines and fields will cold counsel ever come to you."[41]

While these lines may be Christian propaganda against following so heathen a figure, the theme of the ice maiden versus the powers of light is widespread in the North, as reflected in the Finnish *Kalevala*, in which Mistress Louhi of the arctic North battles against the magician god Vainamoinen. Given the nature of the territory, it would seem logical that a female divinity of the land could be depicted in these terms. Skadi may, in passing, have lent her name to *Scandi*navia.

Skuld and the Norns

Isa is the most challenging of the first three runes of Hagal's Aett *(hagalaz, naudiz,* and *isa)*. These staves have been linked by some commentators to the elemental fate goddesses known as the Norns, who are similar to and, some scholars argue, inspired by the Greek Fates. Just as Urd, the crone, represents the past and Verdandi, the mother, is the present, Skuld embodies that which is to come. Skuld, who would correspond to *isa,* was regarded as a singularly hostile Norn. She is the maiden or virgin. Presiding over the future, Skuld's pronouncements on what "has to be" are as rigid and immutable as ice. We must recall that the Norse tended to hold a rather resigned view of the future, regarding it as more fixed than we are generally prepared to accept today. The rigid, incarcerating character of *isa* clearly corresponds well to their notions.

Skuld could be said, in Jungian terms, to embody the shadow side of the virgin archetype. She represents separateness, a lack of engagement, so to speak, with the affairs of human beings, and this very purity makes her fiercely dangerous. This is the quality we allude to when talking of "virgin forest": the untamed, pristine aspect of the wilderness that should be respected as such. There is also a coldness to virginity that is thrown into relief when we think of things sexual and erotic in terms of heat and fire. The connection between extreme cold and a lack of sexual fulfillment is, of course, embodied in the word *frigidity*. For this reason, *isa* does not augur well in friendship, love, or other kinds of partnership, at least until the cold snap has played itself out.

The Broad Bridge

The Old English Rune poem stresses the beguiling aspect of ice—its glistening, gemlike appearance and the beauty of a field covered in frost. And yet there is something sinister in the action of ice as it silently yet irresistibly blankets all life beneath it. Similarly, we must beware of the fatal attraction of things that, however enthralling they may be, conspire to entrap us.

Yet the Norwegian Rune poem also sings *isa*'s praise: As the "broad bridge," ice did have the important function of solidifying stretches of water, thus enabling them to be crossed—no minor convenience in the frozen North. This connects *isa* with Norse mythology's Bifrost Bridge, the mother of all bridges, also known as the rainbow bridge, a mystical pathway that connects Midgard and Ásgard and is guarded by the god Heimdall. When you think about it, a rainbow is merely a vaporized form of water—as doubtless the pagan Norse could observe when the sun shone on their pristine waterfalls—and is ultimately made of the same stuff as ice. Bifrost allows gods to travel to Middle Earth to walk and talk with men and women, and it may similarly allow us glimpses of the domain of the gods. Similarly, harsh experiences can lead to incredible breakthroughs, to insights that are otherwise impossible. In the shamanic tradition, we find there were many acts of asceticism practiced in order to bring about a transcendent state of consciousness, including sitting or lying in snow and ice in a state of trance. The shaman thus passes over into the otherworld. The lesson in this is that elemental extremes, however uncomfortable, are used in a number of cultures to shock the initiate into higher levels of perception in order to awaken us to our senses. This is the type of teaching embodied in *isa*.

Harvesttime: *jera* (Year)

Names: Gmc *jera* (year); **Gothic** *jer/gaar;* **OE** *ger;*
NRP *ar* (harvest); **IRP** *ar* (summer); common root of
modern English "year"

Sound: *y* (as in *year*)

Correspondence: year

OLD ENGLISH RUNE POEM

Harvesttime brings joy
when the goddess Earth
gifts us with her bright fruits.

NORWEGIAN RUNE POEM

Harvesttime brings bounty;
I say that Frothi is generous!

ICELANDIC RUNE POEM

Harvesttime brings profit,
and a high summer
and a ripened field.

VISUALIZATION

A woman bearing the sphere of the earth in her belly stoops to pick the
flowers and fruits of a field.

MEANING

Jera is a rune of gain grounded in effort. Meaning "year," it refers not so much to the full annual cycle as specifically to the harvest season— the growing time when the earth becomes fertile and the fields ripe. This is a sign of generally fruitful conditions, the harvesttime when your efforts come to fruition. *Jera* indicates that you will be blessed with plenty, particularly in matters that have involved much ground work—planting and cultivating—to reach maturity.

Jera comes directly after the three harsh, wintry staves of *hagalaz, naudiz,* and *isa,* thus conveying the sense of relief that accompanies the arrival of spring and summer after cold hard days. It is the return of life, the blossoming of nature, and the bounty of the harvest. *Jera* originally meant "fertile season" or "harvesttime," and we can translate this in modern terms as a fruitful time, crowned with prosperity and success. Now is a particularly favorable moment for harvesting the potential in involvements that have ripened into fullness.

The Rune poems provide the images of earth offering her harvest fruits, flowing from a ripened field. As the *fehu* rune teaches, the earth is the source of all abundance. Here the "ripened field" represents the field of life you have chosen to put your energy into and promises you reward. Your sweat and toil have not been in vain; the fruits are ripening.

The god Frey, praised under the title Frothi in the Norwegian Rune poem, is an earth god whom the Norse invoked for his bountiful generosity. He and his sister Freya are the lord and lady of Norse religion who bestow favor and plenty upon the matter at hand. Growth as well as gain are augured in the area of your life within which this rune falls in a reading.

This is the time when nature reaches a state of fullness, with the sun dispensing its warmth and life-giving energy. Celebrate the bounty of the season and engage in festivity! The "high summer" referred to in the Icelandic Rune poem sums up the quality of the time: Things are at a peak and you should be sure to take advantage of all that is on offer.

This rune is one of nine with no murkstave meanings. However, in rare instances where it seems to relate to a negative cycle of events, it may suggest that you are reaping what you have sown, as the old adage goes. Actions can return to us long after the initial seed was planted, for good or ill. Take action before your garden is overgrown with weeds.

Keywords: Harvest season, growing time, richness and ripeness, fertile season, high summer, full cycle, summer solstice, festivity. (*Note: Jera* is not reversible.)

MYTHS AND LEGENDS

The earth has always been regarded as living and sacred in traditional societies. The Norse were no exception, as the *Prose Edda* makes clear. Scholars have increasingly questioned the status of Snorri Sturluson's account of his pagan predecessors found there, but we can scarcely believe he was deceived when he wrote in the prologue that "they knew the earth was round" and "They looked upon the earth as in some way a living being with a life of its own. They knew it was inconceivably ancient as years go. And by nature powerful; it gave birth to all things and owned all that died."[42]

Among the pieces of evidence advanced for this by Snorri are the facts that water springs from mountain peaks as in low dales; blood runs equally in humans as in birds and beasts; the earth annually sprouts grasses and flowers, followed by the great withering, as feathers and hair sprout and wither on birds and beasts; and grass can grow even on turned soil. Although some of these observations may appear quaint today, we can see this perception of a shared life, encompassing the whole planetary surface, as a precursor of more-modern notions of ecological unity, such as the "living earth" theory of the Gaia hypothesis.

Many contemporary Pagans influenced by, but not working strictly within, the Northern Mysteries celebrate the Wiccan eightfold Wheel of the Year. The seasonal rhythms were central to the Northern world, but what is known of the early Germanic festive calendar actually reveals to us a sixfold annual cycle composed of sixty-day "tides," or double months. These were subdivided into three major festivals. In Iceland there were but two seasons: winter and summer. The Icelandic Rune poem specifically names summer and the fertility of the fields, and this is the time to which the *jera* stave refers. Summer, and especially the solstice, was a time of celebration throughout the ancient world, a pivotal point when the seasonal wheel reaches the apex of its progress, a time of joy and uninhibited revelry. As the wise giant tells Odin in *Vafþrúðnismál* (The Lay of Vathrúdnir), "Summer's sire is delight."[43]

The Lord and Lady

The Celts worshiped the earth as a source of fertility and blessings in the guises of the goddesses Dana and Brigit; the Greeks, Demeter and Persephone; while the Norse venerated the god Frey and his sister Freya as symbols of nature's fruitfulness. Frey and Freya, whose names are really titles meaning "lord" and "lady," are king and queen of the Vanir, the fertility gods, though in an older layer of Norse myth that role was fulfilled by the sea god Njórd and earth goddess Nerthus. Nerthus is often believed especially to represent the earth itself, although her link with island shrines as far afield as the Baltic also suggests a watery association. It is Njórd, by contrast, who embodies the bounty of the ocean, and he was invoked for a good catch at sea.

When the Norwegian Rune poem celebrates the good harvest with the words "I say that Frothi is generous," these lines evidently evoke the Danish king Frothi, who lived during the time of Christ. He has even been interpreted by one academic as a symbol for the "liberality of the Christian savior."* But Frothi himself is regarded in legend as

*Prudence Jones and Nigel Pennick, *A History of Pagan Europe* (London: Routledge, 1995), 144. It is Margaret Clunies Ross who identifies the Frothi of the Norwegian Rune poem with the Danish king Frothi. Because Frothi ruled at the time of Christ, she concludes the following: "So when the 'I' of the Norwegian *Rune Poem* declares, *"harvest is a boon to men;/ I think Frothi was liberal [. . .]* [h]e may not have been unmindful of the 'true' liberality of the Christian God, who caused his son Jesus the son of Frey, and his name is itself a title of Frey's, meaning "lux-uriant,"[44] so mention of him here may be a double entendre. Frey has an intimate connection with the earth. He is typically depicted wield-ing a huge phallus and is associated with his totemic animals, the horse and the pig. In ancient fertility rituals, the god was borne about by his followers in a wagon dispensing blessings and prosperity. He is thus the embodiment of the luxuriant growth that springs from the earth.

Freya, although she dwells in Ásgard (the abode of the Aesir), is actually one of the Vanir (gods of fertility, the land, and magic) and in her various aspects is queen of both. Both she and Frey, who share many similarities, are at the center of many harvest festivities.[45] In Norse myth Freya outlives many of the gods, who will die at Ragnaroc, and her survival reflects in part the regenerative capacities of the land, for we read in *Vǫluspá*'s prophecies that after the destruc-tion "barren fields will bear again."[46] In the Northern Mysteries, she is one face of the Great Goddess.

Brísingamen and *Seithr*

Freya is typically pictured as a gorgeous Norse Aphrodite. To win her famous golden necklace, Brísingamen, she descends—like Persephone or Eurydice in Greek myth—and sleeps with four dwarfs in Svartálfheim (land of the dark elves). Brísingamen may symbolize the harvest sun and the ripening of grains, the golden glow of the "ripened field." The promiscuity of Freya in her aspect as a goddess of orgiastic sex reflects the bounty and indiscriminate gifts of the earth, and in the Old English Rune poem we hear how the earth provides for all (literally "rich and poor alike"), a measure of its greatness and goodness. Freya's worship was widespread and deeply rooted. In one

---

to be born at the time of the *Pax Augusta,* which coincided with Frothi's peace and prosperity in Scandinavia. In the pre-Christian past Frothi may have got sole credit for these achievements, but to the Christian and the 'I' of the poem . . . it is God who has brought about such good fortune." Margaret Clunies Ross, "The Anglo-Saxon and Norse *Rune Poems:* A Comparative Study," *Anglo Saxon England* 19 (1990): 23–39, 33–34.

instance an insult thrown at her by a zealous Christian ("bitch goddess" were the words) initiated a fierce battle in Iceland,[47] an ironic
turn because in Norse mythology the first war in the world was
spurred partly by a jibe offered to her by an uncouth giant.

Freya is in fact a powerful shamaness; she owns a feathered falcon coat and ruled a school of magic known as *seithr,* which involves
trance seership. This alludes to the close link between the energies of
the earth and magic in ancient tradition. Geomancy (primitive divination) is itself a form of earth magic, shamans descend into the earth in
trance, voodoo uses cornflower (grown in the soil) for its magical
vèvès, (ritual symbols), and so on. *Seithr* is again being practiced by
adepts, especially female, in the Northern Mysteries today.

Seemingly less glamorous than Freya, but equally symbolic of the
earth, is Frigga, Odin's wife. In fact, Freya and Frigga were probably
at one time identical figures. Their twinship is revealed by the fact that
Frigga also wears a golden necklace embroidered by dwarfs and she
has to share Odin with her more celebrated alter ego. Frigga is linked
to a number of other goddesses in Norse and other European
mythologies. The list includes Bertha, Brechta, Eastre (after whom
Easter is named), Hlodin, Ostara, and Nerthus. While recent research
has questioned the universality of the Earth Mother figure in antiquity,
she nonetheless has a profound importance for contemporary Pagans.
Duotheists (those who believe in a god and a goddess as coequal partners in creation) don't necessarily have to imagine that there was a
single Great Goddess who was worshiped by everybody everywhere
before the rise of the sky gods. History and, indeed, prehistory are not
that simple. But in psychological (not to mention political) terms, the
difference between a religion within which there is a Goddess or goddesses and one where there is only one God is huge, both for male and
female practitioners. In acknowledging the Goddess in all goddesses
as the natural counterpart of the God in all gods, Pagans seek to
bypass the pathological imbalances manifest in many religious doc-
trines. For her part, the archetypal Earth Mother teaches the path of

respect toward material creation—the body of the earth in whose belly we were forged and to whose soil we inevitably return.

Transition: *eihwaz* **(Yew)**

Names: Gmc *eihuaz* **(yew); Gothic** *aihs/waer;* **OE** *ih* **(yew);
common root of modern English "yew";
NRP and IRP** *yr* **(yew)**

Sound: *i*, *e*, **or** *y* **(as in** *tip, tree,* **and** *yew,* **respectively)**

Correspondence: bow (as in bow and arrow)

OLD ENGLISH RUNE POEM

*Yew has rough bark without
but holds the flame within;
deeply rooted, it graces the land.*

NORWEGIAN RUNE POEM

*Yew is winter's greenest wood;
it splutters when it burns.*

ICELANDIC RUNE POEM

*Yew is a taut bow,
and brittle iron
and the arrow of Fárbauti.*

VISUALIZATION

A twisted yew stands green leafed, with a gaping hollow in its gnarled trunk.

MEANING

Eihwaz is a rune of transition. Representing the yew, a tree of life and death, its presence here signals a major transition close at hand, even that your life may be touched by death. But do not be unduly alarmed; the death may be symbolic, a "dying into life" that marks a shift into a more profound state of being, for *eihwaz* is also a tree of the unending cycle of death and renewal.

Yew has a long-standing association with death and immortality, as evidenced by its place in village churchyards. Yews become hollow in the center as they age, giving them a dark, mysterious appearance. This hollow is a symbolic gateway, a threshold. You are passing through such a gateway. Like the grave, it is an ending; like the womb, it is a beginning.

Similarly, our existence is a series of gateways, an ongoing process of birth, winnowing, and rebirth. The *eihwaz* stave is the thread of continuity. Although the yew has a dark role as an entrance to the underworld, then, it is also a symbol of constant regeneration.

While the breaking down of the customary conditions of your life is a frightening process, this encounter with the dark energies of the underworld may ultimately lead to a dazzling vision of the unity of life and death. Even loss may conceal unsuspected gains within its black robes. Although affirmations may have a hollow ring at the present time, nothing can prevent the eventual return of the light. Let it draw you forward when it beckons.

Keywords: Transition, matters of life and death, death (literal or symbolic), gateway, threshold, a grave, a womb, immortality, everlastingness, regeneration. (*Note: Eihwaz* is not reversible.)

MYTHS AND LEGENDS

Tree lore was widespread across ancient Europe, as countless sources from the Norse, Germanic, and Celtic worlds show. Roman sources also tell us that "the Germanic peoples in central Europe worshipped their gods in forest clearings."[48] In the British Isles and western Europe, the Druids worshiped in *nemetonia,* or sacred groves, and the magical ogam script letters are associated with various trees and plants; in medieval kabbalism, the Tree of Life glyph functions as a mystical map of the cosmos. In the Northern tradition there is, of course, the World Ash, Yggdrasil, that stands at the center of the universe. Yggdrasil is the axis of the nine worlds, the Irminsul, or "central pillar of the world," that holds up the sky.

Although we know Yggdrasil as an ash, it has been suggested that it may originally have been a yew tree, or that yew and ash are doubles of each other. The significant aspects of the yew and the ash are, furthermore, not very difficult to marry: The yew is an evergreen tree that endures summer and winter with little alteration and has long represented the concept of immortality, while Yggdrasil, an ash in later Norse myth, is the World Tree that "was and is and ever shall be." It thus signifies eternity, life everlasting.

The Yew

The yew has a stark aura in early European beliefs. In the Norse and Celtic world it was associated with cults of the dead, including Odin as Lord of the Wild Hunt. Yews were commonly planted at burial sites, and there remain many churchyards in mainland Europe and throughout the British Isles with yew trees at their center. In many cases the yew outdates the cemetery by centuries. In fact, Christian churches were often built on the sites that sacred yew trees already occupied. The yew's role in funerary cults doubtless revolved around the fact that it is evergreen—"winter's greenest wood"—and thus a fitting symbol for immortality. Yew "holds the flame within" in the words of the Old English Rune poem, which suggests both that it burns well as firewood and, because fire can symbolize destruction and regeneration within the cycles of nature, that it symbolizes the immortality of the spirit. The mysterious hollow created within the rough trunk of the tree as it matures also carries connotations of both the grave and the womb (and thus of death and of rebirth). Moreover, ritual human sacrifices in the North often involved the victim's being hanged or immolated on a yew tree.

But most compelling of all, the Icelandic reference to the yew as the "arrow of Fárbauti" not only reminds us that arrows were made of yew but also evokes the name of the giant Fárbauti (meaning "cruel striker"), identified in the *Prose Edda* as Loki's father. Now, Loki's mother was Laufey (meaning "tree island"). She gave birth to Loki after being struck with one of Fárbauti's fiery arrows. Thus the fire that destroys the sap, which is the blood of trees, also clears the way for new growth. This arboreal motif matches the trickster Loki's ambivalent function as a harbinger of both life and death for gods and men.

The Ash

The theme of sacrificial hanging connected to the yew also recalls the shamanic initiation that Odin undergoes on the branches of Yggdrasil as he peers downward into Mímir's Well in his search for the wisdom of the Runes. This symbolic death underlines the fact that death, symbolic or not, is always an initiation. Yggdrasil is the pivot of the nine worlds, the *axis mundi* or central column linking them all. It is a primary symbol of the life force itself, the regenerative aspect of nature that transcends time in its timeless cycles. The motif of the Cosmic Tree is well recognized in comparative mythology as a fundamental concept linked to the notion of a universal axis and spirit pole that bridges the various material and nonmaterial levels of reality. As we saw in the introduction to this book, in ancient shamanistic lore that once stretched across much of Eurasia, the World Tree is the vehicle the shaman rides into the otherworld.

The archaic notion of a tree holding the earth together with its roots, the middle world with its trunk, and the sky with its branches has new relevance today as humanity perilously rediscovers the central supporting role of the tree in the earth's ecology. Our survival depends more than ever upon the greenworld. To revere the forest is to foster life, to destroy it is to bring ruin on us all. In the poem *Vafþrúðnismál,* it is told how a human couple survive Ragnaroc's apocalypse, protected within the trunk of Yggdrasil. After the destruction of the end times, they go on to found a renewed and transformed human race.

The Apples of Immortality

The miraculous apples guarded by the goddess Idunna provide another bridge in Norse myth between trees and immortality. As long as the gods and goddesses consume this fruit, they remain eternally youthful. When Loki, through his shady dealings, allows a giant to steal Idunna's basket, the gods begin to age helplessly and their powers fail them. Without quick action on the part of Odin to pressure Loki to reverse his evil deed, the Aesir might have perished.

Norse beliefs in a human afterlife were varied. Historically, different cults—such as those dedicated to Odin and the Aesir versus those venerating Frey and the Vanir—doubtless held divergent beliefs, and of course these underwent changes over time. The accounts we possess may also reflect Christian influence, although they are embraced as wholly pagan by devotees of the Northern Mysteries today. Viking-age graves do not support the saying "You can't take it with you," for those with status took with them lavish grave goods, such as swords, jewelry, and fine clothes. This was to render them fit for the halls of the gods. Both Odin and Frigga have their halls of immortality into which human beings can be admitted. Odin's hall, Valhalla, is for the brave, while Frigga's hall, Fensalir, reunites faithful lovers. Additionally, Freya has her own hall, named Fólkvangr, where traditionally those she chose to die in battle could find themselves. The shipwrecked are destined to live for eternity in the sea god Njórd's enclosure, called Nóatún and located at the bottom of the ocean. Criminals and other unworthies go to the mist-shrouded world of Hel. Some dead, however, apparently haunt grave mounds. There seems to be some evidence for a belief in reincarnation in the sagas, paralleling the Celtic belief in the transmigration of souls. And finally there is the paradisiacal, golden hall of Gimlé, where, according to *Vǫluspá*'and the *Prose Edda,* "the just" will abide for eternity.

Sacred Play: *pertho* **(Gaming)**

**Names: Gmc *perth;* Gothic: *pairthra/pertra;* OE *pred; peorth;*
exact meaning disputed. (*Note:* There is no *pertho* stave in
the Younger Futhark and therefore no accompanying Norwegian
or Icelandic Rune poem.)**

Sound: *p* **(as in *play*)**

OLD ENGLISH RUNE POEM

Gaming means play and laughter
among the high-spirited who sit
merry together in the mead hall.

VISUALIZATION

Runes spill from a leather pouch onto an ashwood table, while in the background revelers dance and sing in a mead hall.

MEANING

Pertho is one of several mysterious runes whose original identity is elusive. Perhaps this is appropriate for a stave that, most commentators agree, refers to some kind of gaming—specifically a game board, gaming piece, or lot-casting device. This is without doubt a rune of play, fun, pleasure, laughter, and happiness. Enjoyable pursuits in pleasant company are indicated.

Gaming, in terms of both board games and divination systems, was a favorite activity of the Norse and Germanic tribes. The mead hall provided a haven of entertainment with storytelling, feasting, and revelry at regular intervals. We should all take pleasure in the light-hearted, self-gratifying side of life. People sometimes imagine that spirituality and play are incompatible. Norse paganism holds to quite a different perspective, with even enlightenment itself described as the "mead of inspiration." Don't allow anxiety or guilt to cloud your enjoyment of these gifts from the gods.

Board games were specifically linked to divination in the ancient world, and in a Norse context we can draw a parallel with the runes themselves. The runes are both a playful method of self-discovery and a game of knowledge. This leads us on to the notion of sacred play, the idea that all creation is formed from the play of divine consciousness and that we come closest to the spirit of the divine through playfulness of spirit.

This is what the old pagan customs of the feast, fair, and carnival were all about. The times specifically allocated to celebration of the earthy and the sacred in contemporary Paganism are the solstices, solar festivals, and Sabbaths (lunar festivals), along with many important days in between. This rune can also, therefore, indicate your participation in ritual, festivity, or festival life.

Reversed, *pertho* suggests there is some blockage regarding the pleasure principle in your life. This is not helpful to the flow of creative energies. Perhaps you are being too serious and need to lighten up and see the humorous aspects to the game of life. Make a point of allowing yourself to have a good time, though not to the detriment of other areas. This is not, however, a good time to gamble. Be careful to hedge your bets rather than laying too much on the table!

Keywords: Gaming, play, fun, laughter, happiness, entertainment, storytelling, feasting, self-gratification, cultural pursuits, celebration, divination, sacred play, the quest for self-knowledge. *Murkstave:* A lack of gaiety; sadness, melancholy, the need to lighten up and enjoy yourself.

MYTHS AND LEGENDS

In the early days of creation, we are told in *Vŏluspá*, after the Aesir had built their altars, temples, and high-timbered halls and set up forges at the plain of Idavoll, they stopped to relax and enjoy gaming in the ripe meadows:

> *Sitting in meadows   smiling over game-boards,*
> *they never knew   any need of gold.*[49]

This represents a golden age of innocence of the earth. Although it is fated to be short-lived, Idavoll provides us with the ideal of a world where gaming takes precedence over toil and fighting. It is interesting to learn, furthermore, that after Ragnaroc, the final apocalyptic battle of Norse myth, the surviving gods will regroup at Idavoll to consider what has happened in the light of "the ancient runes offered to Odin" and ultimately resume their gaming. As we read in *Vŏluspá:*

> *Later they will find   a wondrous treasure,*
> *gold game boards,   lying in the grass*
> *where they had left them   so long before.*[50]

The theme of an entire cosmogenic cycle of creation, destruction, and renewal being contained within the gaming activities of a group of gods reminds me of the great Indian epic the *Mahabharata,* in which the five sons of King Pandu foolishly gamble away their freedom and shared wife, Draupadi, to the forces of chaos in a dice game. This act provokes a similar cosmic drama of destruction and regeneration. Norse mythology's Indo-European links suggest this may be an echo of an ancient, underlying myth cycle.

The Mead of Inspiration

Another important form of entertainment was storytelling in the mead hall. Indeed, the spiritually enlightened and heightened consciousness of poets was known as the "mead of inspiration." Poetry contained profound themes that related to the religious and ritual life of the culture, yet the storytellers were also popular performers who brought old tales to life for their audience.

Michael Howard links *pertho* with the *wita* (wise man) visiting halls, entertaining, and enlightening his audience. He remarks:

> It is well known that the sacred can be appreciated or experienced through the medium of song and dance. . . . The role of the bard in Celtic society is legendary, and it is evident that in Northern Europe there were wandering shamans who took on a similar role. These Norse bards would not only have been storytellers who related the great sagas to their spell-bound audiences but also teachers of the mysteries, including Runecraft. To the ancient Germanic people the power of ritualised poetry was very influential in magical and spiritual practices. Sacred songs were also an important aspect of shamanic worship and the term covered everything from personal prayers to priestly invocations.[51]

The poets were not only entertainers but adepts in magical arts as well. The fact that Odin was their patron makes it likely that they practiced and preserved runelore. The modern use of the Runes as a divination system is based on an intimately related concept. The Erulian, or runecaster, uses the runestaves not so much to predict or "read fortunes" in the popular sense, but rather to engage in sacred play with the signs, to observe the energies signified by the Runes as they "come into play" in a reading. He or she refines the art of reading the patterns they form in imaginative ways, creating new story lines out of ancient materials.

Games of the Gods

Although, at first glance, gaming in a mead hall and divination ritual
seem poles apart, the ancient kinship of game boards and divination
systems has been amply documented—most notably in Nigel
Pennick's *Games of the Gods: The Origin of Board Games in Magic
and Divination.* We know from Roman historian Tacitus's account
that the Norse were obsessed with both gambling and "the casting of
lots" (that is, fortune-telling). Pennick shows that many common
games, including such well-known examples as chess, snakes and ladders, and mah-jongg, have their roots in ancient divination techniques.

The two-thousand-year-old Indian game *leela,* the original snakes
and ladders, represented the Hindu cosmos in its eight planes and
seventy-two squares, and the roll of the dice reflected one's karma in
action. There are countless equivalent European parallels. The Irish
game *fidchell,* for example, involved a game board of gold with silver pieces similar to a chess board. It had an uneven number of
squares, so that a central square was created upon which the king sat,
surrounded by his forces, assailed from the four sides of the board.
Not just a game, *fidchell* was also regarded as a lesson in strategy and
a divination into the outcome of a battle.[52]

Underlying the Old English Rune poem's simple and rustic image
of warriors at drink and play, therefore, is a web of potential associations. The communal mead hall revelries were festive occasions with
links to the seasonal "wheel of the year" and connected with the activity of the gods, and therefore laughter and feasting also had ritualistic
dimensions. While it is sufficient to read this rune as a simple token of
fun, laughter, and feasting with friends in a familiar and comfortable
environment, *pertho* also provides a commentary on the notion of
sacred play, the principle that play or gaming performs a vital function within the round of earthly experience and that the divine can
reveal itself in a spirit of playfulness. This idea is a fundamental one
in paganism, underlying, as mentioned in the "Meaning" section
above, such festivities as the feast, the fair, and the carnival.

Protection: *algiz* (Elk Sedge)

Names: Gmc *alhiz* **or** *algiz* **(elk); Gothic** *algs/ezec;* **OE** *elux;*
OERP *eolhxsecg* **(elk sedge). (***Note:* **There is no** *algiz* **stave**
in the Younger Futhark and therefore no accompanying
Norwegian or Icelandic Rune poem.)

Sound: *z* (as in *zoo*)

OLD ENGLISH RUNE POEM

Elk sedge grows in the fen,
waxing in the water, grimly wounding;
it burns the blood of those
who would lay hands upon it.

VISUALIZATION

The reflection of an elk bending to drink is framed in a pond flecked
with green sedge.

MEANING

Algiz—literally "elk sedge"—is widely regarded as a stave of magical protection. A similar concept is found in the Celtic world, where
the rowan tree is a symbol of the warding off of unwanted influences,
both physical and metaphysical. When it appears upright in a reading,
this rune assures you that you are protected from any possible danger.

There are many crossroads in the journey of life where danger
presents itself, but *algiz* indicates that you are well prepared to

weather the storm; unseen powers watch over you. Malignant foes, natural catastrophes, disease, random violence, and other negative influences are examples of the possible threats that this rune guards against.

Although *algiz* suggests that you are shielded from harm, it does not counsel complacency. The very presence of this rune in a reading, while it should not make you paranoid, comes as a warning of something against which you must be on your guard. Forewarned is forearmed. Carefully examine any chinks in the armor of your life that could allow danger to enter. Then you can truly go forth with confidence.

On the supernatural front, many magical practices, past and present, are designed to encircle the practitioner and ward off harm. The *algiz* stave can be used in three main ways: as an object of meditative affirmation, as a magical token in spellcraft, and as an excellent amulet when carved on a runestone and hung around one's neck. Armed with such a potent token, you should fear no harm.

Reversed, this rune is somewhat less rosy. Your defenses are down in some area of life and you are vulnerable to danger or attack. Look very carefully to any possible sources of threat and try to eliminate any involvements, patterns, or habits that leave you open to harm. There are perils and pitfalls in life for which you must prepare yourself; do not be caught off guard.

Keywords: Protection, defense, safety from harm, being shielded, magical protection, use of talismans and protective herbs. *Murkstave:* Lack of protection, defenselessness, vulnerability, danger, perils and pitfalls.

MYTHS AND LEGENDS

The exact meaning of the word *algiz* (Anglo-Saxon *eolhxsecg*) is a genuine riddle. It appears to refer to a plant (sedge) and/or an animal (elk). The Old English word *eolhx* is thought to be derived from the common Germanic root *alhiz*, meaning "elk." On the other hand, the word *secg* is the ancestor of the modern English "sedge," though the exact identity of the wetland plant described in the Rune poem is in doubt.

The rune scholar Ralph Elliot guesses it to mean "some sort of sedge or rush, possibly even the Latin *helix,* some 'twisted plant' or 'willow.'"[53] One solution is that perhaps *algiz* was a plant the elk liked to browse on and therefore the sedge came to be known as elk sedge. But another reconstruction of the linguistic roots of *eolhxsecg* suggests that *eolh* may be descended not from *alhiz* but from *algix,* a Germanic root meaning "protection, defense." *Algix* is, in any case, very close to the Germanic name for this rune, *algiz,* and in contemporary divination these various meanings—of sedge, elk, and protection—are generally yoked together. Thus, despite the Rune poem description of *algiz* as a noxious plant, it is also a magical "herb," in the widest sense of the word, that "burns the blood" (in other words, blights or curses) "of those who would lay hands upon it" (that is, anyone who interferes with the runecaster). This association with the elk is strengthened by the shape of the stave, which resembles antlers. Antlers and horns are, of course, powerful symbols of defense and protection in the natural world.

Plant Magic

The use of plant magic, now enjoying something of a renaissance, was common in ancient times, echoed in the later, medieval stereotype of the witch gathering herbs for uses good or ill. Many herbal remedies employed both medicinally and magically in witchcraft have since been "discovered" by science to have healing or inoculating properties. The basis of plant magic is the assumption that if a plant produces physical effects, it could also work on a magical level. This was further underpinned by the belief that plants are powerful, magical entities, spirits, or numina.

The theme of runes being used in magical charms relating to the plant world is a common one in Norse literature. In *Hávamál* (Sayings of the High One), Odin boasts of the various cunning ways he has learned through the lore of the runes. The sixth boon he gained is this:

> *If someone would harm me*
> *by writing runes on a tree root,*

> *the man who wished   I would come to woe*
> *will meet misfortune, not I.*[54]

In *Sigdrífomál* (The Lay of Sigdrífa), the Valkyrie Sigdrífa instructs the hero Sigurd in runelore and teaches him the magical use of the staves.

> *With this sign your horn   can never harm you;*
> *dip a leek in your drink;*
> *then I know   you will never find*
> *death mixed into your mead.*[55]

In both these instances, a plant or plant matter is used in conjunction with a rune: in the first case to curse or blight, in the second to ward off misfortune. The belief in black magic was deeply rooted in the Norse world, and many felt the need to ritually inoculate themselves, so to speak, against such menaces as the hex, curse, baleful eye, and dreaded *draugr* (corpses that, like Haitian zombies, could be reanimated by evil magicians to wreak harm upon the living).

Algiz is still read as a token of protection in contemporary divination and is used as such in the tradition of active magical workings using "rune charms" or "bind runes." A rune charm involves a single rune inscribed on some object, such as an amulet, while a bind rune involves several runes joined together in the one form to create a powerful and binding magical spell.

The Elk

The similarity of the elk's horns to the appearance of this stave strengthens the possible link between the two. The elk or stag was a hugely significant beast to the ancient Germanic and Norse peoples. As object of the hunt, it not only carried the value of its meat and skin but was revered as highly sacred as well. The elk also appears to be a totem animal of magicians and shamans, as preserved in the various horned-god figures found across ancient Europe known collectively as Cernunnos. Indeed, one of Odin's titles is Elgr, meaning elk, and his Germanic equivalent, Woden, was the antlered leader of the Wild Hunt. The Wild Hunt is an ancient theme whose central element is an otherworldly cavalcade through the night skies led by a horned god.

Protective "wards" (magical signs used to ward off misfortune) of various kinds were used to keep from harm the occupants of houses over which the Lord of the Wild Hunt and his otherworldly hounds passed. Michael Howard comments:

> This rune shape has been compared to the old German gesture to ward off evil spirits. The person being threatened held up three fingers with the palm of the hand facing outwards towards the source of alleged evil. This gesture of protection may also be connected with the horned sign used in the Middle Ages as a defence against the evil eye. To make this sign, the first and little fingers are upraised and the other fingers folded in towards the palm. This was a secret sign used for recognition purposes by followers of the medieval witch cult who were traditionally worshippers of the pagan Horned God.[56]

Although clerics demonized horned gods such as Herne, Cernunnos, Pan, and Woden, there is nothing evil about them in the Northern Mysteries or contemporary Paganism. Some may be tricksters or gods of the dead, but they are viewed as representations of the male divinity in his earthly and chthonic (underworldly) aspects. Appeals to horned gods, Odin foremost among them, for protection therefore harmonize perfectly with the spirit of *algiz*.

The Source: *sowulo* (Sun)

Names: Gmc *souulo/ segilan* (sun); Gothic *sauil/sugil;* OE *sigi;* NRP and IRP *sol* (sun)

Sound: *s* (as in *sun*)

Correspondence: sun

OLD ENGLISH RUNE POEM

The sun guides seafarers
who ferry across the fishes' bath
until the seahorse brings them to land.

NORWEGIAN RUNE POEM

Sun is the light of the world;
I bow to its holiness.

ICELANDIC RUNE POEM

Sun is the sky shield,
and a shining radiance,
and the nemesis of ice.

VISUALIZATION

A longship, its billows filled by the wind, sails into the golden orb of the rising sun.

MEANING

Sowulo stands for the sun and is a supremely positive rune. Apart from being the greatest celestial body in the sky and the center of our solar system, the sun has been worshiped across many cultures as an embodiment of divine cosmic energy. In modern terms, we could describe it as the Source or Higher Self, the spark of divine consciousness from which radiates inner light.

Sunlight is the power that causes everything on earth to grow and prosper, and so the sun is a fitting symbol of spiritual power and enlightenment. It also represents the fruitful, incubating force that leads to personal growth and expansion. When you are in contact with the Source, all matters at hand are brightened and illuminated.

Meditation on the sun as a symbol for the Source is a powerful aid to contacting the light and life-giving powers of the cosmos. *Sowulo* is also a token of guidance, of walking in the light. This is a very favorable and positive omen; it is an image of wholeness to treasure in the darker moments of the quest. The sun "guides seafarers," in the words of the Old English Rune poem, and this refers to the role of the Source (or Higher Self) in our lives as a lodestar and lighthouse.

Closing Hagal's Actt—and standing at the opposite extreme of the cycle opened by the wintry staves of *hagalaz, naudiz,* and *isa—sowulo* is regarded as perhaps the most beneficial rune in the Elder Futhark. It is the "icebreaker," the force that smashes the rigid, static powers of winter—both the physical winter and the winters of the soul.

It is, finally, a symbol of enduring enlightenment that in rune magic is considered to have the strength to banish evil. This power was, after all, widely attributed to the sun in Norse mythology, where hostile frost giants and dark elves are turned to stone or perish in its illuminating rays. Similarly, the demons of darkness and doubt that may have plagued you are shriveling away in the light of a new day.

Keywords: The Source, divine cosmic energy, the Higher Self, inner light, spiritual power, enlightenment, guidance, growth and prosperity, brightness, illumination. (*Note: Sowulo* is not reversible.)

MYTHS AND LEGENDS

The central theme of prehistoric Norse religion was, without a doubt, sun worship. The great, glowing orb clearly was and is the source of all that lives and grows. A dominant motif in primitive rock art is the solar disk with related emblems: chariots, ships, and supplicating worshipers. The so-called disk men in such carvings are found in a variety of poses. One of the most common is with arms (either one or both) raised above the head, while another image shows dancing disk men. These figures from archaic times are preserved for us in the act of celebrating the sacred solar disk. Christianity always stigmatized sun worship among pagan peoples as a form of false idolatry, when in fact the sun in paganism was venerated as a physical embodiment of the spiritual principle of limitless light and energy. Living in a frigid landscape swept by extreme winters, the Norse had particular reason to adore the sun, and there is ample evidence of an early cult of sun worship and an enduring reverence for its life-giving power. The great solar festivals of the year marked its progress through the wheel of the four seasons—the "stations of the sun"—thus providing a model for understanding the cyclical nature of earthly life.

It seems some distant echo of sun worship has been preserved in the Norwegian Rune poem, with the line "I bow to its holiness." This verse is, furthermore, one of only two instances in the Rune poems where an "I" occurs, suggestive of deep personal engagement with the great lodestar that lights the heavens. In the Icelandic Rune poem, *sowulo* is "a shining radiance" and "the nemesis of ice." This reminds us of the opposition (and equilibrium) existing in Norse thought between fire and ice. The sun, by melting ice in spring, releases the land from the grip of winter and frees the generative aspects of the life force embodied in the soil to flower.

The Moon's Companion

In the great epic poem *Völuspá*, we hear that shortly after Midgard (Middle Earth, our world) was created,

> *The sun climbed;   the moon's companion*
> *raised its right hand   over heaven's rim.*
> *The sun did not know   where its halls would be set,*
> *the moon did not know   what would be its might.*[57]

It is Odin and his brothers who subsequently set the sun and the other "glowing sparks" in the heavens. This tale is further elaborated in the *Prose Edda,* where Snorri relates how

> a man named Mundilfari has two children. So fair and beautiful were they, he named his son Moon and his daughter Sun, whom he gave in marriage to a man named Glener, Sun. But the gods became wroth at this arrogance, so they took this brother and his sister and set them up in the heavens, and Sun was made to drive the horses of the car of the Sun, which the gods had made to light up the heavens from sparks that flew from Muspellheim.[58]

The reader will note that the sun is feminine here, as it was in ancient Egypt and early Shinto religions. Named in the lore-laden poem *Vafþrúðnismál* as Álfrothul, she was known to the Norse in later times simply as Sunna.

The fundamental role of sun worship in ancient times, coupled with the sun's feminine gender, reminds us that Norse paganism venerated the Goddess as a symbol of the divine Source alongside and perhaps even preceding the male divinities such as Odin and Thór, who triumphed with the rise of the Indo-European sky gods. The later Christian Church, also a sky god–based cult, was particularly hostile to the worship of natural phenomena as incarnations of divinity. They reviled the tendency to acknowledge the female aspects in nature and in the divine that led inevitably to goddess worship.

The Chariot and the Ship

One of the most important images associated with the sun was the solar chariot, the theme of the sun being drawn through the skies by the horses Árvakr (Early Waker) and Alsvithr (All Strong). It is thought that the chariot specifically represents the vehicle that draws the sun during daytime. As the sun is, so to speak, in her element during the day, the chariot becomes a primary symbol connected with Sunna and strengthens the association of the sun as the "solar wheel" that spins through the sky. The great seasonal celebrations marked by the sun's solstices, equinoxes, and other meridian points become the spokes in the wheel. Many practitioners of the Northern Mysteries adopt the solar calendar known in contemporary Paganism as Wheel of the Year (see part 3, "Runecasting," for details).

The sun is also often shown in early depictions drawing a ship, representing its vehicle by night, as illustrated by a scene from the famous Gotland stones from the fifth century. These stones preserve many images of ships beneath whirling disks, complete with rowers, steersmen, and, later, sails. In Norway the custom of burning boats at midsummer survived long into the Christian era. Even the Old English Rune poem verse recalls the link between sun and ship, noting the sun is the savior of seafarers as it leads them to safe harbor. Similarly, the divine Source within will always guide or ferry us to safety in our progress through life. In contemporary Paganism, the sun is widely regarded as a manifestation of the supreme creative and procreative force, a bright embodiment of sacred energy and power.

The Sun's Daughter

There is, finally, an interesting and somewhat mysterious theme that arises in the *Prose Edda, Völuspá,* and *Vafþrúðnismál,* which involves the Sun's daughter. According to the prophetic tradition, the Sun would one day succumb to the great Fenris wolf, who chases her through the heavens at the end times of Ragnaroc. As we can easily imagine, this grim fate spelled the ultimate catastrophe for the Nordic mind, for it signaled the death of the most powerful deity of the natural world. However, the final lines of the major part of the *Prose Edda,* known as "Gylfaginning," tells us that all is not lost, for "the Sun has brought forth a daughter no less lovely than herself, and she rides through the heavens along her mother's course."[59] *Völuspá* states:

> *To the Sun   is born a daughter*
> *Before she dies   in Fenris's jaws.*
> *Her mother's course   this maid shall ride*
> *After the fall   of the mighty gods.*

Similarly, in *Vafþrúðnismál,* Odin tells the giant of the poem's title:

> *Álfrothal, the elf beam,   will bear a fair daughter*
> *before Fenris tears her apart.   This maiden will walk*
> *in her mother's ways   after the gods have been destroyed.*[60]

Here we see the abiding Norse belief that even the greatest of catastrophes will be followed by regeneration and the beginning of a new cycle. Light may be extinguished, but it always manifests again out of even the most encompassing darkness. Therein lies another of *sowulo*'s beneficial lessons.

TÝR'S AETT

The Warrior: *Tiwaz* (the God Týr)

Names: Gmc *Teiuaz* or *Tiw;* Gothic *Teiws/Tyz;* OE *Tiw* or *Tir;* NRP and IRP *Týr*

Sound: *t* (as in *Tuesday*)

Correspondence: Mars

OLD ENGLISH RUNE POEM

Tiw is a sign that spells
confidence to the noble; unfailing,
it holds true through the night clouds.

NORWEGIAN RUNE POEM

Týr is the one-handed of the Aesir;
often has the smith to blow.

ICELANDIC RUNE POEM

Týr is the one-handed god,
and the leavings of the wolf
and ruler of the temple.

VISUALIZATION

The great god Týr leans upon his sword; behind him, a slavering wolf is tethered to a tree stump.

MEANING

Tiwaz is the name of an ancient Scandinavian and Germanic war god, so you may have a fight on your hands. Drawing the *Tiwaz* rune generally signifies opposition that must be faced squarely and with courage. Issues covered by this stave range from the personal to the social, legal, and political. The situation requires strength of conviction and possibly even the carrying out of a sanctified battle or righteous crusade (as opposed to engaging in sheer bloody-mindedness, violence, and conflict). It is particularly important to honor promises at this time.

In Norse myth, Týr (Tiwaz) embodies the principles of justice, bravery, honor, and dedication to a cause higher than the individual self. Corresponding to the Roman god Mars, he relates to the warrior aspect of the human psyche. Though in this global age war and conflict can only lead to disaster, there is still a role for the warrior archetype. On a personal level, we can draw on the strength of the "inner warrior" to carry us through hardship and opposition.

Being a warrior in this fuller sense relates to discipline, courage, tenacity, and principled action. Live your own truth rather than submitting to domination from outside. Yet as a warrior you should also draw on your strength for the benefit of others, defending your friends, family, and community and standing up for those who are too weak to protect themselves. On a planetary level, it is also imperative that we begin turning our warrior energy in defense of our fragile world rather than ceaselessly warring with nature and one another.

In magic, *Tiwaz* is used to invoke and strengthen ourselves in matters requiring courage and bravery. Especially identified with the concept of unswerving justice and its defense against attack from without, *Tiwaz* is often called upon in legal issues. As a "token of faith," the god to whom this rune is sacred is the guardian of oaths and a guiding star of principled behavior that forms a model for action in the world.

Reversed, *Tiwaz* signifies a futile battle or lost cause. Perhaps you are outnumbered and outclassed and need to withdraw in order to preserve your dignity and health, to live to fight another day. Remember, losing a skirmish doesn't mean losing the war. Alternatively, you may be perpetuating a conflict well after its use-by date. Seek resolution and an amnesty in embittered quarrels. Don't misuse the warrior energy or you will become mired in conflict. As the old saying goes, "Live by the sword, die by the sword."

Keywords: A fight, opposition, sanctified battle, righteous crusade, justice, honor, bravery, dedication, promises, oaths of allegiance, the warrior archetype, the spiritual warrior. *Murkstave:* Futile conflict or a lost cause, the misapplication of warrior energy.

MYTHS AND LEGENDS

Tiwaz is the name of the god also known to the Germans as Tiw, and in Old English as Tiw or Tir. Tiwaz was originally the supreme god of old Germanic Europe—a sort of northern European equivalent of the Greek sky god Zeus or the Hebrew Jehovah—whose reign stretches back thousands of years to the Europe of the hunter-gatherers. He was principally a war god and, as a divinity of sky and storm, was associated with the terrible rolling of thunder and flashing of lightning so reminiscent of battle. However, he was no mere meatheaded sword swain but a brave and principled deity who upheld justice, sword lore, and the swearing of oaths.

Tiw's original importance is reflected in the naming of a weekday after him—*Tiwesdaeg,* or Tuesday—but the god's long-standing position as chief deity in the Norse pantheon was shaken by the rise of Odin and Thór. Odin, as warlord and god of wisdom and the dead, replaced Týr as chief of the heavens, while Thór took over the role of general strongman and protector of the gods.

Týr "the One-Handed"

Some traces of the old thunderer's original status are preserved, however, in Norse mythology. Here we see Týr acting as the most heroic and honorable of the gods. In a celebrated episode in the *Prose Edda,* the gods seek to bind the malevolent wolf Fenris by tempting him into a trial of strength. When they approach Fenris with a magical fetter—in the form of ribbon made by the dark elves—the wolf becomes suspicious and demands that one of the gods place an arm in his mouth as "a token of faith." Only Týr is brave enough to meet the demand, and when Fenris finds he has been tricked and bound, he bites off Týr's hand. From this incident Týr came to be known as "the bravest of the gods" and "the one-handed."

This kenning figures in both Scandinavian Rune poems: The Norwegian Rune poem describes Týr as "the one-handed of the Aesir," while the line "often has the smith to blow" refers to the efforts exerted by both the gods and the dark elves to construct a fetter strong enough to bind Fenris. (First the gods make a chain called Laeding, then another named Dromi, then finally they persuade the dark elves to make the magical ribbon or noose known as Gleipnir.) Naming Týr as "the leavings of the wolf" in the Icelandic Rune poem is a wry reference to the god's surviving his encounter with Fenris, while the phrase "ruler of the temple" probably preserves some trace of Týr's original role as the chief of the gods and as a focus of popular worship.

Invoking Týr

There is a *galdr* (incantation, spell) preserved in a famous scene in *Sigdrífomál* (The Lay of Sigdrífa) that directly invokes Týr, and thus the *Tiwaz* rune. The Valkyrie Sigdrífa is instructing the hero Sigurd in the magical art of rune charms. She chants a set of verses, and the first on her list is the following spell:

> *Runes of war know thee   if great thou wilt be*
> *Cut them on hilt of hardened sword—*
> *Some on the brand's back,   some on the shining blade*
> *twice the name of Týr therein.*

The "charging" or consecrating of weapons and other objects in Elder magic involved both the recitation of *galdr* and the carving of runes, as the Eddic sources show. What stave could be more appropriate than *Tiwaz* for the purpose of empowering a sword? As mentioned, this rune is still used today in spells relating to law and justice.

The Constellation of Týr

In the Old English Rune poem, Týr is described as "a sign" (OE *sum*: token, sign) "that spells confidence." This refers to several themes at once. It relates to the aforementioned magical use of *Tiwaz* in bind runes to charge (and therefore strengthen confidence in) a sword. The token of faith that Týr offers to Fenris and the general role of the god in ancient oath-taking rituals also make Týr a sign of confidence. But it is likely that Týr was once represented by a star or constellation, as implied by the last line of the Old English Rune poem: "it holds true through the night clouds." Thus the "sign" of the Rune poem has a stellar aspect.

Several possible stars have been put forward. First, the Icelandic Rune poem correspondence for Týr is given as Mars, appropriately corresponding to the Roman war god's fiery planet. Another possibility is the "Nail of the North," Polaris (the Pole Star), a navigational aid always visible above the horizon in the Northern Hemisphere, which also formed the basis of an immense cult of popular worship. Finally, there is the arrowlike formation composed of Aldebaran (from Taurus), the twin stars of Betelgeuse and Rigel (from Orion), and Sirius (from Canis Major).

The Aldebaran grouping forms an arrow similar to the shape of the *Tiwaz* stave. As Marijane Osborn and Stella Longland comment: "Aldebaran is the bull's eye in Taurus, the bull; the Old Danish name for bull is *tir*. In Old Persian the name for Sirius is Tir, meaning in that language 'an arrow.' Tir, the arrow, hits the bull's eye. It is not possible to explain this coincidence between such distant languages and cultures (though both were sea-faring, star-navigating societies), but it adds greatly to any desire to identify Sirius with Týr."[61]

Whichever of these possibilities is correct, the "token" or "sign" referred to in the Old Englsih Rune poem implies the role of Týr's star or constellation in the heavens, either as a lodestar, a navigational guide, or a sign of the zodiac. From this we have the theme of *Tiwaz* as an unfailing spiritual beacon and guide in our quest.

Birthing: *berkana* (Birch Tree)

**Names: Gmc *berkana* (birch); Gothic *bercna/bern;*
OE *berg* or *beorc;* NRP and IRP *bjarkan* (birch)**

Sound: *b* (as in *birch*)

Correspondence: fir tree

OLD ENGLISH RUNE POEM

*The birch though fruitless
sends out countless shoots;
leafy branches, high crowned,
reach to the sky.*

NORWEGIAN RUNE POEM

*Birch has the greenest-leafed branches;
Loki brought the luck of deceit.*

ICELANDIC RUNE POEM

*Birch is a leafy limb
and a little tree
and a youthful wood.*

VISUALIZATION

A lithe, white birch stretches into the sky, a goddess figure visible in its trunk, her arms uplifted.

MEANING

Berkana is a rune of purification, fertility, and birth—symbolic qualities associated with the birch tree in Northern lore. Drawing this stave doesn't always augur childbirth, although coupled with the *Inguz* (ancestry) rune—particularly in questions relating to pregnancy and fertility—the chances are higher. More often it relates to the inception of a new phase, relationship, or project.

Upright, of course, *berkana* can be a powerful and positive omen for childbirth. It is a "birth rune" that was used to ease labor pangs and was sacred to midwives. Underlying these associations is the image of the birch goddess (known as Bercha or Bertha), an aspect of Mother Earth and thus the Great Goddess herself. You are safe in her hands.

Now is also a favorable time for initiating new beginnings. Be "fruitful" (that is, creative and productive) in all affairs. Push your boundaries to encompass new possibilities. Yet initiate this new growth with the care you would exercise tending a tree. It is important before any major new beginning that you have truly driven out the old. In the Norse and Celtic worlds, birch wands were used as tools of ritual purification. A *birching* (flagellation with birch branches) was designed to release the spirit of the old and thus prepare one for the new.

As the saying goes, every ending is a new beginning. Clear away the deadwood in order to see the new shoots that are growing up around you. Tend and nurture them into fullness and they will bear fruit. Spiritually, *berkana* augurs regrowth after destruction. Culturally and ecologically, it relates to the theme of regeneration. Take part in the processes of renewal.

In rune magic today, *berkana* is also used to bless any new undertaking. The *beorc* stave may be carved in the air with your hand while visualizing success in the matter concerned, or you may carve it on a physical object connected with a specific project. Intent is what counts.

Reversed, *berkana* signals difficulties with initiating new beginnings. It suggests that now may not be the right time to birth this particular project or initiative. Either conditions are hostile to what you conceive of doing or there are inherent problems in your plans. For couples concerned with reproduction, there may be delay or difficulties. Seek appropriate advice.

Keywords: Birth, new beginnings, new projects, fertility, reproduction, pregnancy, purification, driving out the old. *Murkstave:* Difficult beginnings, aborted plans, concerns with reproductive matters.

MYTHS AND LEGENDS

It is likely that the Old English Rune poem's description of the tree actually refers to the gray poplar, as this tree was common in Britain and could easily have been mistaken for birch. But the attributes given to *berkana* in contemporary divination cleave solely to the birch tree, whose symbolism stretches back into ancient Eurasian tree lore. The rune scholar Ralph Elliot writes:

> Berkana . . . literally 'birch twig,' is undoubtedly to be connected with fertility cults, symbolizing the awakening of nature inspired in spring and the birth of new life generally. In many parts of Europe the birch has long played a role in popular beliefs and customs going back beyond Christianity. To promote fruitfulness in men and beasts, birch saplings were placed in houses and stables, and young men were struck with birch twigs. In England there existed an old Cheshire custom of fixing a birch twig over the sweetheart's door on May Day. . . . Such traditions underline the symbolism of the birch and help to account for its choice as a rune-name.[62]

It therefore appears certain that in pagan times the birch had a key role in fertility rites. It could be seen as female, as a manifestation of the fertility of the Great Mother, on the one hand, and probably figured, on the other, as a "phallic pole," or masculine symbol. This is reinforced by the fact that fly agaric *(Amanita muscaria)* mushrooms often grow among the roots of the silver birch, and this "sacred mushroom" was widely seen as representing the union of male and female sexual organs.

Fertility Magic

The affixing of a birch twig over the sweetheart's door on May Day that Elliot mentions is an obvious echo of stave magic connected with seasonal rites. The idea of a tree, wand, or pole as a symbol of fertility is extremely ancient and survives in rural Scandinavia with the maypole celebrations, which often revolve around a birchwood pole.

The maypole enshrines in its innocent form the union of male and female, with the pole being the phallus and the hoop of garlanded flowers the embracing vulva. Such rites were designed to harmonize with the fertilizing forces of nature, both bringing fruitfulness to the individual participating and, by sympathetic magic, transferring across to the fields. As Michael Howard puts it: "In some pagan ceremonies the altar was the naked body of the priestess. In such rituals she would traditionally lie on an improvised bed of birch twigs and wild flowers."[63] In ritual magic the sexual union of priest and priestess is celebrated as the "Great Rite," a symbolic act that marries all opposites and releases an incredible flood of vital energy.

Ritual Purification

Fertility is something we associate particularly with reproduction, but it had a far wider significance in the ancient world. In cultures that celebrated Nature and her cycles, the theme of fertility signified fruitfulness on a number of planes. Think of the word *conceive:* It relates to both the conception and the gestation of an idea in the imagination. The practice described above of young men being struck with birch twigs relates to an older custom of ritual flagellation, with birch wands being used for the purposes of purification. Ritual purification represents the clearing or driving out of the old, thus opening a space for the new. The Celtic and Anglo-Saxon custom of purification with birch twigs had parallels in the classical world with the carnivalesque Roman Saturnalia. In this riotous celebration young men chased people through the streets, striking them with whips called *februa* in an act of ritual cleansing.

The use of birch whips for flagellation in pagan rites is reflected in the later custom of *birching,* a form of corporal punishment employed until quite recently in which criminals were caned, or "birched," with birch branches in order to rid them of their tendencies to wrongdoing.

Help Runes

After cleansing comes renewal or rebirth. Birth itself is, of course, the most obvious symbol of the new issuing forth. In *Sigdrífomál* (The Lay of Sigdrífa) we learn an interesting application of a birth rune for helping a woman through the final stages of childbirth:

> *Help runes shalt thou gather,   if skill thou would gain*
> > *To loosen mother from low-lain child.*
> *Cut they be in hand's hollow   wrapped the joints round about*
> > *Call on the Good Folks' gainsome help.*[64]

But *berkana* signifies not just *literal* birth but also the wider theme of the new sprouting from the soil or womb of the old. Bercha, the birch goddess, is an embodiment of this generative energy and as such represents an aspect of the earth goddess, a fertile aspect of the Great Goddess of antiquity.

It has been noted that when the stave shape takes a rounded rather than angular form, as in the old Anglo-Saxon variant of the script, it resembles a pair of breasts, a common symbol of the Great Mother in antiquity.

Loki's Offspring

It seems strange, perhaps, that Loki should appear in the Norwegian Rune poem verse for this stave, praised, no less, as having "brought the luck of deceit." Loki is, after all, a trickster figure in Norse myth whose antics, while humorous, ultimately prove to be no laughing matter. It is Loki's liaison with a frost giantess that creates the three evil offspring Fenris the wolf, Jormungand the snake, and the hag named Hel, who will eventually overwhelm the world and virtually destroy it. His most treasonous act is to kill the beautiful god Balder, a divinity of light most loved among the gods who symbolizes the powers of runelore, herbal medicine, and foreknowledge. This terrible act signals the beginning of Ragnaroc, the apocalypse in which most of the gods, including Odin and Thór, are doomed to die. What has Loki to do with the green-leafed birch, then?

In fact, Loki himself is born of destruction in the greenworld. In the *Prose Edda* his mother is named as Laufey, meaning "tree island." She gave birth to Loki after being struck with one of the fiery arrows unleashed by his father, the giant Fárbauti. Here we have a commentary on the return of life to woodlands after forest fires, and thus on the theme of rebirth. Moreover, as destructive as Loki appears, we must look to his deeper function in the myths. His ribald humor and provocative manner underlie a classic feature of the trickster: his function as a god of sexuality and even fertility. Across world mythologies, the trickster figure is often depicted wielding a huge phallus, and this exaggeration of the sexual organs is evidenced in Norse mythology by a tale in the *Prose Edda* in which Loki ties one end of a sling to a goat's beard and the other to his testicles, and capers about in order to amuse a giantess. Indeed, Loki's many children—both sinister and fair—are an illustration of one of his primary characteristics: prolific reproduction.

In another tale from the *Prose Edda,* Loki transforms himself into a mare, seduces a colt, and gives birth to the eight-legged steed Sleipnir, Odin's own mount. This myth suggests that he is bisexual or even hermaphroditic in nature, like the birch pole itself with its phallic and vulvic associations. Loki, therefore, can represent the wily and unpredictable force of fertility. And although he proves in the end to be a malignant enemy of the gods, without his traitorous actions the iron-cast order of the nine worlds would never be shaken, the old gods could never die, and new ones would never take their place. While Loki may seem a malignant midwife, he does ultimately herald new birth.

Movement: *ehwaz* (Horse)

Names: Gmc *exuaz* **(horse); Gothic** *egeis/eyz;* **OE** *eh;* **Gothic** *eyz.*
**(*Note:* There is no eh stave in the Younger Futhark
and therefore no accompanying Norwegian or
Icelandic Rune poem.)**

Sound: *e* (as in *equity*)

OLD ENGLISH RUNE POEM

The horse brings joy;
proud on its hooves,
by heroes praised, it is
a solace to the restless.

VISUALIZATION

A white horse gallops on the sand, its mane billowing like sea foam in the wind.

MEANING

Ehwaz literally stands for the horse itself. It signifies movement, mobility, and perhaps a change in locale. Your "horse" represents any "vehicle" that enables a shift from one location to another. Thus your skills, vocation, profession, or guiding star has given you means to make a move to where you need to be. Enjoy your mobility. The time could be ripe for a change in dwelling place, settlement, or even country of residence.

While the *ehwaz* rune can translate as the *need* to move, its mercurial nature can also correspond to the sheer restlessness of spirit that provokes journeying in the first place. Horses are magnificent, restless creatures, not easily tamed. Similarly, travel may be in your blood. This rune may therefore augur a traveler or someone whose routine involves periodic travel.

Another aspect of *ehwaz* is that of working in tandem, which is symbolized by the image of horse and rider. A dynamic interrelationship of opposites results in fluid motion and forward progress. Partnerships on a personal and business level will, where successful, serve to bring the goals of both parties within closer reach. Foster such mutual support where appropriate.

Finally, *ehwaz* can sometimes relate to issues of boundaries, of where and how they are drawn. In sparsely settled parts of the ancient world, a person's estate was measured by how large a circle of land could be covered on horseback in a day. In cases where you are centered and settled in yourself and your abode, this stave could represent having to set boundaries to preserve your personal or professional "territory" from exploitation. Be clear in setting your limits.

Reversed, *ehwaz* indicates you may be stuck in one place and feel the effects on your spirit. Stagnation sets in when we do not follow the creative flow in our lives and move to new ground when appropriate. Horses do not react well to the bridle, and similarly you may resent being forced to tether yourself to one place. Partnerships may be constricting; alternatively, others may not be respecting your boundaries. Assert your freedom!

Keywords: Mobility, journeying, change in locale, travel—one-time or periodic, partnerships, working in tandem, boundaries. *Murkstave:*

Stagnation, the bridle and bit, being stuck, disputes regarding boundaries.

MYTHS AND LEGENDS

Horses are beautiful creatures, long admired for their swiftness and restless grace. Their use by people wrought a revolution upon the ancient world, vastly extending the range, scope, and nature of human activity. It is believed that horses were probably first domesticated around 1800 B.C.E. in the Asian steppes, and of course the greatest implication of this feat was that human beings became far more mobile on land than ever before.

The horse was also one of the most important cult animals of Northern paganism, being associated with the orbits of the sun and moon and functioning as a totem of the earth and fertility gods known as the Vanir. The *Eddas* refer to two horses who draw the sun's chariot, namely Árvakr (Early Waker) and Alsvithr (All Strong). There is mention of two chariots representing night and day, the first of which is drawn by Skinfaxi (Shiny Mane) and the second by Hrímfaxi (Frost Mane). But the most celebrated horse in the Norse myths is Odin's eight-legged steed, Sleipnir, whose origins are outlined below.

Representations of horses, horse-and-rider forms, and Sleipnir-type figures in particular are common in iconography on ancient pictorial stones. For example, one of the Gotland stones from the migration period (third to sixth centuries C.E.) clearly depicts an eight-legged horse whose central four legs intertwine into a Celtic-style knotwork motif. It has been speculated that Sleipnir's eight legs represent the *syzygy* (divine union) of a stallion and mare in one animal. Some commentators then go on to link this stave to the theme of sacred twinship. (For related information, see the *raido* stave on the theme of riding.)

Sleipnir's Stable

The *Prose Edda* tells a delightful and somewhat salacious tale of how Odin's steed, Sleipnir, was sired. Ásgard is built, but the gods have yet to make its boundaries safe against incursions by the mutinous frost and rock giants. One day a builder arrives at its gates and strikes a bargain with the gods in return for his services. He is willing to construct a marvelous wall around Ásgard; if it is completed in a single winter, he will win as his own the goddess Freya, as well as the sun and the moon. On Loki's insistance, the gods—against their better judgment— allow the disguised giant to use his horse, Svadilfari, as a helpmate. This proves to be their undoing, for together the giant and his stallion make alarming progress, and it looks as if Freya and the sun and moon may have to be forfeited.

Incensed, the gods deliver the order to Loki that he must avert the crisis and deliver them from the consequences of their oath. True to his trickster nature, Loki makes off and shapeshifts into the form of a beautiful mare and cavorts seductively in front of the steed Svadilfari, distracting him from his task. Loki then hoofs it into the woods with the stallion in pursuit, and the churlish builder, realizing that he has been tricked, reverts to his original form, that of a rock giant menacing Ásgard. Luckily, Thór returns at that moment from a foray in the east against trolls and cleaves the giant's head in two. Meanwhile, Loki has conceived a colt by Svadilfari. Once born, this colt becomes Odin's lightning steed, Sleipnir.

Vanir Magic

As a cult animal, the horse had a profound role in sacrificial rites, sacred kingship ceremonies, and earth magic. Horses were commonly sacrificed—along with boars and various horned animals—in honor of the fertility gods. This association with the earth-centered Vanir continued for a very long time: there are accounts of magically charged horseflesh being eaten as a type of sacrament into Christian times and also of horse penises being preserved and venerated—all to the horror of clerics. Fragmentary accounts of coronation ceremonies, what is more, suggest a ritual in which the "king" or tribal chieftain mated with a white mare (symbolizing the land) as part of his sacred marriage to the earth deities, of which Loki's cavorting may be a kind of parody.

An example of malefic witchcraft described in *Egils Saga*, which may have been a widespread cultic practice, further underlines the connection between the horse and the land and land spirits. King Eirik Bloodaxe breaks up a sacred Icelandic court, thus casting himself in the role of usurper and provoking Egil's anger. The hero carves runes and sets up a horse's head upon a pole "as a spell to bring down a curse on the king and his wife." He then chants a *galdr* (incantation, spell) that invokes Odin, Frey, and Njórd and "demands that the land spirits drive the king from his realm."[65] Clearly the animal's head is here being used as a boundary marker in a ritual curse connected with the sovereignty of the land. This connection to land spirits and boundary markers returns us to the primary signification of the stave in contemporary divination, in which it usually augurs travel, a change of locale (both boundary-crossing processes), or, sometimes, having one's own boundaries crossed. Needless to say, the rites described above are not practiced in the Northern Mysteries today.

Humanity: *mannaz* (Man)

Names: Gmc *mannaz* (man); Gothic *mannaz/manna*; OE *man*; NRP and IRP *mathr* (man)

Sound: *m* (as in *man*)

Correspondence: man

OLD ENGLISH RUNE POEM

We are each other's mirth
yet must one day take leave,

for the gods will allot
our frail bodies to the earth.

NORWEGIAN RUNE POEM

Man is the waxing of dust;
mighty is the hawk's talon span.

ICELANDIC RUNE POEM

Man is the joy of man
and the increase of dust
and the adorner of ships.

VISUALIZATION

A man and a woman face each other, hands on each other's waist.

MEANING

Mannaz translates as "man" or "humanity." In the runic world vision, humanity is an integral part of the cosmic design. We have been gifted with talents, abilities, and powers to assist us in the journey of life. These faculties are also there to aid us in the quest for happiness and joy. Through self-development we can both benefit ourselves and become more fit vessels to receive the inspiration of the divine realms.

As in American Indian culture, Norse thought sees a unique fate path *(wyrd)* for each individual within the larger web *(ørlog)*. Delving deep into the self leads you to uncover the higher path that exists for you in this life. This is a particularly good time to extend your skills and involvements. Whether your gifts lie in your hands, mind, body, imagination, voice, or spirit, refine and work them like a musician practicing an instrument. Unleashing your creative potential will also begin to invoke reward from the outside world at this time.

This rune is named after Mannaz, an ancestral god who was

known (somewhat chauvinistically) as "the father of the Teutonic people." *Mannaz* is a stave that is also sometimes connected with the god Heimdall, "father of men," and must be understood as the stave of all humanity—of humankind's lot and position within the nine worlds, of the human condition and human potential. Consequently, it embodies the upward thrust of human evolution.

It also signifies the dearness of human beings, one to the other. This rune may sometimes relate to a love affair, partnership, or friendship. Value those around you. As a rune of humanity, *mannaz* also presents the challenge of extending love to other people and planes of being. The existence of family, friends, and community is crucial to your happiness. Our shared mortality should spur us on in developing patience and compassion. On the highest level, this involves the evolution of a genuinely planetary consciousness.

Reversed, *mannaz* may signify that your talents are lying dormant. Make the most of the opportunities that arise while you can. Alternatively, you may be suffering from a lack of humanity (emanating from within or without), misanthropy, or hatred. Concentrate on the virtues of those around you and shun the negative. In the worst-case scenario, *mannaz* as a murkstave may refer to mortality, the sad rite of leave-taking. Process your grief as only you can, but do not ignore the life that continues to flow all around you.

Keywords: Humanity's gifts, talents, ability, and power; human potential and empowerment; inspiration, creativity, compassion, love. *Murkstave:* Dormant talents, misanthropy, hatred, farewells.

MYTHS AND LEGENDS

In Norse mythology, the human realm, Midgard (Middle Earth), is central to the nine worlds. Countless lays and sagas stress the beauty and pleasantness of Midgard. In the celebrated creation account found in *Völuspá* we read how "men's fair dwelling" emerged from the primordial void. After its creation, "Borr's sons" (Odin and his brothers) set about creating the first two human beings, out of a pair of trees named Ask and Embla. This suggests an essential kinship between human beings and other strata of creation, especially the denizens of the greenworld.

The high gods then go on to gift humanity with its primary characteristics:

> *Breath they had not,   nor blood nor senses,*
> *Nor language possessed   nor life-hue:*
> *Odin gave them breath   Hoenir senses,*
> *Blood and life-hue   Lothur gave.*[66]

Thus imbued with the essential ingredients of life—breath, blood, and senses—the human story, the tale of the inhabitation of Midgard by humanity, begins.

In *Rigsðula* (The Song of Rig), which may reflect ancient fertility beliefs and magical practices, we find further elaboration of the development of humanity. There we hear of three human couples who are visited by the divine god Heimdall, guardian of the Bifrost Bridge, which links the domains of gods and men. He shares their beds, thus bestowing upon them the boon of offspring. Although there is a somewhat sinister socializing function to the tale (it explains how the three distinctly stratified social classes arose), such accounts also reveal that in Norse myth, as in many tribal mythologies, human beings were seen as descendants of the gods, the result of an intermarriage of the natural and supernatural planes of existence.

Kith and Kin

Germanic, Norse, and Anglo-Saxon societies valued the ties of kinship and bonds of community above virtually all else. As the Icelandic Rune poem states: *"Mathr er manns gaman"* (Man is the joy of man). The Norse felt that outside the bonds of the community were only misery and defeat. As Odin warns in *Hávamál* (Sayings of the High One):

The pine tree withers   in an open place
neither bark nor needles save it.
How shall a man   hated by everyone
live for very long?[67]

This theme is also explored in the *fehu* and *gebo* runes, but we can note here that social bonds were not merely an emotional and social contract but a legal one. As the rune scholar Maureen Halsall writes: "Germanic kinship bonds were inviolable, making the whole extended family into a kind of psychological unity; betrayal of kinsmen was an unthinkable crime, for which the Germanic law codes provided no recompense."[68]

In contemporary divination, of course, value of community is extended beyond the mere clan or folk group to encompass all of humanity. Humanity—in the sense of our ability to be both human *and* humane—is this stave's lesson.

Humanity's Lot

The Old English Rune poem verse for this stave stresses human mortality, dwelling on the tragedy of leave-taking and the cold recesses of our common grave, the earth. The Scandinavian poems use dust as a symbol of the material from which humanity came and to which it returns, with the Norwegian Rune poem's "mighty is the hawk's talon span" suggesting perhaps some Valkyrie-like bird whose claws finally claim the tiny human life. The Icelandic verse describing man as "the adorner of ships" is ambiguous: Does it refer to the proud seafarers at the helm or a corpse on a flaming burial ship?

However, this is really a rune of human potential, not death. Even though all living beings and the high gods themselves are doomed to die at Ragnaroc, according to *Völuspá* the earth will one day arise anew, "barren fields will bear again," and two symbolic human beings, archetypal lovers named Líf and Lifthraser (probably derived from the root *lif,* meaning "life"), survive the purgation. In the *Prose Edda* it is said that they find shelter within the trunk of the World Tree,

Yggdrasil, during the destruction and then reemerge to people Midgard again. Then shall begin an age of peace, with the bright god Balder, champion of herbal medicine and runelore, sitting on Ásgard's throne. Thus, once again, humanity's fate is shown to be linked with the greenworld from which we arose. Only through oneness with the World Tree can we hope to survive. Outside its bark there is only ruin. And in this oneness with creation lies hope, for in Middle Earth, as in all the other realms sustained by Yggdrasil, death is always followed by rebirth.

The Unconscious: *laguz* (Water)

Names: Gmc *laguz* (water); Gothic *lagus/laaz*; OE *lago*; NRP and IRP *logr* (water); common root of modern English "lagoon"

Sound: *l* (as in *lake*)

Correspondence: lake

OLD ENGLISH RUNE POEM

Water to land folk seems never-ending
when they set sail on a heaving ship;
the huge waves overwhelm them
and the seahorse won't heed the bridle.

NORWEGIAN RUNE POEM

Water falls free from the mountain;
gold trinkets are so highly prized.

Water wells from the spring
and the great geyser
and the land of fish.

VISUALIZATION

The sails of a longship rise upon a ruffled sea under the full moon.

MEANING

Laguz represents water—the sea, a waterfall, or a lake—and can beto-ken a journey by water. Water-going voyages, especially the infamous raiding missions by longship, were a classic feature of Viking life. This meaning can still hold true, and if this rune is accompanied by *raido* or *ehwaz*, it often signals a journey and perhaps a trip literally overseas.

However, on a deeper level, water is linked with the lunar realm of emotion, sensibility, feeling, and flow. These fluid forces are the true "waters of life," and the more profound journey signified by this rune is the one inward to the depths of the self. Thus *laguz* is most often associated with the process of discovering the hidden springs of our inner life.

In esoteric terms, the true voyage is one of self-discovery that leads us into the primordial realm, the "churning waters" of the depths of the psyche. Its mythological inhabitants—including the monsters and demons of the watery deep—become the drives, desires, compulsions, and complexes that the runecaster seeks to identify and understand.

Either way, the waters of life are welling up from within and tak-ing you with them on their course. Now is the time to journey fear-lessly through emotional rapids, waterfalls, warm streams, ice floes, and deep tidal waters. Hold steady on your course. You may at times feel out of control and at the mercy of the current. In such moments it is best not to resist the tide, for fighting a force stronger than your conscious mind only leads to exhaustion.

Reversed, *laguz* signifies blockages or perils on your journey. As far as physical travel is concerned, this is a difficult time, with nothing seeming to flow in the right direction. The journey within, too, may be beset by difficulties. Beware of being swamped by the titanic forces of the unconscious. Some stones are best left unturned, at least until the appropriate time. You should allow emotion to express itself freely, but don't wallow. When out of your depth, seek solid ground as quickly as possible.

Keywords: Journey by water, travel overseas, journey inward, depths of the self, metaphysical insight. *Murkstave:* Blockages, perils, titanic forces, the danger of the unconscious.

MYTHS AND LEGENDS

In the older layers of Germanic mythology, water figures as both the source of life and the death-dealing force that leads us to the gates of the underworld. As a life-giving elixir, water manifests in sacred springs, wells, and rivers. Well worship was common among the Norse, as it was with the Celts, and is a beautiful honoring of the waters of life. Ornate goods, including pieces made of gold, were often cast into a swamp, lake, or well as an offering to the deities. The idea here is that we return to the gods a proportion of the goods that have been bestowed upon us only by dint of their generosity. By so doing, we participate in the greater flow of the surrounding world. As the Icelandic Rune poem implies, water falls freely, like the gift of life, yet people often place the highest value on meaningless material trinkets.

It is sometimes stated that there is no rune relating to the moon. However, *laguz* is the true lunar stave. After all, it is the secret influence of the moon that governs the tides, just as *laguz* embodies the forces that rule our inner life. This stave, therefore, can relate to the secret or hidden things that govern the tides of our emotional experience. Water is truly alive, an energetic substance that spirals and dances its way through many elemental states and facets of the ecosystem. It embodies the very substance of the life force and is one of the most profound mysteries in Paganism past and present. We see this in the importance of the goddess symbols of the well, cauldron, and cup from which the god Odin drinks and receives enlightenment and inspiration. As we will see below, water is associated with a number of other mythological themes.

The Fishes' Bath

The ocean is a fertile yet more ambivalent vortex of water's primal powers, an abode of demons and monsters. Its king was the old sea god Aegir—member of a generation of gods even more ancient than the Vanir fertility deities—who received sacrifices in the form of prisoners to distract him from his fetish for wreaking ships. His wife, Ran, also delighted in snatching sailors from the decks with her "drowning net" and dragging them down to her coral caves "where mead flowed as freely as in Valhalla."[69]

The underworldly citadel of the dead at the bottom of the sea is preserved in later Norse myth with the figure of the sea god Njörd, who lives in a hall on the ocean floor known as Nóatún (enclosure of ships) to which seafarers go after their death. Njörd's first wife was Nerthus, a goddess worshiped, among other places, on an island shrine in Frisia, and for whom sacrificial victims were also drowned. A related theme can be seen in the Slavonic Rusalki, water nymphs inhabiting rivers and lakes who loved to lure travelers to their death by drowning. Obviously, journeys by water held special perils, and there were many spells for calming the ocean's rages and ensuring safe passage. One of the spells Odin recounts in the *Runatal* is this:

> *I know a ninth: if I ever need*
> *To save my ship in a storm,*
> *It will quiet the wind   and calm the waves,*
> *Soothing the sea.*[70]

And in *Sigdrífomál* (The Lay of Sigdrífa) we learn:

> *Sea runes good at need   learned in ship's saving;*
> *For the good health of   the swimming horse,*
> *On the stern cut them   cut them on the rudder blade,*
> *And set flame the shaven oar.*
> *How so big the sea hills   how so deep the blue beneath*
> *Hail from the main   and comest thou home.*[71]

Finally, Njórd's son Frey possessed a celebrated ship known as *Skíthbladnir* (Wooden Blade)—the tale of how it was fashioned for him by the same sons of the dwarf Ivaldi, who made Odin his spear, Gugnir, is told in the tenth-century tale *Grímnismál* (The Lay of Grimnir)—and other references suggest that the famous Viking-ship burials were a Vanir cult. So in total we find in ancient Norse myth the symbol of the funeral or processional ship that leads the soul into the underworld.

The Collective Unconscious

The association of water with the nether realms of Germanic and Norse cosmography causes this stave to be identified in contemporary divination with the unconscious (in the Jungian sense), the oceanic realm of the universal or collective underworld. Jung's understanding of the unconscious, which he identified with the esoteric element of water, was actually based in part on ancient cross-cultural traditions, including that of the Germanic netherworld, so the marriage of concepts is quite appropriate. The anarchic character of these realms as it strikes the inexperienced traveler may be read in the Old English Rune poem lines: "The huge waves overwhelm them and the seahorse won't heed the bridle." The currents or vortices of the personality are underpinned by transpersonal forces beyond conscious control. Jung himself discovered the perils of the unconscious when beset by visions that precipitated a mental breakdown. But this experience ultimately gave way to a reborn self and a more profound sense of wholeness.

Here, the fertility aspect of water is also of relevance, for the safe return from the depths of self-analysis—which parallels the archetypal myth of the hero's descent to and return from the under-world—accomplishes the rejuvenation of life. By descending into the dark depths, we can discover the secret, life-giving springs of wonder and inspiration that lie within the self. A prime Norse model for this theme is Odin's return from Mímir's Well with the wisdom of the Runes.

Sexuality: *Inguz* (The God Ing)

Names: Gmc *inguz* (Ing); Gothic *iggws/enguz;* OE *inc.* (*Note:* There is no *Ing* stave in the Younger Futhark and therefore no accompanying Norwegian or Icelandic Rune poem.)

Sound: *ng* (as in *sing*)

OLD ENGLISH RUNE POEM

Ing, first seen by the East Danes,
later rode his wagon away
eastward over the waves;
thus was the great god named.

VISUALIZATION

The fertility god Ing, on a golden wagon, returns westward to a spring-like landscape.

MEANING

Inguz is a rune of sexuality, fertility, family lines, and ancestry. In the immediate sense it is like Wilhelm Reich's *orgone* (sexual life force energy) bursting through the seams. Pleasure and gratification are augured. Yet ultimately, this rune turns our attention to the great river of life flowing from the ancestral past through the sexual act into the present and on to future generations.

Norse paganism encourages us in our enjoyment of sexuality. Earthly life and its fruits are there to be relished, and this rune counsels you to take pleasure in and express your sexual self with confidence. It is healthy to feel at home in our body and be aware of our erotic nature. At the same time, *Inguz* promotes growth in the matters at hand. It is an empowering, fertilizing rune.

Not that the appearance of *Inguz* means you may abandon everything in the pursuit of pleasure. This is a very dynamic and multifaceted rune that brings a sense of continuity and connection within the unfolding fabric of life. It prompts us to dig deep to seek out the roots of the current issue. What is the larger context of what is occurring to you, be it pleasure or pain? How does it fit into the big picture? What is the ultimate source of what you are experiencing?

This rune relies to a greater extent than others on the staves surrounding it in a reading. One of the reasons is that *Inguz*, like the sexual act, embodies in itself a great mystery. Out of the materials of the past spring new, innovative forms that cannot be predicted from the sum of their parts. As some commentators have noted, the stave shape of *Inguz* resembles the structure of DNA as it spirals through the generations.

Ing in later times came to be regarded as a type of legendary ancestor, and tribes were named after him, such as the *Ing*wine (Danes) and *Inga*evones (a Germanic tribe on the Baltic coast), and, some even claim, *Eng*land itself (after the Angles)—hence, Ing's celebrated role as an ancestral god. Finally, just as *berkana* can relate to motherhood, *Inguz* can relate to men's mysteries such as potency, strength, support, protection, and fatherhood.

Keywords: Sexuality, fertility, family lines, ancestry, orgone, sexual energy, river of life, fertilizing force, bodily awareness, erotic confidence. (*Note: Inguz* is not reversible.)

MYTHS AND LEGENDS

The god Ing was an ancient fertility god and early folk hero of the Scandinavian peninsula. He is depicted in the Rune poem as riding in a wagon, and such figures were a widespread fertility motif in Northern lands. In particular, a cart bearing a fertility god crowned, reigning, and dispensing blessings as he traveled around the countryside is common in chronicles of Norse life. Such figureheads could be both gods and goddesses, according to time and place, but were especially connected with the cult of the Vanir. An early example of a ritual procession in Denmark, described by Tacitus, involves the cult of the goddess Nerthus, one of whose titles is Terra Mater (Mother Earth). Oxen drew her wagon through the land, and her arrival occasioned a kind of brief summer of love, with the setting aside of all weapons "while the people gave themselves up to feasting."[72] Nerthus herself was sometimes said to be Frey's lover, and Frey often figured in similar festivities, replete with the giant phallus with which he is traditionally portrayed.

Indeed, Frey (a gnomish god with a huge penis) is also sometimes pictured in Norse literature being transported around in his wagon to bless the land in spring. In *Flateyjarbók* (Ólaf's Saga) there is a comic tale in which the god's image is taken around the farms of Sweden in a vehicle drawn by oxen, attended by a beautiful young priestess playing the part of his wife.[73] A member of the processional impersonates Frey and acts out his seduction of his wife, which results in her bearing a child. Such accounts clearly echo old pagan fertility customs in which the human lover becomes a consort of the goddess and thus himself becomes a god. Frey was sometimes called Ingi-Frey and has been identified with Ing; these rites are directly relevant to this stave. Frey, furthermore, shares this fertility aspect with his sister, the sex goddess Freya, so *Inguz* may be regarded as her rune too.

Warp and Weft

In the *Skáldskaparmál* (Poetic Diction) section of the *Prose Edda*, the gods are described as "the race of Ingi-Frey," suggesting that the paternity of the Aesir may once have been attributed not to Odin but to Frey. Medieval genealogies frequently began with fertility gods being placed at their head, reflecting much more ancient tribal genealogies. Consequently, this stave is associated with the passing down of life through the generations, with kinship ties, and with inherited characteristics and family trees.

Members of the Vanir—particularly Frey and Freya—relate to several runes, including *fehu, jera,* and *ehwaz.* The images of the primordial cow, agricultural year, and fleet-hoofed horse all allude to their gnomish, agrarian nature. They also figure, more tangentially, in *laguz,* as the life-giving aspect of water, and pervade all three *aettir.* An elven race is the best description of the Vanir, and the name of their domain, Ljossálfheim, is literally "the land of the light elves." These earth deities embody the procreative energies of the soil, leaf, flower, fish, bird, and human being. Their realm is the plane of sensual pleasure, of carnal passions, an earthly bower of bliss.

Yet the Vanir are no mere garden gnomes. In *Völuspá* it is told how, in the world's first war, between the Aesir and the Vanir, the latter prevail by virtue of their magic and conduct a truce. In the *Prose Edda,* Frey seems on intimate terms with the Aesir and often kicks up his heels in Ásgard. He is no less amorous a character than his sister, a theme especially underlined by the central theme of the epic poems *For Scírnis* (Skirnir's Journey) and *Skirnismál* (Lay of Skirnir). Here the Vanir's lord becomes enamored of Gerd, a giantess and daughter of Gymer and Orboda. He becomes so full of grief and foul of looks that his father, Njórd, notices. Frey's servant Skirnir is sent on a mission to court Gerd for the smitten god. She agrees to join with Frey, but he must agree to wait nine whole nights. In his torment, this period seems interminable. Frey ruminates with these words:

> *Long is one night,   long are two nights;*
> *How can I hold out for three?*

> *Oft to me one month   seemed less*
> *Than this half night of love.*

There is a sensual side here that underlies the earthy disposition of the Vanir. In general, the pagan gods and goddesses—Heimdall, Njórd, Freya, and Odin being chief among them—revel in the carnal side of experience. What this speaks of to us is that the deities of Norse paganism are not neutered or ascetic gods. Sexuality is its own deity, and its simultaneous beauty, vitality, and raging glory plays itself out at all levels of creation. *Inguz* is, similarly, an orgiastic rune, a stave of the eruption, expression, and channeling of sexuality.

The Double Helix

Several contemporary runic commentators note that the Anglo-Saxon form of the rune resembles the double helix of the DNA strand, the vehicle for the transmission of the genetic constituents of life from time immemorial to the present day and into the future, described by the quantum physicist Paul Davies as "two coils entwined in mutual embrace." Certainly it is a complex, potent, and archetypal sign that is well employed when worn as a fertility talisman.

There is, however, the matter of bloodlines, which have a powerful role in Northern thought, though one that needs to be tempered with much wisdom. It is true that the Norse believed in ancestral spirits, fetches (a term that also conveys the sense of a familiar or doppleganger), and the *hamingja* (a kind of personal guardian spirit and higher being). In one respect, then, the bloodlines are vessels of genetic, familial, tribal, and spiritual heritage. Yet in a multicultural world, we have to see ourselves as members of a greater human family tree. Even the personal "fetch" of the icy North, for instance, can be likened to the Indian *devas*, Chinese *shen ming*, Persian *jinn*, Arabic genie, and Western genius—all of these terms referring to entities that both accompany and in some sense are aspects of the person who cultivates them.

Inguz can also be linked to cellular memory, the powerful patterns locked within our innermost constitution, which, we are increasingly reminded, play a huge, unacknowledged part in our lives. Certain magical rites in the Northern Mysteries are designed to transform the flow of this vital energy through the body, and in part 3, "Rune-casting," you can read about the development in the twentieth century of a school of runic yoga. There can be no greater transgression, from a contemporary Pagan perspective, however, than either racially moti-vated hate, on the one hand, or, on the other, the "scientific" manipu-lation of genetic materials (in plants and animals) by biotechnical companies intent on profit. *Inguz* is indeed an emblem of the need to respect all life at its most fundamental level.

Light of the Gods: *dagaz* (Daybreak)

Names: Gmc *dagaz* (day); Gothic *dags/daaz*; OE *tag*. (*Note:* There is no *dagaz* stave in the Younger Futhark and therefore no accompanying Norwegian or Icelandic Rune poem.)

Sound: *d* (as in *dawn*)

OLD EПGLİSH RVПE POEM

Day is the gods' messenger;
the light of the gods grants ecstasy,
good hope, and a boon to all.

VISUALIZATIOΠ

Dawn breaks over an eastern hillside, brightening fields, forests, and fjords.

MEANING

Dagaz means "day" and represents the sun's rays and thus our connection with the world of light. Whereas *sowulo* (the rune of the sun itself) refers to the Source, *dagaz* is widely regarded in contemporary divination as a rune of earthly blessings and the dawning of spiritual enlightenment. You are "walking in the light," and this fills each facet of your life with warmth and illumination.

The "light of the gods" is a cross-cultural concept referring to the higher consciousness that human awareness can break into at certain moments. Such flashes of insight, sometimes called peak experiences, reveal the profound unity and beauty of existence and are glimpses into the higher orders of the spirit. The ultimate goal is to enjoy this ecstatic state in every moment of existence, though most of us have been conditioned to believe we must settle for less.

Dagaz can also mean "day" in the sense of a cycle of time that encompasses both day and night. It is especially associated with the transitional zones of twilight and dawn, and consequently with the shift from an old state or condition to a new one. You may, therefore, be in a period of transition in which a long night of the soul is melting in the light of a new day.

In Norse paganism, the solar qualities of beauty and light falling to earth find embodiment in Balder, a radiant god reminiscent of more familiar figures such as Krishna and Christ. Killed in Ragnaroc, Balder's return "brings an end to sorrow," a new age. This can be read as a metaphor for the way in which the light often seems to be eclipsed, whether on a personal, cultural, or global level. This shadow side is, however, only one face of an eternal cycle of days and nights. Dawn is now approaching. Arise and dance the dance of renewal.

Keywords: Day, the sun's rays, world of light, divine messages, blessings, enlightenment, the light of the gods, insight, peak experiences, "a day," a cycle of time, transitional zones, the dance of renewal. (*Note: Dagaz* is not reversible.)

MYTHS AND LEGENDS

The Anglo-Saxon name *daeg* recalls the Norse Dag, a mythological figure who traveled daily across the sky in a chariot pulled by the horse Skinfaxi, "whose shiny mane lit up the world." Day, light, and sun were and are of special significance in the North, as the *sowulo* rune demonstrates. Winter's severity makes the sun's fertile rays all the more adored for those few brief months. The literature of the *Eddas* is full of praise for the virtues of day and the warmth of the sun on one's back. In *Vafþrúðnismál* (The Lay of Vathrúdnir), the giant Vathrúdnir questions Odin: "What is the horse called who climbs the heavens / drawing behind him day?" Odin answers:

> *"That is the horse   Shiny-Mane,*
> *who brings the brightness of day;*
> *he is considered the best of his kind—*
> *the light never leaves his mane."* [74]

Skinfaxi, or Shiny Mane, may be "the best of his kind" owing to the splendor of his mane, which obviously represents the rays of the sun, but that does not mean that night is evil in nature. Vathrúdnir then asks Odin: "What horse comes eastward / climbing the sky / to give sweet night to the gods?" Odin replies:

> *"Hrimfaxi, Frost-Mane,   draws forth night,*
> *giving pleasure to the gods;*
> *drops of foam   fall from his bridle—*
> *that is the dew of dawn."* [75]

Here day and night are seen as complementary pairs that together make up the total round of each terrestrial day. This cyclical and time-keeping function is further elaborated when Odin in return asks Vathrúdnir: "Whence came day which looks down on men, / night and the waning moon?" The giant responds:

> *"The Shining One   is Day's father,*
> *Night is a giant's daughter.*
> *The new and waning moons   were made by the gods*
> *so that men could measure time."* [76]

In this dialogue we see illustrated the dual concepts of day as *the world when illuminated under the sun's rays* and as *a cycle of time* encompassing day and night and symbolizing a round of events. Such a pattern can be observed in the very shape of the *dagaz* rune, which begins as a full line on the left that dwindles to a point at the center, and returns to fullness on the right-hand side.

Balder's Return

The story of Balder, a prominent solar god from Norse myth, further illuminates this aspect of the *dagaz* stave. Balder is a god of light, "radiantly handsome," and considered the most beautiful of all the Aesir and Vanir. He has runes carved on his tongue (signifying a rune master), is a god of herbal medicine and white magic, and can see the future—barring his own fate. Balder's presence lights up Ásgard like the rays of the sun, but over time his prescient dreams, which have always been radiant, become nightmares auguring disaster.

Odin and the other gods know that the death of Balder will spell catastrophe, as predicted in ancient prophecy. But they are unable to prevent the trickster Loki from fooling Balder's brother, Hoder—who is, by contrast, a blind and gloomy god of darkness—into killing the beautiful god. This terrible event brings about Ragnaroc. However, after the great battle Balder is released from the underworld, and as we read in the great prophetic poem *Völuspá*:

> *Barren fields   will bear again,*
> *Balder's return   brings an end to sorrow.* [77]

Here we see the classic cyclical myth of a solar god, a god of light, murdered and darkness reigning for a period of time. For after Balder's death, darkness falls and the twilight of the gods ensues.

Then comes the ultimate triumph of darkness: Fimbulwinter—three winters when "the sun turns black," with no summer. Finally, however, the light returns in the form of Balder, with all the images of dawn. The earth is "green once more," "barren fields bear fruit," and two human beings who have survived the apocalypse return to repopulate the world, feeding on "the morning dew."[78]

After Ragnaroc

This beautiful regeneration motif can become a powerful symbol for our times on several levels: personally, socially, and ecologically. Even if, as with Balder, a shadow falls upon us, the inner psychological meaning of the myth is that the higher lore of the soul Balder embodies will always return. Life always returns, like dawn after the darkest hour, and we are part of its flow. Similarly, societies undergo periods of rise and fall, crisis and transformation. Certainly the Norse seemed to ken the demise of their own culture, sensing the death of the old gods, though a resurgence is now under way and the runes carved on Balder's tongue are again finding ears for their secrets.

What is no secret is that the earth is under severe duress from the pressure of human expansion and exploitation. Midgard is ailing, and the health of each one of us is linked to it. As long as we remain out of alignment with the golden mean of balance found in nature, we invite the unraveling of the fabric of life, within which each of us is a thread. If the picture formed by this tapestry gets darker, uglier, more frayed, this will be reflected holistically in each of our lives. Each of us carries a personal shadow, but if we allow them to grow unchecked like a wolf in the woods, the shadows we collectively cast will lock in a suicidal embrace. Much has already been destroyed or, in Tolkien's words regarding his mythical kingdom of Numinor, has "passed into shadow." Yet something remains; all is not lost. Thus, the need for personal and collective healing—Balder's herb lore and white magic—becomes ever more pressing.

Home: *othila* (Ancestral Hall)

Names: Gmc *othila,* also *ethel* (landed property); Gothic *othal/utal;* OE *odil.* (*Note:* There is no *othila* stave in the Younger Futhark and therefore no accompanying Norwegian or Icelandic Rune poem.)

Sound: *o* (as in *home*)

OLD ENGLISH RUNE POEM

Home is loved by all
who prosper there in peace
and enjoy a frequent harvest.

VISUALIZATION

An ancestral hall sits on a golden plain, its doors open and smoke rising from the chimney.

MEANING

Othila signifies *home,* in several senses of the word. Literally, it refers to property, an estate or possessions. Practical associations of this rune include homecoming and buying or inheriting a house or another major possession. It can also signify gaining a sense of place or perhaps coming to feel at home within yourself. This last aspect points to *othila*'s symbolic, psychological, or spiritual meanings. It is, in total, a profoundly grounding and affirming rune.

As the Old English Rune poem suggests, *othila* conveys a blessing: "Home is loved by all" sings the praises not just of a physical dwelling but of a more profound sense of place as well. To "prosper" there provides an image of contentment, and the "frequent harvest" means reaping the fruit of our efforts. This theme also recalls the first rune, *fehu* (Abundance), returning us to the beginning of the Futhark sequence, like a wheel in motion.

As a rune of inheritance, *othila* also represents the raw ingredients that you are gifted to work with in life: the condition into which you are born, the materials and possibilities at your disposal—in short, your lot in life. It is interesting to note that the form of this stave incorporates the *Inguz* rune in its upper two thirds and the *gebo* rune in its lower two thirds, suggesting that which is gifted to us—for better or worse—from the generations that have gone before. The choice of what to make with these basic building blocks is yours, however.

In spiritual discipline, *othila* represents being content within the self, of coming home to your own still center of being. In a world where everybody chases the dragons of material wealth and sensory stimulation, this stave teaches the value of our truest possession: the haven within.

Reversed, *othila* may suggest you are being left out in the cold in some respect. There may be problems over inheritance or connected with your home ground. Your efforts to create a haven are encountering difficulty. Perhaps you feel alienated and displaced or of no fixed abode materially or spiritually. Think long and hard about where you truly belong and what kind of environment will feed the center of your being. Follow your heart, either consolidating your current position or moving to a more tenable space. Nurture and nourish yourself.

Keywords: Home, property, inherited estate, homecoming, buying a house, a sense of home, contentment, plenty, good harvest, one's lot in life. *Murkstave:* Problems over inheritance, being left out in the cold, displacement, alienation, homelessness.

MYTHS AND LEGENDS

As with most tribal cultures, the family, extended family, clan, and community of the early Norse and Germanic peoples were close-knit structures that tied the lives of individual members into a cohesive whole. The bonds of community could be as oppressive as they were no doubt fulfilling, however, as illustrated by the somewhat regimented class structure depicted in the *Eddas*.

The tripartite model of society was viewed as having been established by the gods. In *Rigsðula* (The Song of Rig) we read how Rig, another guise of the god Heimdall (guardian of Bifrost, the rainbow bridge linking Midgard to the upperworlds), fathered the three classes of human beings. This set the pattern for the lives men and women were to lead. The thralls, or serfs, received the grimmest lot. Manual laborers who were never freed, they had no patron god, though doubtless they believed in a plethora of supernatural beings. On earth, however, they had to make do with rude, stinking huts, sleeping under the same roof as their domestic animals. The larger peasant class were somewhat better off. They had Thór as their patron and in the Viking period tended to live in dwellings consisting off "two or more buildings—a pair of parallel long-houses sometimes supplemented by a barn or two, making a three- or even four-sided complex with a court-yard in the middle."[79] This type of structure is known to archaeologists as an *oppidum* (pl. *oppida*). Then there was the class of "earls," really aristocratic warlords who lived refined lives in fine halls, with their retainers, treasure hoards, ships, and estates passed from father to son. Odin was their patron, and they sought his favor through exploits in battle.

You had to work within what had been dictated by fate and make the best of your lot in such a society. We are lucky to have more mobility in our society but, similarly, must make the most of the possibilities at our disposal.

House and Lands

As we know, by Viking times the Scandinavians had become very acquisitive, raiding, trading, and bringing back goods to their own family holdings in their homelands. The condition of your estate (in the Viking age, this was often a holding shared by a large, extended family) was important on a symbolic, as well as material, level. It pays to recall that there was a formal distinction in Norse culture between fixed and movable property. In *Grettir's Saga,* for instance, it is told how two brothers, Thórgrim and Thórgeir, divide an estate: "Þorgrim took the movable property and Þorgeir the lands." There is a clear contrast of this kind operating between *othila* and *fehu.* This, the last of the Elder Futhark runes, is one of house and lands, while the first stave, with its evocation of wealth as a consolation to all, suggests "movable" rather than ancestral wealth.

The image of a person's estate as the receptacle of his or her fortunes is nicely illustrated in one of the most famous of Norse sagas. In *Eiríks saga rauða* (Erik the Red's Saga), it is related how the wandering priestess Thórbjorg, whose prophetic role and ritual attire are discussed in the introduction, is welcomed by the householder Thórkel and given fine food and utensils to eat with. After the meal he gets around to asking her "what she thought of the household there and of men's state and condition." The seeress is clearly being consulted for her psychic powers to give a reading on the fate of Thórkel's estate and fortunes. She later tells him that although he will enjoy success in Greenland, his future lies in Iceland, and she prophesies great good fortune for him there in terms that remind us of the Old English Rune poem's image of the prospering householder.

For some people, living a spiritual life involves renouncing material goods and prosperity in favor of a more ascetic existence. Certainly we are an overly materialistic civilization and, untempered, this greed is likely to prove our undoing. We must, however, be aware that for the pagan Norse, conditions were very different. In a landscape of fjords and inlets, where even gentle plains could be virtually unpassable in winter, farmhouses nestling into hillsides with grass roofs and smoking chimneys represented a very real form of security against extremely hostile conditions. All human beings throughout the ages have sought to make a home in an ever changing world, however much we are all mere travelers passing through. This rune provides a contrast with the rune *raido,* then, which refers to the importance of leaving the familiar behind and striking out in the world. Everything, after all, has its season.

Obviously, for us in the modern West the challenges of daily life are quite different from conditions two thousand years ago, but for me the very Northern sense of home and belonging that is found especially in the Norse sagas is not without its inspiration. (As I write, heavy snow has blanketed much of the country, and farmers are laying reserves of hay on the fields to provide succor for their cattle. Outside a cold rain is falling and the wind's chilly blasts whistle through the eaves. I have just been brought a much appreciated mug of tea, and my son lies tucked under his bedcovers, asleep.) Strip away all the trappings of our modern-day lives and our hopes and fears are not so different from those of our ancestors. Home offers many comforts. Who does not seek to prosper there in peace, enjoying a frequent harvest?

Gimlé: The Hall of Gold

Michael Howard offers a beautiful interpretation of *othila* as home in another sense, it being "the end of the seeker's journey through the runic alphabet." He writes:

> It is the goal which the seeker has sought so hard for. It is the sacred grove in the centre of the forest which the traveller reaches after walking along the woodland path. In some of the classical mysteries the aspirant is led through many ordeals until he reaches an empty room which is the inner sanctum of the temple. In other versions the initiate travels through a maze and finds at its centre a mirror in which is reflected his or her image.[80]

Here *othila* becomes home in the sense of the true seat of the self.

As far as our ultimate resting place (if there is such a thing), in Norse mythology the final abode is a hall named Gimlé that is "fairer than the sun," according to the great prophetic poem *Vǫluspá*. Thatched with gold, Gimlé is where the surviving gods regroup after Ragnaroc. It is also where deserving people will dwell "to the end of time," enjoying complete happiness. Reminiscent of the Celtic world's Tir na nÓg, land of eternal youth, it is the Northern Tradition's everlasting paradise and harvest home. In spiritual discipline, it may be used as a visualization of the temple of the Higher Self that each of us carries within. For many it also nurses hopes for repatriation with their loved ones in the netherworld when their own journey is done.

Part 3

RUNECASTING

He who would read   the sacred runes
        given by the gods,
        that Odin set down
        and the sage stained with colour
is well advised   to waste no words.

HÁVAMÁL (SAYINGS OF THE HIGH ONE),
POEMS OF THE "ELDER EDDA"

This final part of *Nordic Runes* presents a complete system of runic divination that will be of use and inspiration to the novice and advanced practitioner alike. In the section "The Art of Runecasting," the reader will find outlined the steps for creating, charging, casting, and spreading the magical staves of the Elder Futhark alphabet. The section "Spreads and Castings" provides five methods of utilizing your runestaves, including write-ups of real-life consultations that reveal how the Runes may be interpreted in the context of common human cares and concerns. You might like to turn straight to these sections in order to begin the practical divination work. However, first addressed are some matters that will be of interest to those curious about the hows and the whys of contemporary runic divination. The pages directly following, "Re-membering the Tradition," outline how Runes have become popular again, including elements as diverse as the revival of Germanic folklore and J. R. R. Tolkien's fantasy fictions. The next section, entitled "The Theory of Runic Divination," explores the question of why runecasting should actually work. Here we contemplate theories of chaos, synchronicity, and the unconscious.

RE-MEMBERING
THE TRADITION

The revival of Runes as a fully fledged divinatory system is a relatively recent phenomenon, although, as we will see, runic scripts have not lain entirely dormant over the last thousand years. The decline of the tradition is generally dated from about the tenth century, from which time it suffered under the general suppression of pagan practices carried out by the Christian Church. The question is, to what extent did the persecution achieve its aims? The problem we face here is that history is written by the victors, and little if any concrete evidence exists of an organized network of rune guilds or the like surviving the conquest. It is often implied in standard histories that Christianization proceeded very rapidly in the North, sweeping aside the old ways in barely one hundred years. Certainly, on the surface at least, conversion seems to have taken hold with alarming speed. Around the tenth century, most of the Northern lands were subject to intense missionary effort. Local rulers and the kings of emerging nation-states such as Sweden, Denmark, and Iceland saw both political and economic benefit in converting to the increasingly cosmopolitan faith their southern neighbors had come to embrace. Monasteries were set up and supported by local patronage, and through them the entire Church apparatus was introduced.

Denmark was Christianized under Harald Gormsson in 950, while in 998 King Olaf Tryggvason established it as the official religion of Norway by armed force. Olave Scotkonung attempted a similar feat in

Sweden in the first two and a half decades of the tenth century. In Iceland, Christianity was imposed after an infamous bribe made to the law-speaker Thorgeirr in the year 1000. By the twelfth century, the *gothi* (priests of a tribe or clan) who gathered at the Thing (parliamentary assembly) had welcomed two Catholic bishops, of Skalholt and of Holar, to Iceland's venerated Althing (parliament). The new religion was clearly on the rise. However, progress was by no means even, or meekly accepted. In Norway, where pagan temples were sacked, there are accounts of attempted conversions of pagan priests with the use of torture and mutilation, and there, as in Denmark, pagans fought against their Christian persecutors. Denmark even reverted to paganism as its official religion in 988 under Harald's son, Swein, who drove his father from his native land. Similarly, in Sweden there was a reversion to paganism around the year 1060, with the bishops of Sigtuna and Skara being expelled from the country. It was, indeed, not until the 1120s that Swedish resistance was crushed by the Norwegian king Sigmund, and with Sweden the last pagan kingdom in the North fell.

By the twelfth to thirteenth centuries, however, there is little doubt that the alien faith had managed to establish itself with exceptional vigor. But to what extent might a continuance of the old ways have survived in families of noble lineage, on the one hand, and in conservative rural communities, on the other?

It seems very likely there was some measure of accommodation on both sides. We have only to look at the *Eddas* and Norse sagas to see that the educated Icelandic and Norwegian classes retained an interest in their native culture and the religion of the Elder days. While these documents, as seen in part 1, often had underlying Christian agendas, they suggest that the exploits of the old gods and mythological heroes were accorded high status both as supposed histories and as shared stories in much of the North. In a region where ancestor worship had flourished for centuries, if not millennia, the beliefs of one's forefathers could not be entirely erased from the collective memory. Even in the courts of Christian kings, preserving some record of the glories of the past was given a degree of priority, as the sagas show. The Norwegian and Icelandic Rune poems further demonstrate that this interest applied to runes as well, and given their late dates and the conscious use of pagan themes, they may be viewed as products of an early form of Neopaganism. What the common people felt is less easily judged, for we are talking in the main about a largely illiterate population of serfs whose thoughts writers of the time were not much concerned with recording. But some folkways certainly survived, in the case of runes, including grave markers, decorative features, and some remnants of ancient spellcraft. Perverse confirmation of the continuance of the magical use of runes may be found in an edict from Iceland, from as late as 1639, in which their use was defined as witchcraft and therefore illegal.[1]

By and large, however, it goes without saying that the arrival of Christianity in the North was the doom of the organized system of runelore, evidence for which we surveyed in the first part of this book. The oral tradition may have continued in whispers and echoes in story and fable, but the survival of a more formal apparatus for the transmission of runelore seems unlikely. So were the Christians entirely successful in their pogrom? Paradoxically, and with delicious irony, it is the early courtly or monastic collections of literature and related Northern lore that are the foremost sources for any revival of rune magic and divination tradition today. Some scholars have even argued that runelore as we know it must be viewed as of late Viking–age vintage, as if the complex webs of significance we have been exploring in this book were of purely literary invention, a kind of precursor to Gothic romance. Moreover, one or two medievalists have even gone so far as to suggest that the monasteries *contributed* to the survival of the script, via the illuminated pages of the manuscript tradition. But from a magical point of view, the smattering of runes we find there surely represents a rather limited and ornamental use. Again, it is from the rich well of Norse literature, not in a few runes scribbled in the margins of history, that a fully operational system of runic divination can be recovered, for those who choose to draw upon it.

It has been claimed by some esoteric authors that the Elder lore survived intact in the countryside in Sweden and Norway. This is probably an exaggeration and should have some qualification. As we will see in the last section of this book, "A Final Word: The Rune Revival," more than one writer in the popular sphere has claimed initiatory knowledge conferred by secret orders of this kind. This is not necessarily a lie, but neither is it the whole truth. Unhappily, it strikes at an issue that dogs the entire contemporary Pagan community, and deserves some explanation here. As we will see below, folklorists have for more than a hundred years been fostering the revival of ancient folk practices on the Scandinavian peninsula, from the sort of groups that stage mock longship funerals to occultists with more magical agendas. Some of the latter like to make out that they are vastly more ancient and authentic than they in fact are, although I think their role is an important one. In any case, these are the types of societies that some contemporary authors are likely to be talking about.

This is not a problem limited to the Northern Mysteries. In England more than one of the "ancient festivals" and apparently antique rites performed in village greens are believed by tourists and contemporary Pagans alike to be unbroken survivals from the distant past. Of course, some elements may be avowedly ancient, but recent research by historians such as Ronald Hutton of Bristol University (author of *The Triumph of the Moon: A Study of Modern Pagan Witchcraft*) suggest that they date to much more recent efforts to *revive* ancient pagan customs by nineteenth- and early-twentieth-century folklorists and anthropologists. Such revelations are dispiriting, and indeed some of the recent critiques of Wicca, in particular, and its claims to antiquity are downright disturbing. Aidan Kelly basically concludes in his two-part investigation *Crafting the Art of Magic* that Wicca as we know it is largely a modern creation put together by the movement's father, Gerald Gardner. Kelly describes Gardner as "devious" and, although still professing a personal affiliation to Wicca, raises serious reservations as to the truth of its claims. Hutton, while praising Gardner as a creative genius, gives the reader equal pause for thought. He talks of the danger of Pagan fundamentalism—

a mentality whereby Neopagans cling to historical inaccuracies with a vigor similar to that of fundamentalist Christians in denial over the theory of evolution. In her 1998 book, *Druid, Shaman, Priest: Metaphors of Celtic Paganism*, Leslie Ellen Jones sets out to show just how much of present-day Druidism is a modern construct (or perhaps an accretion of projections springing from outside sources dating as far back as the ancient Greek historians). Similar reservations can be applied to the extravagant claims of some adepts of the Northern Tradition.

Yet, in my estimation, a middle path exists between abject gullibility and mocking cynicism regarding the "Elder ways." Yes, much of contemporary Paganism, whether of the North, South, East, or West, has been recovered in recent times, albeit in many cases from genuinely ancient remnants. But, then, what belief system is not an amalgamation of ideas from across time and space? What we know of Christianity today bears little resemblance to its early or even medieval manifestations. Taoism had many forms and interpretations. Likewise Buddhism. Belief systems always do. Modern Paganism in all its varieties harks back to the most ancient times, but its form is in reality the product of a long accumulation of influences. What modern Paganism really does is provide a medium, in the common form of the ceremonial circle, within which threads and traces of ancient ways can be reclaimed. It is about a set of philosophies or practices — such as animism, animal totemism, seasonal celebration, chanting, and spellcraft — that share a common ancestry in shamanism and have surfaced far and wide and in many cultural guises across the centuries. If the ways have been broken, it is because their practitioners were persecuted. My own opinion is that rather than having to mount everything in an antique frame, we should recognize that Pagan tradition consists of a variety of subtle and subversive threads woven through history. Each of us, even in as simple an act as picking up the Runes, is a weaver in its ongoing renewal.

Moreover, as to the subject of this book, runes have never entirely lost their magic or charm. As the Icelandic laws show, their (presumably magical) use was widespread enough as late as the seventeenth century to provoke hostile legislation. The use of *bauta* (memorial) stones continued in Gotland until the 1700s. In the sphere of learned interest, the early Swedish nationalist Johannes Bureus (1568–1652) wrote several treatises on runes, including a novel system of "adulrunes" and his own esoteric system based on correspondences with the kabbalah. Despite claiming to be a devout Christian, he still managed to provoke the ire of the Church, his immunity to prosecution (or worse) ensured only through royal connections.[2] Finally, runes occasionally crossed over into the spellcraft of High Ceremonial Magic, which abounded in the Hermetic climate of mainland Europe in the early modern period. Although these seem to have been exceptional cases rather than the rule, they provide a venerable precedent for the incorporation of the staves into mainstream occultism.

Moving on to the folkloric and nationalistic movements flourishing in Scandinavia and Germany in the early nineteenth to the twentieth century, we can see that it is here that the most direct roots of the contemporary revival may be found. The year 1811 saw the establishment in Sweden of the Gotiska Forbundet (Gothic League). This was, of course, the era of the brothers Grimm and of Goethe. Although many remember the Grimms for their captivating children's stories, replete with echoes of ancient myth and saga, the brothers were also serious scholars who sought to understand and systematize Germanic heritage. After them, no educated person could simply dismiss folk- and fairy tales as nonsense. With Goethe, one of the greatest literary figures of the European world, it became possible to talk about local and vernacular literature as something to be set alongside the lofty Greek or Roman classics. And over the course of the nineteenth century, the "Gothic" past was increasingly seen in a romantic light, with many members of the intelligentsia recognizing it as the birthright of the northern European world. For better or worse, a pan-Germanic consciousness was gradually taking shape. Most famously, perhaps, Richard Wagner made the saga of the cursed treasure hoard of the

Nibelungen the centerpiece of his grand Ring Cycle. The theme of the Ring was gleaned by Wagner from the Icelandic *Volsunga Saga* and Germanic folklore; in the former we have, of course, the story of the hero Sigurd being instructed by the Valkyrie Brunhild in the arts of runelore. When Eugene Grasset (1841–1917), a Swiss-French illustrator, designed a poster for the opening of *La Valkyrie* at the Paris Opera in 1880, it depicted Odin armed with a spear and decorated with runes.[3]

By this time a renewal of interest in the magical aspects of runes, both exoteric and esoteric, was surfacing in scholarly and folkloric movements in Germany and the Scandinavian peninsula. On the one side, there was a growing interest in mythology and primitive religion as fields of study, with a particular emphasis on those with common Indo-European underpinnings; on the other, mystical societies began to form that were intent on actively reclaiming such eclipsed cultural traditions. Many were occult or esoteric societies—the word *occult* here simply meaning "hidden" and referring to a concern with uncovering higher truth. If there is a dark side to the revival of runes as magical sigils, it lies not in the stereotypical Christian images of the doomed rune magus plying his black arts for personal gain, but rather in the nationalistic tendencies of some of the movement's founders.

It was out of the mystical experiences of the German occultist Guido von List in the early decades of the twentieth century that the first modern attempt to recover the occult meanings of the runic script and to resurrect the Runes as an esoteric system was initiated. List (1848–1919) was a reactionary romantic who adopted the aristocratic prefix "von" despite lacking noble genealogy. He has been described by his biographer and translator Stephen Flowers as a "doctrinaire racist,"[4] for List shared the fascination of his time with a (real or imagined) founding Germanic culture, and over the course of his life his mystical revelations were interlaced with a less laudable involvement in right-wing political movements. With hindsight, the self-conscious Aryanism of much of his writing makes for painful reading. However, List died almost two decades before the National Socialists came to power, and to speak of him in the same breath as Nazism is therefore anachronistic. Hospitalized in 1902 for an eye operation, he spent eleven months blindfolded, and in this condition he claimed to experience a series of visions inspired by Odin that revealed to him the "secrets of the runes."[5] His system is based on eighteen verses from the "Runatal" section of the Eddic poem *Hávamál* (Sayings of the High One), where Odin relates the *galdr* (spells, incantations) he has learned at Mímir's Well. This is a somewhat different approach from most contemporary divination in the English-speaking world, where the twenty-four staves of the Elder Futhark are used, as presented in part 2. (The *Hávamál* verses are still sometimes used as keys in rune magic, but their direct relevance to individual runes in divination is generally considered to be minor.)

Guido von List's Armanen Runes

RUNES	NAMES	VALUES ASSIGNED BY VON LIST
ᚠ	*fa, feh, feo*	fire generation, fire borer, property, livestock; to grow, wander, destroy; the primordial word; arising, being
ᚢ	*ur*	eternity, primal fire, primal light, primal generation, aurochs, resurrection
ᚦ	*thorr, thurs*	thunder, thunderbolt, lightning flash, a threatening sign but also thorn of life (phallus)
ᚨ	*os, as, ask, ast*	mouth, arising, ash, ashes, the power of speech, spiritual power working through speech, bursting fetters
ᚱ	*rit, reith, rath*	red, wheel, right, the solar wheel, the primal fire, God itself, exalted introspective awareness of the Aryans
ᚴ	*ka, kuan, ka*	World Tree, Aryan tribal tree, feminine principle (*kuan*), the All in a purely sexual sense, blood, highest possession
ᚼ	*hagal*	to enclose, the All-hedge, hail, to destroy, introspective consciousness, to bear qualities of God within
ᚿ	*nuath, noth*	need, compulsion of fate, organic causality of all phenomena, constraint of clearly recognized way

RUNES	NAMES	VALUES ASSIGNED BY von LIST
$\mid$	*is, ire, iron*	iron, doubtless consciousness of personal power, all life obedient to the compelling will
λ	*ar, sun, ar-yans*	nobles, the sun and light to destroy spiritual and physical darkness, doubt, uncertainty, primal fire, God
H	*sol, sal, sul, si*	sun, salvation, victory, column, school, the conquering energy of the creative spirit
$\uparrow$	*tyr, tar, turn*	to turn, conceal, cap of concealment, to generate, reborn phoenix spirit of young sun god
B	*bar, beor*	birth, the eternal life in which human life is one day, predestination in the greatest sense
r	*laf, lagu, logr*	primal law, defeat, life, downfall, intuitive knowledge of all organic essence, laws of nature, Aryan sacred teachings
Y	*man, mon*	moon, to mother, to increase, empty or dead, sanctified sign of propagation of human race, *ma* as mothering
λ	*yr, eur*	iris, bow, rainbow, yew-wood bow, error, anger, inverted man rune, mutability of the moon (feminine essence)
Y	*eh*	law, horse, court, marriage, the concept of lasting love on the basis of marriage, two bound by the primal law of life
$\oplus$ X	*fyrfos, ge*	fyrfos or hooked cross or the gea, geo, earth, giver of life; the first: a sign of nuptially bound deities, dyad of spiritual/physical power; the second: a primal root for life

List's ideas were ultimately published in a book entitled *Das Geheimnis der Runen* (The Secrets of the Runes) in 1908. Although flawed by Aryan supremacism and its false assumptions, like so much of the pseudoscholarship into early Germanic mysticism of that time, his work and that of other early runologists did thrust runes into the arena of occult and esoteric studies. Less edifying was the adoption of the Armanen runes by the Nazi party, most notoriously in the insignia of the SS, composed of a doubling of List's "Sol" rune (the Elder Futhark's *sowulo*).[6] This conjures up the whole sordid matter of the connection between runes and Nazism. It is true that the Third Reich tried to manipulate ancient Germanic symbolism, as it did so much else. It is important, however, to remain skeptical about the assumption that esoteric runology in the period, even in Germany, was necessarily complicit with Nazism. In the 1920s the mystic Friedrich Marby evolved a set of exercises called *Runengymnastik* (rune gymnastics), a technique further developed by Siegfried Kummer, published in a tome in the early 1930s entitled *Runenyoga.*[7] Marby was arrested in 1936 and sent to Dachau, and spent more than eight years in concentration camps. So rune magicians who crossed the party line suffered persecution along with other nonconformists under the Third Reich.

As Prudence Jones and Nigel Pennick comment in *A History of Pagan Europe,* "It is often written that Hitler's regime in Germany . . . was pagan in inspiration, but this is untrue. Hitler's rise to power came into being when the Catholic party supported the Nazis in the Reichstag in 1933, enabling Nazi seizure of power."[8] The point is an important one, for the taint of Nazism has led many mainstream scholars to stridently disassociate themselves from both esoteric runology and the value of our pagan heritage. The rabidly antimagical rune scholar R. I. Page, for instance, wrote in his influential little 1973 tract *Runes:*

> In the fiction of late medieval Scandinavia the employment of runes for magical formula became a commonplace. This belief, that the runes were magical, attracts the fluffy-minded in modern times (just as, incidentally, it appealed to the Teutonic mysticism of some Nazi supporters in the 1930's). Our age shows a lamentable tendency to flee from reason, common sense and practicality into the realms of superstition and fantasy, and the runes have been taken up into this. Indeed it is possible for a modern writer, asserting the value of runes for divination today, to define them as 'a mirror for the magic of our unknown selves' and 'an instrument for tuning into our own wisdom.'[9]

In fact, Norse myths involving runes — many dating to at least the tenth century — are not merely late medieval, reflecting, as we saw in part 1 a genuinely ancient tradition. Indeed, the deepest layers of Norse and Germanic myth point to a broad-based, Indo-European stratum of religious belief. The demon of Nazism that Page raises also needs to be squarely faced, then banished once and for all. Once again, the Third Reich misappropriated runic and other occult materials for its own sordid ends, a cynical manipulation that provokes disgust in contemporary runic practitioners. But the gross and nationalistic distortions of paganism practiced in Hitler's Germany no more reflect the Northern Tradition's central beliefs than the Crusades, Inquisition, and witch burnings did Christ's.

However, some seek to condemn the revival of Northern paganism on just these grounds. One of the foremost authorities on Norse religion, Hilda Davidson, writes:

> It is useless to attempt to recreate it [that is, Northern pagan religion] as a living way of faith, as some have attempted to do, relentlessly shutting their eyes to the problems and striving to see the old religion in clear lines and bright colours. The attempts of Nazi Germany to recreate non-existent Aryan religion belonging to the heroic past and its hideous consequences should be sufficient warning against such attempts to catch a fallen star and return it to the heavens again.[10]

Davidson's researches have been useful to many in the rune revival, and it is perhaps ungracious to note that her line here is uncomfortably reminiscent of Hitler's own words in 1941: "It seems to me that nothing would be more foolish than to re-establish the worship of Wotan. Our old mythology ceased to be viable when Christianity implanted itself."[11]

Yet re-enthrone Odin and Freya many people subsequently have: the Pagan faith Asatru is an official religion of Iceland, and the wider revival of contemporary Paganism is recognized and protected under the United Nations Charter of Religious Freedom. At its best, the Northern Mysteries schools of contemporary Paganism seek to restore the spiritual heritage of the Northern world to life. As we saw in part 1, the early Norse materials, from arcane wisdom verse to Viking saga, are a store of immense practical and esoteric wisdom. They exist quite apart from more recent, nationalistic manipulations of "pan-Germanic" culture. Although influenced by medievalism and Christianity, through the cultural treasure of the poems and sagas we catch glimpses of an ancient stratum of northern European lore, itself intermingled with a still older Indo-European wisdom tradition and native shamanic traditions. When we draw on runes, we are actually accessing this well of vast ancestral wisdom, pictured in Norse tradition as the waters of Mímir's Well.

TOLKIEN AND COMPANY

Today few people associate runes with anything particularly sinister. In the immediate postwar decades, however, the field of ancient Germanic religion and magic was still strongly tarnished by association with Hitler's regime. The postwar climate in England was particularly hostile to anything remotely "Germanic"—even sausages with German-sounding names—though scholarship into Anglo-Saxon runes, especially in the epigraphical tradition, remained a staple of Old English studies at prestigious universities. On another front, divination itself remained an obscure practice ignored by most except the superstitious, or students of anthropology, until quite recently. Even C. G. Jung kept quiet his researches into the theory of synchronicity until the early 1950s.[12] Yet through the fifties, sixties, and seventies a consensus was slowly emerging among scholars that the original uses and practices associated with runes were magico-religious in nature, involving rituals of spellcasting and divination.

As far as the popular field is concerned, J. R. R. Tolkien's fantasy fictions proved to be something of a watershed, contributing to the aura of charm, mystery, and magic surrounding runes in the popular imagination. Tolkien was a professor of Anglo-Saxon and philology, translator of epics, and illustrator as well as a best-selling author. Over the course of his life, he became proficient in approximately a dozen languages, having begun inventing his own tongues and scripts from an early age. As a lover, along with fellow "inklings" C. S. Lewis and W. H. Auden, of everything "Northern," Tolkien had a special interest in runes. The very roots of his fictional mythology, subsequently published in 1977 as *The Silmarillion,* and the many volumes of the *Book of Lost Tales,* were profoundly influenced by Norse myth, with the idea of Middle-earth itself derived from the Midgard of the Norse nine-world model.

When *The Hobbit* was published in 1937, its cover was ringed by Anglo-Saxon runes. Readers of *The Hobbit* will recognize these lines from the opening monograph of that work: "Runes were old letters originally used for cutting or scratching on wood, stone, or metal, and so were thin and angular. At the time of this tale only the Dwarves made regular use of them, especially for private or secret records. Their runes are in this book represented by English runes, which are known now to few people."[13]

In other words, Tolkien "translates" his Dwarf runes by using the twenty-nine- to thirty-one-stave version of the Anglo-Saxon Futhark, which evolved in England around the beginning of the ninth century and whose first twenty-four letters are none other than "our" runes — the Elder Futhark script.

Like the Futharks, the "Dwarf runes," more properly known as Moon Runes, or the Runes of Erebor, are treated as magical sigils of power and mystery that Gandalf, as a wizard, retained the skill to interpret. How they gained this title is explained to Bilbo by Elrond (himself a rune master), when the adventuring hobbit first visits the Last Homely House East of the Sea:

> "Moon-letters are rune-letters, but you cannot see them," said Elrond, "not when you look straight at them. They can only be seen when the moon shines behind them, and what is more, with the more cunning sort it must be a moon of the same shape and season as the day when they were written. The dwarves invented them and wrote

them with silver pens, as your friends could tell you. These must
have been written on a midsummer's eve in a crescent moon, a long
while ago."[14]

When *The Hobbit* achieved great popularity and the publisher
requested a sequel, Tolkien began the saga that would come to be
known as *The Lord of the Rings*. For this, more than a row of Moon
Runes would be required, and Tolkien furnished his trilogy—actually
a sextet—with several magical alphabets, including the fifty-eight-
stave Angerthas rune script. Many of these staves are based on genuine runes, including the Elder Futhark. Examples include: ᚠ, ᚦ, ᚲ,
ᚨ, ᚱ, ᚷ, ᚹ, ᚺ, ᛇ, ᛏ, and ᛊ.

In *The Return of the King*, we read that the Lady Eowyn gifts
Merry with an ancient horn on which "there were set runes of great
virtue,"[15] and there is ample evidence to support the claim that Tolkien
drew on elements of the magical as well as epigraphical traditions.
The wizard Gandalf, for example, signs himself with the rune ᚠ,
which reminds us of Odin's rune in the Elder Futhark: ᚨ. The com-
parison seems justified in light of the similarities between the characters. Odin is, in Norse myth, a magician who sits upon his shaman's
throne in Ásgard. When he walks abroad, he is disguised in a blue
robe, with a felt hat pulled low over his missing eye, and is armed
with a magic spear or staff.[16] Gandalf is described in nearly identical
terms in the following poem from *The Fellowship of the Ring:*

> *A lord of wisdom throned he sat,*
> *Swift in anger, quick to laugh;*
> *An old man in a battered hat*
> *Who leaned upon a thorny staff.*[17]

To adopt Odin's own rune for Gandalf would have been a dead
giveaway, but the similarity suggests that Tolkien had contemplated
the morphology of meaningful names attached to the Futharks.
Indeed, the Old English, Norwegian, and Icelandic Rune poems were
squarely within his sphere of interest. Another possible, though cryp-

tic, reference along similar lines may be divined in the scene where the Lady Galadriel presents gifts to the Company of the Ring in the forest of Lothlorien. We read that the gray wooden box given to Sam-the-gardener has a silver rune set into the lid. Galadriel says: "Here is set G for Galadriel." In the original Elder Futhark script, as we saw, the *gebo* rune represents the sound *g*, and its meaning is "gift." It seems that Tolkien was making a kind of educated joke here.

The likelihood that Tolkien contemplated the traditional runic meanings, and therefore the wider system of reference of which they form a part, becomes a certainty when we note that he composed lists of meaningful names for his own "invented" runestaves. Thus, we read of Quenyan, a flowing script that can also be represented by the Angerthas runes, in Appendix E of *The Return of the King*:

In all modes [of Quenyan] each letter and sign had a name; but these names were devised to fit or describe the phonetic uses in each particular mode. It was, however, often felt desirable, especially in describing the uses of the letters in other modes, to have a name for each letter in itself as a shape. For this purpose the Quenyan "full names" were commonly employed, even when they referred to uses peculiar to Quenya. Each "full name" was an actual word in Quenya that contained the letter in question. Where possible it was the first sound of the word; but where the sound or the combination expressed did not occur initially it followed immediately after the initial vowel. The names of the letters in the table were (1) *tinco* metal, *parma* book, *calma* lamp, *quesse* feather; (2) *ando* gate, *umbar* fate, *anga* iron, *ungwe* spider's web; (3) *thule* spirit, *formen* north, *harma* treasure (or *aha* rage), *hwesta* breeze; (4) *anto* mouth, *ampa* hook, *unque* a hollow; (5) *numen* west, *malta* gold, *noldo* (older *ngoldo*) one of the kindred of the Nordor, *nwalme* (older *ngwalme*) torment; (6) *ore* heart (inner mind), *vala* angelic power, *anna* gift, *vilya* air, sky (older *wilya*); *romen* east, *arda* region, *lambe* tongue, *alda* tree; *silme* light, *silme nuquerna* (s reversed) are sunlight (or *esse* name), are *nuquerna*; *hyarmen* south, *hwesta sindarinwa*, *yanta* bridge, *ure* heat.[18]

Here we find a miscellany of terms that remind us irresistibly of
the enigmatic Futharks: there is a division into sets, recalling the role
of the *aettir;* apparently mundane objects sit alongside natural forces,
heavenly bodies, and abstract concepts. Some runes refer to beings or
races, others are symbolic; there are even lacunae (lost meanings) in
the list.

Of course, Tolkien was a conservative and devoutly Catholic by
upbringing *and* conviction; he certainly was no occultist or runecaster.
However, pagan themes did fire his imagination, and most of the elements present in his mythology can be traced to Norse and Celtic literature. After all, the central piece of *The Lord of the Rings,* the story
of a magically potent ring and its destructive effects, is an old Norse
theme, found in the *Volsunga Saga,* where Loki's conniving
unleashes the curse of the Ring of Andvari. Wagner, of course,
adapted it for his famous opera (though Tolkien "held in contempt"[19]
his treatment of the Ring Cycle). Interestingly, the first rune in both
the Elder Futhark and the Anglo-Saxon rune scripts—the source of
Tolkien's Moon Runes—is *fehu.* As my commentary on this rune in
part 2 reveals, in the medieval Scandinavian Rune poems, *fehu* refers
to the gold ring of Andvari that Loki gave as wergild (blood money)
for the slaying of Otter. Otter himself is a creature from Norse myth
somewhat reminiscent of Gollum (whose name is derived from
golem, a Hebrew word denoting the homunculus created for evil purposes by sorcerers in kabbalistic rituals). Both characters are
shapeshifters who are equally at home in water and on land and whose
fates revolve around a cursed ring. Thus the rune meanings we find in
"Runestaves" are more than incidental to Tolkien's fictions, and many
other parallels can be drawn between his fictional universe and
themes from the well of runelore.

The immense and ongoing popularity of Tolkien's fiction—one
has only to think of the success of the film trilogy directed by New
Zealander Peter Jackson—has undoubtedly had an impact on the
reception of runes within an English-speaking audience. In terms of
the popular imagination, it may have helped place them more squarely

in a world of magic and mystery, of wizards, witches, dwarfs, elves, ents, and hobbits, rather than anything less savory. Certainly, Tolkien's virtual founding of the genre of modern fantasy has provided fertile ground for minds of a magical, as opposed to fanatic, bent. Many popular spin-offs in this domain, such as the popular sword-and-sorcery-style Warhammer series, employ runic-type sigils that possess names and meaningful values and function in an overtly magical way within the conventions of role-playing games. Although these areas have little direct application to the Northern Mysteries, it is interesting to speculate on whether they may inspire the upcoming generation, even unconsciously, to gravitate toward the Elder lore.

THE THEORY OF
RUNIC DIVINATION

Since you have picked up this book, you probably don't have a problem with the idea that "randomly" generated runes can carry hidden meanings or messages. But why on earth should they? Traditional cultures have long held to the notion that omens occur in the natural world, signs that spontaneously arise and betoken some fortune or misfortune in the human realm. There are many examples of this, from the passive divining of signs in the natural world—such as the Celtic belief that a flock of ravens landing on the roof of a dwelling augurs death for someone within—to more active and inventive technical systems. In an oracle reading, signs of this kind are consciously sought and evoked by utilizing a created system such as the Runes, which aims to reflect all the forces, currents, and energies at work in the world of human experience. And underlying the sign there is always an image.

While some oracles, such as the I Ching, are composed primarily of text—oracular poems with interpretations—that advises the reader, sometimes cryptically, at the heart of divination systems across the globe are images. Even the I Ching's oracular poems are ultimately grounded in the primary images of the oracle, such as the Well or Cauldron. Indeed, according to Chinese tradition, the images have primacy. Tarot has been preserved simply as a set of images around which a large body of interpretations have clustered, and in my book *Ogam: The Celtic Oracle of the Trees*, the ancient alphabet of the Irish

Druids is shown to possess oracular images and its own cryptic poetic code.

Similarly, the runestaves are signs accompanied by an image (often implied by their name) and a text (the poems). These images are highlighted in the visualizations in part 2 of this book. While culturally rooted, their symbolism transcends time and space and addresses us in the here and now with their ancestral wisdom. Through them we can recover, to its full function as a mnemonic system of correspondences, the body of divinatory signs from the stock of traditional Norse and Germanic tradition. As we saw in part 1, the Rune poems and their web of correspondences in Norse myth and literature show the deeper significations of the signs. But can the universe really choose the correct runes for us at the time of consultation, thus providing the key to the resolution of a crisis?

In modern divination, the Runes may be used in "fortune-telling" by some, but for most commentators the purpose of their use is self-development and the acquisition of esoteric knowledge. This is sometimes referred to as *image* or *archetype work.* As to how or why such a process should work, despite divergences of approach by various commentators, there is a basic unity of perspective. It is perhaps fitting to start our brief discussion of the subject with the most popular of runic guidebooks, Ralph Blum's *New Book of Runes,* a familiar authority to many. In the preface, Dr. Martin D. Rayner posits an interesting theory on the subject of meaningful coincidence. "Perhaps these Rune interpretations are simply so evocative that each contains *some* point which can be accepted as relevant to *some* part of what is happening at the limits of consciousness any day, any time, to anyone," he writes. Now, chance and psychological projection are the common or garden-variety explanations given by those who suspect that divination reflects nothing more than the desire of those who practice it to uncover meaningful messages. Dr. Rayner, however, goes on to submit the following question for contemplation: "Can there be other factors that distort the expected randomness of Rune selection so as to provide a language by which the subconscious makes itself and its expectations known? For myself, I maintain an open mind, reminding myself that observations should not be discounted simply because their underlying mechanisms have not yet been satisfactorily explained."[20]

The term for which Rayner is searching is surely *synchronicity*, for the reading of the Runes as an oracle text—along similar lines to the tarot, the I Ching, and a host of other contemporary examples—is founded on the notion of meaningful coincidence, as C. G. Jung defined *synchronicity*. Synchronicity itself implies that there is an inherent pattern-forming tendency in the universe, which means that the macrocosm will be reflected in the microcosm, moment by moment.

This idea is not as offbeat as it sounds to the uninitiated, even in scientific terms. The physicists F. David Peat and David Bohm (a former student of Einstein's) have produced particularly significant research on the synchronistic nature of quantum phenomena. Their collaborative works, such as *Science, Order, and Creativity* and *The Turbulent Mirror,* have been concerned with unraveling the philosophical implications of the collapse of the materialistic Western empirical model. This has in turn prompted a complementary revaluation of other, older cultural worldviews. In *Synchronicity: The Bridge between Matter and Mind,* Peat discusses the I Ching in light of David Bohm's concept of quantum "enfolding":

> When the I Ching is cast, an image is created or unfolded of the particular moment in time which included the questioner, the question, and all that surrounds him or her. Just as in quantum physics the observer, or questioner, is included within the general description of reality, so is the questioner irreducibly linked to the divination. The microcosm of this meaningful instant is represented by a particular hexagram, within which are contained the balance of yin and yang. In a sense, therefore, the moment of divination and the hexagram that is obtained are an image of the seed out of which the future is born.[21]

Bohm's vision comes remarkably close to the esoteric when he claims that there is an "enfolded" or "implicate order" that may be credited with a pattern-forming tendency and that the "explicate order" (what we would call the material world) is merely a creative expression or "unfolding" of the implicate order. Quantum physics and chaos theory occupy a rapidly evolving field, but it is no exaggeration to state that far from being outmoded and superstitious, the synchronistic outlook of runecasting accords rather well with the cutting-edge insights of the emerging New Physics.

Synchronicity's primary importance in relation to divination is that the "random" appearance of signs in a reading is indicative of forces underlying the surface of events. Interpreting their configuration in a casting illuminates the flow of events from the past to the present and into the future. This flow is not necessarily fixed: The point of charting it is to see how we may alter or improve the possible outcomes of a given situation. A fruitful parallel can be drawn between the modern notion of synchronicity and the functioning of *ørlog* (fate or destiny) within the Web of Wyrd, as it is understood in ancient Norse conceptual reality. What is exciting about this parallel is that in recent years the notion of synchronicity has extended itself well beyond the circles of Jungian psychology and magical adepts, as the passage quoted above indicates. Synchronicity may be at the root of the mysterious way in which subatomic particles can "track" each other without any physical link, and in the aforementioned book, F. David Peat evokes it to explain many processes, from the creation of the cosmos to the principles underlying evolution.

Another suggestion sometimes made about runes is that they were originally a body of sacred sounds, even more primal than the later chants that eventually became the Rune poems. Each sound corresponds to and invokes a certain energy. This is a notion of magical sympathy or correspondence. Stephen Flowers writes in *Runes and Magic:* "Scripts are widely used in the execution of magical operations, but it is never clear in the most archaic stages to what extent the forms of the letters themselves contain power and to what extent they are pure abstractions for the *sound* which is believed to contain power.[22]

The fact that the Elder Futhark has three rows of eight runes each (the *aettir*) encourages us to think of each *aett* as an "octave" in a kind of esoteric or occult scale. A single stave is like a note within that scale, while several runes together form a chord.

Freya Asswyn has no doubt that the origin of the runic signs lies in "a series of sounds related to natural forces," and she has produced a haunting set of chants of rune names and other traditional materials. According to her: "Sound was a paralinguistic way of communicating. Gradually, particular sounds were connected with specific sigils and became concepts."[23] Whether or not this is true, we can take the point that alphabets in general embody a series of sounds—that, of course, is their distinguishing feature. Root sounds certainly underlie individual runes, though these shifted over time, and as with the Celtic ogam, they could be used to organize higher concepts. The importance of sound in mystical traditions—such as the sacred monosyllables and mantras of Tibetan Buddhism—is well known, and it is possible to develop similar practices using runes. You can experiment by chanting these syllables, which are provided along with the rune names in "Runestaves," or, if you prefer, sing the names associated with each rune. Like all chants, singing the rune names bypasses the critical, rational mind and leads us deep into the domain of the intuitive.

As we have seen, while the Runes are a tool of self-development, they are also part of a traditional cultural framework. They exist within, and embody, an ancestral heritage. To many runecasters, the lessons in the traditional runic system are no less important than the direct personal significance of a divination. The Runes are keys opening doorways in the collective knowledge of the North, symbolized by Mímir's Well. As we have seen, some knowledge and understanding of the traditional Norse nine-world system is vital for the practice of runic divination. Indeed, the Runes are a perfect tool for the reflection of Norse wisdom and associated concepts such as the actions of the Norns and the Web of Wyrd. Runes are threads or chords in the web that are "chimed," so to speak, in the act of divination, enabling us to realize the archetypal content of our individual experiences. This is designed to be an empowering and enlightening experience, shedding the "light of the gods" upon our situation. Some writers in the Rune revival, Edred Thorsson, Tony Willis, and Freya Asswyn especially, are concerned with the Runes as a vehicle for this cultural heritage; for others, the Runes have a more universal significance.

Not only do the runic signs form a type of sacred text within the revival of the Northern Mysteries, but they are also gaining an increasing following in the much wider movement of contemporary Paganism. As anthropologist Tanya Luhrmann notes in *Persuasions of the Witch's Craft: Ritual Magic in Contemporary England:* "There is a growing interest in magic which draws its symbology from the old Germanic and Icelandic tales, and the corpus of Norse mythology."[24] The search for a living continuation of the "old ways" by modern-day practitioners creates a desire to capture the spirit of ancient paganism through a modern way of belief and being that attempts to tune in to the rhythms of the elements.

We can conclude, then, that the nature of runic divination depends partly on the emphasis of the caster and the interpretations with which he or she is working. Not every runecaster will choose to follow all of the interpretations or practices in the foregoing. Obviously a person seeking pragmatic information through a future-oriented spread using a short list of divinatory correspondences will generate a fortune-telling-type prediction. In such a reading the emphasis is material and the signs received will be interpreted literally.

On the other hand, if you are seeking a mirror of their situation in the web world of traditional runic associations—and work by contemplating the image and the Rune poem verses attached to each stave—you will engage *the traditional elements* in far greater depth. Even then the character of the reading can, of course, vary. Some readers may focus on archetype or image work, which tends to give the interpretation a psychological or psychospiritual orientation. For others, the reading may be a type of storytelling using the traditional symbols and attached narratives. Here the ancient tales and poetic images from the *Eddas* and other texts from the Northern world take on a personal bearing, as if the runecaster had somehow entered into the web world itself. The individual follows the signs like threads in a maze of significations, creating a personal story line composed of the runic texts that can be related to events in the life of the quester. Still others engage the Runes more as an aid to intuition and psychical development. Working with runes on a regular basis, particularly if you are doing readings for others, will certainly enhance your intuition and help trigger dormant psychic and precognitive abilities.

Of course, the main focus of most runework remains self-analysis and investigation of the factors underlying challenging personal situations. Indeed, the most popular aspect of runecasting in modern times has been self-development and what may be called self-help. Some people may see the Runes as a vehicle for communicating with their "personal guide" (a concept paralleled in Norse tradition by the *hamingja,* or ancestral guiding spirit), their Higher Self, or perhaps the God or Goddess, in whatever form people choose to worship them. Such New Age adaptations of an age-old system have opened many interesting doors. In fact, in many ways the term *New Age* is a misnomer. Many things referred to as New Age, often somewhat derisively, are actually ancient practices and techniques. The phrase came into English with William Blake, who took the concept from the Swedish mystic Swedenborg, and so the idea has a more noble lineage than first appearances suggest. But in any case, everything must move with the times. Of what use is an esoteric system if it does not address us in the here and now with insightful and practical knowledge?

While some commentators may stray far from the verifiable wisdom of traditional runelore—using the staves as too fluid a symbol system, attaching almost any set of truisms or assemblage of New Age teachings to them—it pays to keep a sense of fun, of "sacred play" in connection to the Runes. Sacred play, as Ϝ (the *pertho* rune) illustrates, is the notion that the sacred can reveal itself in a spirit of play. Now, when engaging the synchronicity concept to generate a set of meaningful signs, we are actually interacting with the universe at a profound level. But one should not suppose that the seeking and gaining of truth in this way is always a process of the utmost seriousness and piety. Books of runes are systems of "oracular play," as several authors point out. We should always make an effort to approach the Runes in a spirit of respect but remain light of heart in doing so. It is, indeed, possible to see the universe itself as a manifestation of a type of cosmic humor, even if it seems at times that the joke is on us. It is often said of the Vikings that they laughed at death, and in this at least they may be taken as a model to be emulated. To become bowed by fatalism and negativity aids nobody in his or her quest for personal development. Aside from anything else, runes, in my experience, are fun.

Used correctly, the Runes can become a powerful aid and ally, illuminating for us regions of our experience that are often hidden from our own view. By making underlying patterns conscious, we can identify problem areas and work on the level of the actual energy blockage. At the same time, you will often find the Runes encouraging you to celebrate the good fortune you have. Along with the boon of good counsel, they encourage us to dance the way of the world.

THE ART OF
RUNECASTING

 his section of *Nordic Runes* presents a system for both understanding and practicing the art of runecasting. Now, in this book the term *runecasting* is used in a general sense to mean divination using runes. However, in contemporary circles you will find that it is often used more specifically for the practice of randomly tossing runes onto a white cloth and observing the pattern of their fall. This technique is the most spontaneous, unstructured, and, in a sense, primal form of runic divination. But there are also many runic "spreads" similar to those used for tarot cards. One of the simplest involves the three positions of past, present, and future. Here we lay down the runes one after the other and then read the meaning of the staves in conjunction with their positions in the layout.

Those unfamiliar with the practice of runecasting might well ask what it takes to be able to read runes successfully. Must we be clairvoyant or psychic? Are some readers more naturally gifted than others? There is really no single answer to such questions. It depends in part on what the object of the reading (and the reader) is. In *Nordic Runes* we are concerned with more than mere fortune-telling. Divination, as discussed earlier, is about uncovering the kernel of higher truth in a situation, the quotient of undiluted reality, so that the caster is able to make more fully informed decisions. Above and beyond these practical terms, it also involves a quest for meaning and understanding. There is, of course, a role in divination for reading the future. But its place is alongside an overall analysis of the trends occurring in a person's life, which involve matters of the past and present as much as the future. For pure future reading, it is probably best to consult a gifted clairvoyant or psychic.

This means, crucially, that a person need not be a natural seer to divine successfully. Runes, like other divination systems, will increase your intuition and, with time and patience, enhance your access to higher degrees of perception. And the qualities that make a good reader or caster are ultimately the same that working with runes fosters—insight, understanding, self-knowledge, compassion, strength, endurance, self-mastery, and rapport with the great mysteries of life. Often people first approach divination systems in the spirit of sensationalism, perhaps to test or experiment or to prove a technique to be true or false, but a crucial facet of the divining process is that it is an interactive affair. You get out of the process as much as you are prepared to put in, whether reading for yourself or having the Runes interpreted by others.

How, essentially, does runic divination work on a practical level? The fall of a rune into a particular "position" in a layout is the key to oracle reading with runes. Edred Thorsson, commenting on how these two elements interrelate to generate a reading, provides two useful technical terms for describing the dynamics of the procedure: "Runecasting, like any precise system of divination—I Ching, Tarot, astrology—is based on the apparently random superimposition of 'meaningful elements' over 'meaningful fields.' From the combination and interrelationships of those combinations, the full interpretation is read."[25]

In other words, a rune is meaningful in itself, and that meaning takes on its special relevance depending on its position in a spread— to which we could add the situation of the person drawing the runes as the third element. Such is the basic technical foundation of runic divination.

Once we grasp the essential simplicity of the process, it becomes clear that all we need to do is be receptive to what the reading offers.

The runes organize themselves into a meaningful pattern; our role is to interpret their message to us (or to the person for whom we are reading—often known in divinatory language as the querent). Focusing the mind and preparing the spirit for what is generally a profound reflective process is the best note upon which to begin. With time you will develop a unique sense of space that unfolds and deepens with each occasion as you are preparing to divine. It is a relaxed, open, and somewhat detached state that is pervaded by peace and calm. What we are essentially doing at this stage is creating a type of sacred space within which to enter the divining process, a safe and nourishing place to which we return again and again and which becomes more pronounced with time.

Divination is like looking in a mirror, searching beyond the narcissistic images that the ego reflects for us when we think of ourselves in material terms in order to show things as they really are. Runes are symbols that reflect back to us the progression of stages and states we are passing through, allowing us to assess ourselves with a rare objectivity that is also profoundly sensitive to our subjective perceptions. For the Runes map reality and show us our place within it. They allow the seeker to identify the emotional, spiritual, and material landscape he or she is passing through and help counsel what is the best attitude or response under the circumstances. Runes are, at the same time, guides to action rather than absolute arbiters. Fate is fluid and we should see ourselves as destiny's children rather than its servants. Now, before turning back to the reading process, let us look more closely at some of the techniques that have been developed to facilitate our work with the Runes.

MAKING AND CHARGING YOUR RUNES

As we saw in part 1, "Runelore," there are few concrete references to runic divination in the historical sources. Therefore, the account by Tacitus in which the Roman historian describes a Germanic lot-casting rite has become a key document in reconstructing runecasting ritual. Ritual is important in that it provides steps to follow and focuses us on the special character of the art in which we are engaging. Let us look again at the picture Tacitus sketches of the art of "sortilege" among the Germanii:

> To divination and lot-casting they pay the greatest attention. Their method of casting lots is very simple. They lop a branch from a fruit bearing tree and cut it into slices, which they mark with distinguishing signs (Latin: *notae*) and scatter at random without order on a white cloth. Then the priest of the community . . . invokes the gods and, with eyes lifted to the sky, picks up three slices of wood, one at a time, and interprets them according to the signs previously marked upon them.[26]

Various references to rune*staves* in the source materials also suggest that the authentic runes of old were actually carved onto twigs, with ocher or even blood then used as ink (hence, Old Norse as *hlaut-teine*—"lot twig" or "blood twig," as mentioned in "Runelore"). Needless to say, it is not necessary to follow such clues to the letter of the law. Today small stones or pottery tablets—including the mass-produced variety that Edred Thorsson dismisses as "rune cookies"— are used in place of lot twigs. Many practitioners already possess such sets, but it is ultimately desirable for you to make your own runes out of stone, pottery, or wood, and similarly to inscribe them personally. This process personalizes the stones and infuses them with your unique energy. You can also turn the whole process into a type of ritual by meditating deeply on the meaning of each rune as you inscribe it.

Your runestones should be kept in a special, ritually "secluded" space, just as in Chinese tradition the I Ching should always be placed on the top shelf of a bookcase lest the *shen ming* (divinatory spirits) be offended. It is desirable that before their first use runes be "charged" in some way: this may involve a period of meditation on the signs and the consecration of the runestones at a sacred site of one kind or another. The aim here is to both personalize and empower the stones. We should remember that animism—the belief that spiritual power can reside in material objects—is a feature of contemporary Paganism, and thus we have the practice of activating the stones so that they become in some sense "alive." Imbuing the runestones with living potency also charges them for related talismanic and ritual magic purposes. Sometimes people put a runestone under their pillow each night until they have worked through the entire sequence, so as to inscribe the meanings in the subconscious mind, or even mark them on a baked cookie or bun and ceremonially eat them, so as to literally ingest the energy of the stave.

Another way of consecrating runestones is to expose them to the various elemental forces of which they are tokens: sun, ice, hail, fire, and so on. This also serves to reinforce their connection to the powers inherent in these elements.

CREATING A POUCH AND CASTING CLOTH

Tradition does not directly state that runes should be kept in a small leather or cloth pouch, but given the materials on hand at the time, there is no doubt that this would have been the way to store and carry anything precious and talismanic. Indeed, in *Eiríks saga rauða* (Erik the Red's Saga), found in part 1, the description of the Sami priestess Thórbjorg, last surviving member of nine sisters, tells how "round her middle she wore a belt of touchwood, and on it was a big skin pouch in which she kept those charms of hers which she needed for her magic."[27] Of course, rune twigs may sometimes have been ritually destroyed after use, but the difficulty of creating a new set for each act of consultation would have made this a less than everyday event.

While your runestones should thus generally be kept in a cloth or leather bag, the actual casting requires a ceremonial white cloth, as described by Tacitus. This could be cotton, linen, silk, or some other precious material, but it should not be synthetic. It should also be kept clean, both literally and ritually. Some runecasters mark the cloth with divisions that map different "spheres" of existence, and the staves are then interpreted in light of the areas into which they have fallen, which act like positions in a spread, but this is not necessary for the spreads and castings set forth in this book.

INVOCATION

We read in Tacitus's account that before divination, the priest "invokes the gods." Few actual invocation formulas have been preserved in historical accounts. However, there is ample documentation of gods and goddesses such as Odin, Thór, Frey, Njórd, and Freya being invoked in rituals of protection and vengeance and in oath taking.[28] In contemporary divination, as of old, it is customary to offer up some invocation or chant at the commencement of casting. It should be remembered that in certain respects the "gods" of ancient belief are understood as symbolic entities representing certain functions or forces in the self or nature. While the energies referred to are objectively real, we personify them in cultural terms to provide us with a graspable symbol or model. Thus an invocation to Odin, for example, is partly a call to the prophetic, poetic, and oracular source of inspiration itself—which can be viewed both as a quality of self and as an external agent that "visits" one.

Such chants are designed to charge the space in which the divination occurs, thus creating a symbolic enclosure, a magical circle dedicated to the work at hand, within which the "gods" arise. The chant below is designed to invoke Odin in his role as master of runes, divination, and magic.

Hail to thee, Odin, All Father,
master of magic, mystery, and might.

Guardian and gifter of runelore,
Lend me your one, burning eye.

Odin! Thee I call, thee I invoke
In thine aspect of Grímnir, the Hooded One!

By the Norns' nail, by Bragi's tongue,
By Sleipnir's jaw teeth and the neb of the night owl,
By blood, by bone, by kinsfolk gone before,
Thee I call, thee I invoke!

Come, All Father, into this circle
To bless and consecrate
The casting that is to be performed.

Although Odin is the archgod of divination, some readers may prefer to invoke the Goddess, in one or another of her aspects. There is actually a description of a divination ritual from *Eiríks saga rauða* (Erik the Red's Saga) that involves a Northern variant of the great contemporary Pagan rite of circle casting, a ritual derived from Ceremonial Magic. In this powerful story it is performed by the shamaness Thórbjorg, who is working in the *seithr* tradition, and the account is so beautiful that I have included it in its entirety here.

[Thórbjorg] was fitted out with the apparatus she needed to perform her spells. She asked for such women to be found as knew the lore that was necessary for performing the spell and bore the name *Varblokur*, Spiritlocks. But no such women were to be found, so there was a search made right through the house to find whether anyone was versed in these matters.

"I am unversed in magic," was Gudrid's reply, "neither am I a prophetess, yet Halldis my foster mother taught me in Iceland the lore [or "chant"] that she called Varblokur."

"Then you are wiser than I dared hope," said Thórbjorg.

"But this is the kind of lore and proceeding I feel I cannot assist in," said Gudrid, "for I am a Christian woman."

"Yet it might happen," said Thórbjorg, "that you could prove helpful to people in this affair, and still no worse a woman than before. Still, I leave it to Thórkel to procure me the things I need here."

Thórkel [the master of the house] now pressed Gudrid hard, till she said she would do as he wished. The women now formed a circle all around, while Thórbjorg took up her seat on the spell platform. Gudrid recited the chant so beautifully and well that no one present could say they had ever heard the chant recited by a lovelier voice. The seeress thanked her for her chant, saying that she had attracted many spirits who thought it lovely to lend ear to the chant—spirits "who hold aloof from us and pay us no heed. And now many things stand revealed to me that earlier were hidden from me and from others."

The seeress then prophesies, telling the gathered company of the trials they will overcome and the good fortune that awaits them.

While we do not know the exact words of the chant, we can easily guess the deity to which the whole occasion may have been dedicated. Freya is the mistress of the school of magic known as *seithr*, which Thórbjorg was practicing, and the goddess is a powerful shamaness and seer in her own right. Although she is not directly associated with the Runes, Norse myth reveals several divine female figures as teachers of runecraft and practitioners of seership. Freya is famed for having taught magic to the gods of the Aesir and as such is a useful figure to invoke, for those who feel rapport with her. The following chant is in the spirit of traditional spellcraft, for those who wish to so consecrate their divination ritual.

> *Hail to thee, Freya, Queen of the Aesir,*
> *Queen of Vanir, fair Lady of Álfheim.*
> *Mistress of magic, Mother of Midgard;*
> *By the sovereign power of* seithr
> *And strength of Brísingamen*
> *Lend me your insight in this my rite.*
>
> *Freya! Great Goddess! Thee I call, thee I invoke!*
> *Surround me in your feathered cloak*
> *That I may see through the nine worlds*

From the roots to the trunk to the tips
Of the holy tree. Freya, gift your secrets to me!

Freya! Thee I call, thee I invoke:
By wheel of wagon and cat's light paw,
On wings of falcon, from dark veins of soil,
By day's golden light and night's black toil.

Come, Queen of All, into this circle
And bless the casting that is to be performed.

Those who prefer less sonorous rituals may substitute words of a personal significance. The important point with ritual is focus and intent. It is also vital to be comfortable with the forms that you use. The traditional formulas are there mainly to link us with the past and to enhance the potency of a chant through repetition and the resonance this creates through the nine worlds. If you have your own guardians or protectors, offer up a prayer to them instead, or simply form an intent, without the need for spoken words.

Instructions for generating a magical ritual would not be complete without a few words of caution. However one understands the nature of ancient gods, invoking them should not be undertaken in the wrong frame of mind. By this I mean that the elements of ritual outlined above, designed to ensure ritual purity, should be respected, and divination should be avoided when a person is in an angry, upset, or cajoling state of mind. This might seem to defeat the purpose of divination, as people often turn to the Runes or other oracles when embroiled in a personal crisis. The point is not that we cannot take our troubles to the Runes—this is one of the very reasons the "runes of good help" are to be employed. The important thing is that we should not put on the oracle the burden of responding in a predetermined way. When we go into a reading expecting, even demanding, a desired outcome, the results can often be unpleasant. Moreover, casually invoking ancient gods using traditional spellcraft formulas awakens forces that, while full of illumination, are best dealt with when in a ritually pure state of being.

As an example, I once carried out a tarot reading under less than ideal circumstances and the results were somewhat sobering for those concerned. The occasion was a small gathering, where a couple whom I had recently met pressed me to give them a reading. Unhappily, people had been drinking, and I have a rule that divination should never be mixed with alcohol. However, as the woman concerned would soon be leaving the area, another opportunity might not have presented itself for some time. It was a somewhat stormy night and I personally felt that the elements seemed disturbed, but out of courtesy I obliged. What follows sounds like something from a rather tasteless horror movie, but here is what happened: The cards were laid out on a table, and the first to be turned over, crossing the querent, was the Tower. This tarot card is usually considered bad for lovers, with its depiction of two figures (a man and a woman) falling in opposite directions from the turret of a crumbling tower that has been struck by lightning. As I set about explaining the card, a terrifying flash of lightning illuminated the dimly lit room through an overhead skylight, and a great peel of thunder drowned out my words. The poor fellow in the couple leaped up from his chair, and in the next moment a gust of wind somehow smashed open the back door of the house, and a second later the door into the room in which we sat was also flung open, sending in a chill blast and all but scattering the cards.

I am not suggesting that undertaking the reading at that time invoked the thunderclap, but the timing was certainly unpleasantly synchronistic and was not lost on those present. The lesson I took from it is never to do a reading, not even out of a false sense of politeness, if you have any qualms about it. It will not bestow any favors on the recipients.

Having made this rather dramatic proviso, I would like to point out that the vast majority of readings are, in my experience, very edifying occasions indeed, and I have sometimes had people approach me after months, or even years, with accounts of just how accurate or helpful the Runes turned out to be. With a few basic ground rules in place, your experience is certain to be equally fulfilling. Remember that tradition states the Runes were given in order to help, not hinder, us in our progress.

SPREADS AND CASTINGS

Τ here are dozens of spreads and casting techniques available for use, some of them standard forms, others unique creations. Furthermore, you may want to innovate along the way. Runes may occasionally be pulled from their pouch to fit positions inspired by the needs of the moment, so that a novel spread is created in an instant.

A spread is a layout of runes according to a preset pattern of positions. A runecasting involves tossing runes onto a cloth (which may be divided into segments or "meaningful fields")—although, unless otherwise stated, the term *casting* is used here in the general sense to cover both spreads and castings. Presented in what follows are five specific examples: four spreads and one casting. You will find a list of meanings provided for each position in the spread given, followed by a sample reading in which we can observe the interrelationship of runic sign and position. Note that a spread is read in the order that the positions have been numbered (see below), although after they are laid out you may wish to look at the interrelationships among all the runes, regardless of order. This brings us to the subject of the relative position of a rune—in other words, how it relates to runes around it: There are no hard and fast rules here, but obviously, if a reading has a particular overall theme, a rune's relative position will affect how we read it in the layout. If the spread involves positions such as past, present, and future, for instance, the runes in these positions might take on a special significance. For instance, *isa* in the present followed by *sowulo* in the future would tend to indicate the current misfortune being melted away by a new light that will enter the situation in the future. Further, a rather ambiguous rune, such as *Inguz,* is clarified by the runes in its immediate vicinity, especially when the spread itself contains a clear sequence of events or allows us to easily observe the development of a particular theme.

Finally, a few words on reversed runes: A rune is considered reversed when, though placed faceup to show the side with the stave, the stave itself remains upside down. Runes that are the same both upside down and right side up have no reversed, or murkstave, meanings. Some people consider a rune to be reversed when it comes out of the pouch facedown (so that you see the back of the stone rather than the side with the stave on it). In my opinion, if a rune is facedown, the best thing to do is simply to turn it over from left to right so as not to risk accidentally reversing it. I do not take a facedown rune to be a token of a murkstave meaning. Nine of the runes, in fact, have no murkstave meanings, so how would it be possible to read any of these nine as reversed if they came out facedown? If a particular position in a spread refers to negative issues (see, for example, the seventh position in the Rune Master's spread below), then a rune in that position is said to be "ill-aspected"—that is, we consider its reversed meaning, even if it is not reversed (presuming, of course, the rune is reversible!).

The readings are written up from castings in which the querent (the person for whom the casting is being performed) was encouraged to take the active part in interpretation. These write-ups aim to reflect as much as possible these men and women's subjective interpretations of the layouts or castings and to show how the signs are interpreted to function within actual readings.

THE THREE NORNS SPREAD

A common and simple rune spread involves three runes that are laid out one after the other to represent past, present, and future. These positions correspond to the role of the three Norns, who, in Norse mythology, rule over what "has passed, is passing, and is to come." The variation below is a four-stave spread, where we first draw a rune to define the overall issue of the divination:

	First position: the issue	
Second position: the roots of the issue	Third position: present events	Fourth position: the likely outcome

This elementary spread can be quite revealing. Remember, runes are multifaceted, and an apparently simple lineup can contain many layers of hidden meaning. It also has the virtue of being easy to learn and remember: a day-to-day layout, as it were. As always, however, we should not become fatalistic about the Runes' advice or apparent predictions, as with any other oracle system, for the future should always be regarded as flexible rather than set in concrete. Runes give promptings and deep counsel, but their interpretation should be complemented by our own intuition and healthily developed sense of free will.

Sample Reading

Jane, a healer, decided to consult the Runes because she felt she had reached an impasse in her search for a livable home and personal sense of place. Two years earlier she had ended a seven-year relationship with her partner (with whom she was then living) and a year later moved from a pleasant home in a semirural locale to the midst of a large city. She had hoped to find an apartment that would provide a sense of warmth and security but had failed after several shifts. Living in the city was necessary because Jane was undertaking part-time studies, and she had hopes for a stimulating new life with the increased access to opportunities city life afforded her. However, she was beginning to despair of finding a living environment that fulfilled her deeper needs. She consulted the Runes, with this result:

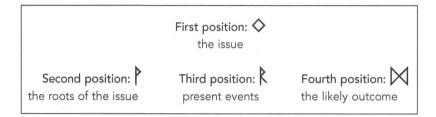

First position: ◇
the issue

Second position: ᚹ
the roots of the issue

Third position: ᚱ
present events

Fourth position: ᛝ
the likely outcome

The issue: ◇ (*Inguz:* Sexuality)

None of the significations of the *Inguz* rune resonated for Jane until she came to its festivity aspect. A strict vegetarian, animal rights campaigner, and champion of causes, Jane felt that she might have lost some sense of spontaneous fun and the ability to celebrate life. She interpreted the occurrence of the *Inguz* rune as a reminder of what she had been telling herself along these lines. It was time to lighten up and allow her fertile, vital energy to express itself more freely.

The roots of the issue: ᚹ (*wunjo:* Bliss)

The second rune was far easier for Jane to interpret. As far as the abandoned partnership was concerned, she was tentatively seeking to restore a friendship with her ex-partner and had been allowing herself, at this remove from the affair, to recall its happier moments, which she felt to be a constructive process. The Old English Rune poem verse for this stave reads:

> *Joy comes to you who know no sorrow,*
> *blessed with gain and plenty,*
> *content in a strong community.*

Also, though she felt the move away from living in a smaller community was necessary, she missed the sense of place and familiarity it had provided. She associated those times with simplicity and security. Thus *wunjo* well described Jane's past in contrast to the present.

Present events: ᚱ (*raido:* Rhythm)

Unraveling the associations of this rune proved highly meaningful to Jane. The Old English Rune poem verse for *raido* reads:

> *Riding is easy for heroes*
> *inside a hall; it's much harder astride a strong horse*
> *pounding the great mile paths.*

Jane felt that this perfectly reflected her present circumstance. When still "inside a hall" (a reference, she felt, to her previous life), things were "soft" (that is, easy and comfortable), but she had been feeling confined and even suffocated. Now she was "astride . . . the great mile paths" of a city, fending for herself in the wider world, outside her comfort zone.

Yet in this rune she recognized a challenge that she felt she must face. The image of the "strong horse" struck a particular chord with her, as she had grown up on a farm surrounded by horses and fondly remembered her childhood rapport with these animals. When told that some of *raido*'s divinatory significations were "going places, rhythm, movement," she felt that this well summed up her current phase of existence. While she might not hope to achieve a sense of place in the immediate future, she was in a phase of progress and had a sense of momentum to her life that had been lacking in her previous existence. The image of a rider firmly in the saddle of a striding horse was interpreted as her staying centered within the flux of her current existence.

The likely outcome: ᛞ (*dagaz:* Light of the Gods)

> *Day is the gods' messenger;*
> *the light of the gods grants ecstasy,*
> *good hope, and a boon to all.*

This stave corresponded to Jane's hopes for the future. Although she was reconciled to the outer aspects of her current situation, she stated that she had recently felt her world to have darkened. The *dagaz* rune represents literally "day," but also "a day": a cycle of light and dark followed by a new dawn. Some commentators interpret the helixlike shape of the rune as representing light dwindling to a point of utter darkness and then reappearing and brightening again.

This grabbed Jane's attention. She was comforted to think of her current circumstances as a phase within the wider path of her life, but was beginning to wonder when the sense of inner light would return to the situation. *Dagaz* seemed to her confirmation that there was light at the end of the tunnel. This conclusion led her back to *Inguz* and reaffirmed her sense that she needed to lighten up, to recover her enjoyment and celebration of life.

THE WHEEL OF THE YEAR SPREADS

The Wheel of the Year is the seasonal cycle commonly celebrated in contemporary Paganism. The following readings involve overlaying the points of the Wheel of the Year with runes, thus creating a divinatory analysis of an entire annual cycle. (*Note:* The sacred calendars reproduced below are based on the general system of festival dates used in contemporary Paganism. They are not specifically of the Northern Tradition. For a discussion of the Germanic and Norse calendars, see the *jera* rune.)

Two variants are offered here: the Four Seasons Spread and the Eightfold Wheel Spread. What this allows is for us to chart our progress through an entire year, with more or less detail, depending on whether we choose to use the Four Seasons or the Eightfold Wheel Spread.

The Four Seasons Spread involves the four major seasonal points of the year, which I have given under their Norse titles, with the more general terms used in contemporary Paganism included in parentheses. These solar festivals are based on the proximity of the sun to Earth and are more universal and ancient than the fire festivals, which reflect Celtic agricultural cycles. Arriving at a "Northern" calendar that fits with the wider contemporary Pagan fire festivals is difficult, furthermore, so in the Eightfold Wheel Spread I have used the more familiar Celtic terms. Different Northern Mysteries groups have found their own solutions to this problem, so I will leave this matter to the discretion of the reader. Needless to say, it is a simple matter to adjust these spreads to your system of personal preference. In both spreads, the Southern Hemisphere dates are shown in parentheses: in the Southern Hemisphere the direction of the wheel is reversed.

Please note that these two spreads are best used as a kind of chart against which to measure the unfolding of events and the challenges they bring. You will tend to find that the runes pulled using these spreads correspond very closely to the unfolding of your life path. Yet runes are multifaceted and seldom conform to our exact expectations, so don't be alarmed if a negative-seeming rune appears in the future: it doesn't necessarily correspond to what your fears might tell you. Also, the point of the Runes is to learn to meld your future creatively. A "negative" omen gives you the opportunity to anticipate a difficulty and take action to avoid or amend difficulties in the future.

The Four Seasons Spread

In the Four Seasons Spread we simply lay out four runes, starting with the next season that begins nearest to the day of the reading. This creates a seasonal forecast giving indications of the basic character of each of the four quarters ahead. (Remember, runecasting should always be regarded as giving indications of trends rather than immutable predictions, where the future is concerned.)

Alternatively, you might choose to place the first rune on the marker for the solstice or equinox just passed and allocate the following three to the spaces representing the next three seasons. That way you can illuminate the issues of the recent past, which are sometimes just as obscure to us as the future. The Four Seasons Spread that appears below shows the seasonal points upon which the runes should be placed.

	Midsummer	
	(Summer Solstice)	
	June 22 (December 22)	
Ostara		Shedding
(Spring Equinox)		(Autumn Equinox)
March 22 (September 22)		September 22 (March 22)
	Yule	
	(Winter Solstice)	
	December 22 (June 22)	

The Eightfold Wheel Spread

Similar principles apply to the Eightfold Wheel Spread as to the spread above. You simply lay out eight runes, from the current or upcoming season till the end of a full annual cycle. This variant merely supplies more detail than the Four Seasons Spread.

The Eightfold Wheel Spread also creates more scope for turning back the process a season or two and therefore gaining insight into the events of the recent past. For example, it may be Midsummer, yet you may lay down the first rune for the past Spring Equinox. This means that you can see the threads running through the past quarter, from Spring Equinox to Beltane, into the present Summer Solstice, and into the future, beginning with Lughnasa.

Midsummer
(Summer Solstice)
June 22 (December 22)

Beltane   Lughnasa
May 1 (November 1)   August 1 (February 1)

Ostara   Shedding
(Spring Equinox)   (Autumn Equinox)
March 22 (September 22)   September 22 (March 22)

Imbolc   Samhain
February 1 (August 1)   November 1 (May 1)

Yule
(Winter Solstice)
December 22 (June 22)

Sample Reading

The sample reading presented below is based on the Eightfold Wheel Spread, though the same principle can be applied to the Four Seasons Spread. Which one you choose depends on the volume of information you are seeking. Both can be powerful, although the latter is, of course, simpler.

This reading was performed for a couple who had recently conceived their first child. Although they were in a strong relationship and were not unhappy about the event, there were many practical considerations stemming from their decision to continue with the pregnancy. There were emotional challenges along with financial considerations. Uncertain exactly how the next year would shape up, they decided to consult the Runes for guidance, using the Eightfold Wheel Spread. This is how the Runes responded (note that the wheel turns, and is therefore read, in a clockwise direction—i.e., from left to right):

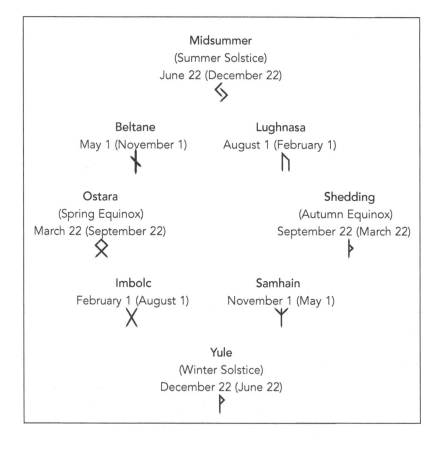

Yule: ᛈ (*wunjo:* Bliss)

At the time of the reading, the Winter Solstice lay a month ahead. For most expecting parents, the impending arrival of a child carries a mixture of emotions, but the appearance of *wunjo* here reflected the aspect of mysterious and transcendent joy that Caitlin and Finn were experiencing. This stave simply appeared to be saying: "For now, just allow yourself to feel joyful over this great occasion."

Imbolc: ᚷ (*gebo:* Exchange)

Gebo in *Imbolc* intimates that the couple's partnership has every prospect of enduring and strengthening in the near future, with a probable deepening of the sense of the contribution each could make to the other and to the child. There is also the sense that fertility is one of the great gifts of life and that this rune complements the message of the previous one.

Ostara: ᛟ (*othila:* Home)

By the Spring Equinox, Caitlin would be five months pregnant. *Othila* suggests the importance of domestic matters and the maintaining of the home front. Pregnancy may make women especially sensitive to the state of the home environment, and already the couple were talking of things to be done around the place to prepare for the new arrival. Both would likely find their energies turning "inward" as time progressed.

Beltane: ᚾ (*naudiz:* Constraint)

Naudiz in Beltane suggests a phase in which Caitlin and Finn would most likely be focused on their needs and the necessities of life. With Caitlin seven and one-half months pregnant, her bodily and emotional needs would be growing along with the swelling in her womb. She and Finn would be responding to practical matters: the necessities of the situation.

Midsummer: ᛃ (*jera:* Harvesttime)

The appearance of *jera* at Midsummer is a beautiful emblem of birth approaching. *Jera* is the harvest rune, representing the time when "the bright Earth gifts us all her fruits." With the sun at its zenith and a child ripening in Caitlin's womb, the couple would await the beginning of a new life (in more ways than one). This would also be the time to begin capitalizing on their preparations and arrangements for the birth and the days ahead.

Lughnasa: ᚢ (*urox:* Challenge)
The ancient festival day of Lughnasa falls in the very week in which the baby is due. The appearance of *urox*, the stave of the wild ox, suggested to Finn and Caitlin that the child would be a boy. Of course, any newborn infant erupts into its parents' life with a great deal of gusto, and not a little disruption, but both partners intuitively felt (without preference) that the child would be male (which subsequently proved to be the case).

Shedding: ᚦ (*thurisaz:* Misfortune)
Thurisaz at the autumnal equinox, by which time the baby would be seven weeks old, suggested a period of adjustment and attendant difficulties. The disruptive image of a giant could translate into either the demanding character of the newborn infant or certain shadow aspects arising in the parents in response to this new situation. *Thurisaz* can sometimes signal female health issues and could augur the challenging phase of the postnatal period. Finally, difficulties with institutions could arise.

Samhain: ᛉ (*algiz:* Protection)
Any trials, however, look set to be overcome by Samhain. By this time the child would be fourteen weeks old and the parents beginning to get into the rhythm of parenting. *Algiz* is a strong sign of protection, suggesting a consolidation of their relationship and the presence of favorable influences warding off negativity. As the commentary on *algiz* reassures us, "fear no harm."

THE NINE-WORLD SPREAD

The Nine-World Spread is particularly good for unraveling the elements of a knotty issue or giving a full analysis of all the components of your overall life situation. It is best for psychological, or psychospiritual, self-analysis, providing a mirror to the underlying threads in your character and situation. It is not so useful as a solely predictive spread or one applied to purely "practical" issues.

A particular strength of this spread is that it allows you insight into how—consciously or unconsciously—you are creating the reality you are living. Of course, some elements of our reality are preexisting structures that only somebody in a delusional state would imagine he or she had personally created. But other elements are there because we are attracting them to us, whether or not we are aware of the process. The aim of this reading is to make that knowledge conscious.

This spread works on the nine-world model of Norse mythology, there being nine worlds to the Norse mythological system, as we saw in part 1. These worlds can be related to aspects of the human psyche and certain archetypal forces with which we interrelate; the central column can be seen to correspond to the Eastern system of chakras. Ljossálfheim, for instance, is the world of the light elves in Norse myth. They can be identified with spirit guides and higher guiding forces that bring us to our creative expression, and this position corresponds to the throat chakra, the chakra of our self-expression.

	Ásgard	
	Ljossálfheim	
Vanaheim		Muspellheim
	Midgard	
Niflheim		Jotunheim
	Svartálfheim	
	Hel	

Ásgard

As the world of the high gods, this position represents the Higher Self, the divine will, and how we stand in relation to these aspects. It represents what the higher powers wish for us in a situation and so can also relate to the best possible future that we can create for ourselves. Ásgard is the source of universal intelligence, divine consciousness, and enlightenment. In Eastern terms, it corresponds to the crown chakra.

Ljossálfheim

As the world of the light elves, Ljossálfheim provides a bridge between Ásgard and Midgard. In other words, it relates to our creativity and powers of manifestation. It teaches us about our ability to find novel solutions to problems, both practical and more abstract, and thus relates to thought, in the highest sense of the word. At this level, what we think is what we manifest, for material reality reflects our state of mind. Ljossálfheim is also where our spirit guides reside, the intermediary forces that inspire and advise us. It corresponds to the throat chakra.

Vanaheim

As the world of the fertility gods, Vanaheim represents our connection to the waters of life, and it therefore corresponds to feeling and emotion. This sphere can relate to actual biological fertility in a question specific to that issue but most commonly refers to the wellsprings of our innermost feelings and how we express them. Our health in this area determines what will flourish and grow and what will wither and die in the emotional landscape of our lives. Fundamentally, then, Vanaheim relates to the feeling of love.

Muspellheim

As the world of fire giants, Muspellheim relates to our primal passions, in the sense both of the things that drive us (to survive or succeed or conquer) and of that which we feel most passionately about. This may take the form of a fiery dedication to a particular path or passionate love or lust for another. Fire, of course, has two aspects: that which nurtures and protects and that which burns and consumes. The fiery sword is double-edged!

Midgard

As the world of Middle Earth (our world), Midgard relates to our humanity, both in the sense of the degree to which we are living out our potential and regarding our relationship to others. This is our center, from which self-empowerment emanates, and it is the measure of our self-realization. The ideal is to achieve our highest possible potential. Midgard is also where we are tested in relation to others, especially in our ability to express and extend our humanity to our fellow human beings. It corresponds to the heart chakra.

Niflheim

As the world of fog and mist, Niflheim relates to our confusions, illusions, and delusions. It refers to those things that we see cloudily, as if in a fog. This could be due to exterior conditions but may also signal where we are imagining things, for better or worse, and are in need of a more objective outlook. Fantasy, psychological projection, and at worst grandiosity and paranoia are possible issues. It is the negative aspect of the forces that spring from Vanaheim and shows us the influences that may lead us astray.

Jotunheim

As the world of the hostile frost giants, Jotunheim relates to the unconscious forces (drives, desires, compulsions) that overtake us. It shows us where we are being compelled, as opposed to acting from our own stable center. On a personal level, it relates to blindness and ignorance and how these create stumbling blocks in our lives. In the outer world, these forces harden into brutality, and as such this position can relate to hostile people or giant institutions with which we have to contend. Along with Svartálfheim, the world below, it corresponds to the sexual chakra.

Svartálfheim

As a world of the dark elves, Svartálfheim relates to the instinctive life of sensation. It is the being-in-nowness enjoyed by animals and nature spirits. It is vital to a sense of connection to the energies of the earth and to spontaneous action that is not filtered through the intellect. While this is also an important bridge to the world of the unconscious, in its negative aspects it can lead us into unthinking habits that may, at worst, be labeled vices. It corresponds to the sexual chakra.

Hel

As the realm of the deepest underworld, Hel corresponds to the modern psychological notion of the unconscious. The unconscious is on the one hand the storehouse of repressed personal materials (suppressed memories, experiences, desires, and the like) that we cast into the shadows of our conscious reality. But it is also the shadow plane, home to the archetypal formations that arise from the deep. We are not consciously aware of this "imagal" realm, which generates many of the experiences that surround us. Making it conscious is imperative, however, as our repetitive cycles and deepest psychological conflicts originate here. It corresponds to the lower chakra.

Sample Reading

Natalie, a woman in her thirties, felt she had reached something of a crisis or impasse in her relationship with her partner, Tobias. Tensions between the pair had become almost unbearable. Natalie had believed for some time that they would be better off living apart but balked at actually making the move, partly for financial reasons. She was involved in part-time work and studying photography, her great passion. Tobias had a small but successful business exporting ornamental sculpture and tended to pay the lion's share of the bills.

Recently they had fallen into a pattern of bitter arguments and recrimination. Tobias, often fueled by more than "a few drinks," became demanding and overbearing, in Natalie's estimation; his resentment at having to support her financially would also surface.

These fights had become more frequent and emotionally violent. Natalie found herself realizing that she had to move out and find her own space, both for her own sake and for the relationship. Yet she felt that she and Tobias still cherished each other when all was said and done, and the prospect of striking out on her own filled her with insecurity. She consulted the Runes, using the Nine-World Spread, in an attempt to get to the bottom of her own role in the unfolding drama.

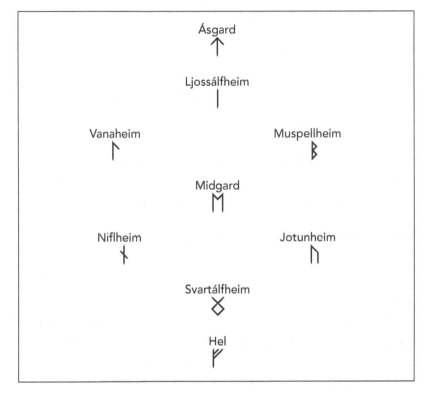

Ásgard: ↑ (*Tiwaz:* the Warrior)
Tiwaz in Ásgard suggests that this is a time that must be governed by truth and a fearless facing of the facts. It will be necessary for Natalie to access the inner warrior in order to confront the nature of the problems she faces. She must also be objective and impartial to ensure that the sword hanging above her relationship with Tobias is wielded with fairness and justice.

Ljossálfheim: | (*isa:* Danger)

Isa in Ljossálfheim suggests a blockage between the world of the gods (or Higher Self) and the practical, day-to-day world of Midgard. Ljossálfheim, as the world of the light elves, is supposed to bridge that gap, but it is frozen and paralyzed by the inert and static energy of *isa* (ice). This dams the flow of inspiration and creativity; it freezes the throat chakra and stunts our full self-expression. Artistically, Natalie had yet to fully find her voice.

Vanaheim: ↑ (*laguz:* the Unconscious)

Laguz in Vanaheim is a very strong combination, for Vanaheim is the world of flow and fertility, where the waters of life reside, the wellspring of our feelings and emotions. To have *laguz* (a stave of water) here is a sympathetic placement. It certainly indicates a rapport on Natalie's behalf with her inner life. There could be a tendency, however, to get bogged down in emotion and be overwhelmed by ferocious currents, as was happening in her love life.

Muspellheim: ᛒ (*berkana:* Birthing)

Berkana in Muspellheim is another potent placement. Muspellheim governs passions, which in Natalie's case could relate to her relationship with Tobias and love of photography. She was, through her part-time course and creative activities, without doubt in a phase of inception. (This seemed, at the present time, a more fitting interpretation to her than any suggestion of childbearing). She wanted above all else to begin birthing her conceptual ideas.

Midgard: ᛗ (*ehwaz:* Movement)

Ehwaz in Midgard was a very appropriate summation of Natalie's life situation and personal relations at the present time. She was in a phase of movement, contemplating a shift to another abode in order to get some space and change the boundaries of the relationship. She felt acutely the need to make a move. At this stage, however, what she needed was the practical and financial vehicle that would get her there.

Niflheim: ᚾ (*naudiz:* Constraint)

Naudiz in Niflheim pinpoints the problem in this equation. Natalie's greatest fears related to the issues of need and necessity—survival in the real world. Her sense of how she would accomplish this was hazy and somewhat constricted by negativity. Her relationship was supporting these needs at the present time and beyond that she felt uncertain and not a little fearful.

Jotunheim: ᚢ (*urox:* Challenge)

Urox in Jotunheim, however, reinforced the need to take action. Jotunheim is the dangerous and giantine realm of chaos and violence. To have the aggressive and testing wild ox placed here reflected the increasingly fraught emotional atmosphere of Natalie and Tobias's relationship. Both partners had become like bulls in each other's china shop, and the situation seemed to be spinning more and more out of control.

Svartálfheim: ᛟ (*othila:* Home)

Othila reversed in Svartálfheim underlines this urgency even more sharply. The only reversed rune in the reading, it signifies a hall or house, here literally turned on its head. Natalie related its placement in Svartálfheim to the fact that instinctively she was a homemaker who loved the sensual and nurturing qualities of a pleasant, aesthetic home environment. She and Tobias shared that, but negative undercurrents had welled up and upset its equilibrium.

Hel: ᚠ (*fehu:* Abundance)

Fehu in Hel, finally, appeared at the root of the whole cycle that Natalie felt herself to be living out. *Fehu* relates to wealth, money, or gold and to have it here, buried in Hel, seemed in her mind to show the underlying cause of the impasse. She had lost her independence and become reliant on Tobias, and the whole situation was undermining their confidence in each other. This reinforced for her the need to strike out and establish her own life for herself, with hope that this move would also prove positive for her long-term relationship with Tobias, whom she dearly loved.

THE RUNE MASTER'S SPREAD

This layout is not specifically connected to the Runes. In fact, it is a tarot spread adapted here for use with runes (and renamed as such). I like it so much that I included it in my *Ogam: The Celtic Oracle of the Trees* as the Druidical Spread. This illustrates the principle that spreads from other systems—such as tarot, ogam, and others of the many oracles available today—can be adapted for runic divination. If you have a favorite tarot or other spread, experiment with adapting it to the runic field.

With time and practice, you will find that the different positions in the Rune Master's Spread interrelate in many ways. The upper positions define the higher, symbolic value of past, present, and future experience, while the middle row illustrates a time line of events from the past into the present and future. The bottom row reveals the hidden influences, for better or worse, at work in a situation.

Another way of looking at this is that the left-hand "cross" of staves is the past page or chapter in the book of your life, the central column is the present, and the right-hand side shows the nexus of future events, like a page about to unfold. These three areas, too, can be seen as being ruled by the three Norns.

```
                          6


        9                                      10
    1       2                 3             4       5
        7                                      8
```

First position: distant past   Sixth position: overall theme

Second position: recent past   Seventh position: blockages

Third position: present   Eighth position: guides and helpers

Fourth position: near future   Ninth position: past theme

Fifth position: further future   Tenth position: future theme

Sample Reading

Jeff was at a major transition in his life. He had worked as an investment banker in an overseas company for a number of years, commuting between London and New York. Despite favorable remuneration, he had become disillusioned with his lifestyle. Being offered a higher position in the company and a raise should have been an occasion for joy. Instead, he had felt trapped and even a little desperate at the prospect. He felt his own life was slipping away without his really feeling fulfilled in his profession, and the inner conflict over the new position highlighted this.

In fact, instead of accepting the offered position, he decided to return to the town of his birth and to a more satisfying lifestyle. This he did and with his savings set up a small business of his own, connected to the film industry. The venture was not entirely successful, however, so he chose to dissolve the company. He then began a string of modest part-time jobs, focusing not so much on work as on his own time and interests. However, two major issues confronted Jeff. He still did not know what he wanted to do and his funds were dwindling.

Jeff's feeling was that after years in the soulless corporate sector, he wanted to do something helpful and meaningful. He had recently encountered people and ideas of a spiritual nature and felt himself connected to a strong spiritual source. Ideally, he would like to be involved in a truly progressive and enlightened project or enterprise. The only immediate prospect of any tangible kind on the horizon, however, lay with a friend who wanted him to become involved with an equestrian farm. He had also become increasingly interested in the Runes and contemplated the possibility of reading commercially for others. But this was, at the time, an experimental idea. Jeff posed his dilemma to the Runes. The result:

First position: distant past ᛏ
Second position: recent past ᚢ
Third position: present ᛊ
Fourth position: near future ᛃ
Fifth position: further future ᚱ
Sixth position: overall theme ᚷ
Seventh position: blockages ᛟ
Eighth position: guides and helpers ᛞ
Ninth position: past theme ᛚ
Tenth position: future theme ᛦ

1. Distant past: ↑ (*Tiwaz:* the Warrior)

Jeff identified this rune with the warlike energies of his previous career in finance, which, although a world of tooth and claw, had also provided him with a sense of strength and position. As a qualified lawyer, the rune of *Tiwaz* (with its connections to "troth," or "truth") was suggestive to him of his original vocation, one from which he had turned away.

2. Recent past: ᚢ (*urox:* Challenge)

Urox is a rune of challenge, and the recent past had certainly held that for Jeff. After leaving his safe position, he had had a series of trials of strength. His brush with the film industry had put him into contact with an aggressive and conflictual environment against which he had struggled, ultimately in vain. And his quest for a more meaningful vocation had certainly led him into a major rite of passage.

3. Present: ᛊ (*sowulo:* the Source)

The appearance of *sowulo* in the center of the time line of events was a comfort to Jeff and confirmed the fact that despite the challenges in his life, he felt that light was being shed on his circumstances and that he was closer to sources of inner illumination, more comfortable in himself, and thus lighter and more "on track" than ever before. He now felt a much stronger sense of rapport with what he termed universal energy.

4. Near future: ᛃ (*jera:* Harvesttime)

Jera's placement in the near future had two distinct angles for Jeff. As a rune of harvest, it corresponded to his hope that in the near future his efforts and undertakings would start to bear fruit and that a firm direction would open up. He also regarded it as a possible message not to become too insecure about the future, as the earth goddess "gifts all her bright fruits," representing the potential for developing fields of involvement and making material gains in the months that lay ahead.

5. Further future: ᚱ (*raido:* Rhythm)

Raido, too, falling in the position of the "further future," suggested two distinct readings. On the one hand, as a rune of action in the world it could signal a channel ultimately opening for Jeff's skills and talents. This is, at the same time, specifically a rune of movement and momentum, implying either that he would need to take the initiative or that his future vocation would involve much movement or travel. Or could this be an augury relating to the equestrian enterprise a friend was offering?

6. Overall theme: ᚷ (*gebo:* Exchange)

The overall theme of the reading is embodied in *gebo,* and Jeff felt he had a clear understanding of its importance. His ultimate goal was to find a vocation in which he could gift his talents and energies and receive in return a sense of reward and fulfillment. The primary meaning of *gebo* as a rune of exchange corresponded perfectly with this in his mind.

7. Blockages: ᛟ (*othila:* Home)

Othila turned up reversed in this reading in the position relating to blockages. As a rune of property and "home" (in all senses), its appearance made perfect sense. Jeff had recently invested in an apartment, with an agreement involving an initial deposit and finance to be arranged subsequently. Subsequently, however, his latest job had ended, and suddenly he had to convince a bank to grant him a mortgage. His investment in the apartment was under threat, perfectly reflected, in his eyes, by the upside-down *othila* stave.

8. Guides and helpers: ᛞ (*dagaz:* Light of the Gods)

The appearance of this stave represented another boost for Jeff. As with the *sowulo* rune in the third position, it appears to indicate a strong connection to the world of light. Jeff had been consciously attempting to connect to his higher (or spirit) guides and felt that this rune was an affirmation of this fact.

9. Past theme: ᛚ (*laguz:* the Unconscious)

Laguz is a rune of the feeling realm and of the unconscious. This in many ways summed up the recent chapter of Jeff's life, for after a very concrete and rational career, he was now focusing more on the nonmaterial and intuitive levels of reality. Still, this has its own tests and trials, and *laguz* also warns of the dangers of being swamped by the waters of the unconscious: probably very appropriate advice.

10. Future theme: ᛉ (*algiz:* Protection)

The last rune carried a note of warning to Jeff. Although he felt a sense of connection with the light, darkness was still very much present for him and his current existence was not a secure one. *Algiz's* appearing reversed here strongly suggests the need to take care in the near future, lest the rigors of surviving in the real world rise up to swallow Jeff's newfound idealism and hope. He believed, however, that he could heed the substance of this admonition while still remaining optimistic about the future. (Today Jeff is working in a well-paid, high governmental position that he finds both meaningful and fulfilling.)

FREE RUNECASTING

The runecastings above are based on the placement of runes upon a particular position, from which its meaning is established. This is the most common type of divination practiced today with runes, tarot cards, and so on. In ancient cultures, however, divination was often a far more spontaneous art, based on such apparently unstructured forms as patterns in cracked mud, cloud formations, and bird flight. The following runecasting is based on a similar, free method of divination. It is an advanced technique.

Here the whole set of runestones is thrown in front of the caster (preferably onto a white cloth). Some of the runes fall faceup, some facedown. The facedown runes are put to one side. Among the remaining runes, the reader looks for a "master rune": that is, a shape formed by their overall configuration. If one appears, the individual runes are then straightened—so as to accentuate the master rune—and interpreted as a sequence, from past to future. Such a method is much more variable than standard divination and highly dependent on individual intuition. It is recommended as a good way of developing a nonstructured, intuitive art of runecasting. If no master rune appears, you can still look at the overall pattern and interrelationship of the runes one to another. The runes that have fallen in the center are the central concerns, while those on the fringes are more distant elements. Remember, however, that there is no simple formula for this type of divination.

Sample Reading

Victor is a musician skilled in a number of instruments. Involved in quite a diverse range of musical projects, he had also built up a home studio of recording and sampling equipment. While working at a music festival in another city, he received the devastating news that his studio had been broken into and his equipment stolen. This came on top of a number of other cruel blows that had rained on him in recent months, including a breakup with his partner and a nervous breakdown. After the initial shock wore off, he went through a process of considerable soul-searching as to how he could recover from this misfortune. Was there any kind of message in this blow to his aspirations? Could anything of benefit be redeemed from the loss?

Victor posed this question to the Runes. First he drew a single rune from the pouch to signify the overall theme of his current challenge, sight unseen, which was *fehu*. Then he threw in front of him the remaining stones, which landed in a sort of fanned-out flute. When the facedown runes were eliminated, those remaining seemed to Victor—an experienced runecaster—to form an elongated *isa* stave. This he deemed to be the master rune, which appears in a runecasting as a stave shape that is revealed among the randomly cast runes. This rune is then read as the overall theme of the reading. As a stave of difficulty, misfortune, and danger, *isa* appeared to be quite appropriate. Victor intuitively felt that the lower runes in the line of thrown runes—those nearest to him—represented the roots of the problem and that each rune down the line represented an unfolding of his *wyrd*, or individual fate, in this situation.

Rune sequence: The theme rune is fehu. *The runes forming the* isa *master rune, read from the bottom up (i.e., from those closest to the runecaster to those farthest away), were:* isa, naudiz, hagalaz, Inguz, dagaz, jera, eihwaz, *and* berkana.

Vincent interpreted pulling *fehu* as signaling that the overall theme of the reading was the issue of abundance in his life. He had for a long time been fighting with the tension between the integrity of the creative process and the commercialization of music in the material world. While he wished to make money in order to liberate his plans and ambitions, he despised gross materialism. He interpreted *fehu*'s appearance as indicating that his relationship with abundance and plenty may have been blocked on some level, leading to a disturbing series of events of which the loss of equipment was merely the latest and most serious. How could this negative pattern be reversed?

The master rune, *isa,* seemed to reinforce this feeling. *Isa* is a rune of severe hardship and misfortune, ruled by the unsympathetic Norn Skuld. *Isa* tends to relate to intractable conditions or complexes that harden into major trials in our fate paths and tends to be quite difficult to overcome. But even more revealing, and incredibly synchronistic, is that the bottom three runes, *hagalaz, naudiz,* and the *isa* stave — corresponding to the three Norns, Urd, Verdandi, and Skuld — appear in their exact Futhark order. Not only did the *isa* stave occupy the root position of the reading, but it was in its traditional sequence of three as well, and the entire spread formed a master *isa* rune! This powerful manifestation communicates in no uncertain terms the influence of the Norns in Vincent's life, in this case in a most challenging configuration. What he faced was nothing short of a major karmic challenge to be overcome.

The next three runes seemed to indicate the way ahead. *Inguz* and *dagaz* are runes of vitality and light. They suggest vital energy and divine illumination. This combination — of personal energy and "the light of the gods" — is just the necessary combination to break the grip of this negative manifestation of the nornic influence. This is confirmed by the next rune: *jera,* harvesttime. *Jera* actually follows the three nornic runes in the Futhark sequence, and its appearance here indicates that *Inguz*'s fertilizing influence fulfills itself after the time cycle represented by *dagaz.* A new light dawns and brings with it growth, fullness, and festivity. Although Vincent must exert effort *(Inguz)* and cultivate inner light *(dagaz)* to escape the current cycle, the possibilities look very promising.

Finally, the pairing of *eihwaz* with *berkana* shows the necessity for movement to initiate a transition into a phase of new beginnings and the inception of new projects. *Eihwaz* is a rune of movement, of extending ourselves beyond our established boundaries. Here an aspect of the past is finally and fully shed so as to make way for a new reality. *Berkana* fulfills this beautifully. As a rune of "birching," it suggests purifying oneself by putting the past behind and embracing the new. It is also a rune of fruitfulness and of the birthing of one's conceptions, whatever form they may take. Ultimately, therefore, the entire reading shows a regenerative movement in Vincent's life from being stuck in the icy grip of the Norns' hostile influence to unleashing his creative energy and entering into a new phase of possibilities and abundance.

A FINAL WORD:
THE RUNE REVIVAL

In this book we have followed the Elder Futhark Runes from their roots in the runelore of the first centuries C.E. through various developments to the present day. We've gathered not only the runestaves of the Elder Futhark and their various names and correspondences, but also a complete set of interpretations of the meaning of the staves themselves, sourced uniquely in the actual texts that survive from an ancient wisdom tradition. And we've examined aspects of the spreading and casting of runes that should guide you to the point of being able to innovate your own approach, including the creation of novel spreads and castings, where appropriate or necessary. But even with these tools and information, you may wish to explore the wider world of runecasting.

In the following pages, I have provided a brief survey of some of the major commentators of the Rune revival, along with the advantages and drawbacks of their "books of Runes" to your growing understanding of the Runes and your developing interpretive skill.

As far as the divinatory approach to Runes goes, the early 1980s were the watershed years. Marijane Osborn and Stella Longland's *Rune Games*, published in 1982, offers a unique blend of scholarship (with valuable work on the Old English Rune poem) and imaginative insight. Osborn had read Old English literature for her doctorate at Oxford and in conjunction with Longland set about creating a set of activities or games designed to access the "consciousness-altering wisdom" of the runic signs. She claimed—here and in various published essays—that the Old English Rune poem was actually a set of "oracular verses" and that this function could be reclaimed for present-day users. It is worth repeating here a passage also reproduced in part 1 of this book:

> The art of divination has many forms, but because we consider "The Rune Poem" to be a series of oracular utterances it is divination by oracles that concerns us here. . . .
>
> In a creative way oracles, by their use of analogy and symbol, paradox and ambiguity, stimulate the individual's imagination in new directions so that he can, if he is able, perceive his relationship with the outside world in a different way and so change his future. . . . The contribution the oracle makes is to provide an enigmatic utterance which can trigger unused creative potentials. . . .
>
> The possibility of change through self-analysis is the real "magical" quality of fortune-telling systems, which could more aptly be called "fortune-making" systems.[1]

To this end, the authors compare the Runes with the I Ching and tarot, stating: " 'The Rune Poem' offers a fresh approach to the problems of individuality and existence that arises directly from the experience of peoples from the Northern latitudes."[2] The commentaries on the Old English Rune poem are the most sophisticated to be found within the corpus of contemporary oracular literature, but strangely, the Scandinavian poems are all but ignored. The use of the Runes in divination was a primary object of the work, but divination was understood by the authors in a special sense: not as fortune-telling but directed to the end of self-knowledge and "to trigger unused creative potentials."[3] Not the most accessible text for most readers in terms of content or layout, *Rune Games* remains a sort of forgotten classic prophetic of and feeding into the more popular approaches that followed. If you should chance upon it in a secondhand bookshop, don't pass it up.

Ralph Blum's *Book of Runes,* also first published in 1982 and republished in 1991 as the *New Book of Runes,* and Edred Thorsson's *Futhark: A Handbook of Rune Magic* are two other early offerings that can be taken as representative of the wildly divergent poles of contemporary runic interpretation.

Blum can be counted as a member of the "human potential" movement, approaching the Runes from a psychological and spiritual perspective, with a liberal dash of New Age philosophy. His *Book of Runes* acknowledges the influence of "a unique course" entitled The Oracular Tradition taught by Dr. Allan W. Anderson at the Department of Religious Studies, San Diego State University. The course focused on the I Ching as, in Anderson's words, "the only systematic sacred text we possess," and later Blum was to turn to I Ching consultation in order to fill in the gaps of the less obviously systematic runic oracle.[4] To the great outrage of traditionalists, of whom Thorsson has been the most blunt, Blum spontaneously divined the order of his Runes, blithely disregarding the ancient Elder Futhark sequence. Moreover, the interpretations offered for certain staves woefully ignore the Rune poems and other historical sources, with virtually no reference to ancient Norse literature. In *At the Well of Wyrd,* Thorsson pointedly speaks of the "bastardisations" of the tradition and names Blum as a chief "offender."[5] Blum, however, has been something of a hit with the public, and his works have been the best-selling of all popular commentators'.

Thorsson represents the pole of the Rune revival, which draws on the German "rune masters" of the early- to mid-twentieth-century German occult revival, and in particular the work of Guido von List. However, whereas List worked with an eighteen-stave variant of the Elder Futhark, basing his interpretation of each runic sign on a set of verses from the ancient Norse poem *Hávamál,* Thorsson used the standard twenty-four-stave Elder Futhark, with reference to the Old English and Scandinavian poems (and other materials of Germanic and Norse provenance). His own treatment of the runic signs is mystically inspired, yet also underpinned by doctoral researches in

Germanic religion and folk beliefs. Thorsson was instrumental in setting up the Rune Gild in Austin, Texas, in 1980, which has since become an international association that aims at "scientific" as well as magical study of the Runes.

In *Futhark*, Thorsson sets forth to purge the Runes of "foreign" elements—by which is meant Judaic-Christian glosses. But lest this be misunderstood, he condemns the simplification inherent in the conscription of runes by the National Socialists, stating that "during the Nazi regime all things 'Germanic' were mobilised and perverted towards manipulative ends."[6] His subsequent work, *Runelore*, offers an interesting set of historical researches into the history of the script from the Elder age to the present day. An unwary reader might infer from this book the existence of an underground tradition of rune gilds surviving in secrecy over the centuries, which Thorsson does not, however, actually claim. In fact, Thorsson endorses what he calls scientific (that is, scholarly or academic) runology and points to areas that deserve further research, such as the work of Johannes Bureus. Thorsson's best runic divination text was, however, released under the title *At the Well of Wyrd: A Handbook of Runic Divination* in 1988. It is a very workable book, a manual specifically designed for the purposes of divination. It is also graced by the fact that the Teutonic mysticism of Thorsson's earlier works has softened in tone and that Thorsson's commentaries on each rune are prefaced by his own versions of the three Rune poems.

Like Thorsson, who has also written a book on ogam, two British authors, Michael Howard and Nigel Pennick, have displayed a more general concern with magical scripts. Michael Howard, who wrote *Runes and Other Magical Alphabets*, published in 1978, is a contemporary Pagan author well known for his editorship of *The Cauldron*, one of the longest-lived magazines of the Wiccan and Celtic pagan world.[7] His most popular contribution to our subject, *The Wisdom of the Runes*, was published in 1985 and provides a sort of middle ground between the extremes of Blum and Thorsson. Traditionalist to the extent that he prefixes his interpretations with the appropriate Old

English Rune poem verses, Howard provides a well-researched and very readable lead-in to the overall field and a meandering commentary through what he calls the Woodland Path: the conjectural meanings of the individual staves in "heathen" thought. Nigel Pennick, a writer whose general interest in alphabetic mysticism and related subjects is reflected in several tomes devoted to the Runes and to ogam, was the second writer to engage the wider sphere of sacred alphabets. In *The Secret Lore of Runes and Other Ancient Alphabets*, Pennick inquires into the whole tradition of esoteric uses of ancient scripts: Hebrew, Greek, Runes, ogam, magical, and alchemical alphabets. Pennick followed up *Secret Lore* with *Secrets of the Runes* in 1992. Some of the material is gleaned from the previous work, but this text deepens and extends his consideration of the Norse sources, with translations from Icelandic literature and the Old English Rune poem. This is also a primer in the Northern Tradition rather than a straightforward divination manual. Of the Runes' place within that tradition, Pennick writes: "If [runes] are to have any value at all, both meanings and the magical uses of the runes must relate to present conditions. Of course, whilst there are some meanings that will never be appropriate for certain runes, they must always be understood in terms of present conditions. This creative, non-dogmatic approach is a characteristic aspect of the Northern Tradition today, as it was in past times."[8]

Pennick's later *Complete Illustrated Guide to Runes* is probably the finest overall study to date on the phenomenon of the Rune revival. Almost every conceivable aspect of the "tradition," from the Elder age to the present day, is brought into sharp focus, and a number of runic scripts other than the Futhark are considered for their divinatory potential: Anglo-Saxon, Northumbrian, Younger Futhark, Gothic, Medieval, and Armenian. If there is a shortcoming to this approach, it is that individual scripts, such as the Elder Futhark, are not explored in any real depth, leaving the reader with a bit of a smorgasbord of meanings.

In 1988 Freya Asswyn's *Leaves of Yggdrasil* contributed the first goddess-centered approach to the runic oracle. A self-proclaimed priestess of Woden, Asswyn consciously sets out to restore the system of *seithr,* a magical tradition connected with her namesake, the goddess Freya, who in Norse myth is said to have instructed Odin in the art of Vanir magic. Much of Asswyn's commentary is directed toward magical workings, as opposed to simple divination, although these two branches are closely linked. Another feature of her work is a more in-depth emphasis on Norse mythology than that found in most other commentaries, including many original insights into the web of resonances that the staves embody within the nine-world system of Norse thought. *Leaves of Yggdrasil* was updated and republished by Llewellyn in 1998 as *Northern Mysteries and Magic: Runes, Gods and Feminine Powers* with an accompanying CD, which includes haunting chants or *galdr* (spells, incantations) based on Norse lays such as *Völuspá, Hávamál* (Sayings of the High One), and *Sigdrífomál* (The Lay of Sigdrífa).

Kenneth Meadows, in his 1996 work *Rune Power,* is another author—along with Tony Willis—who lays claims to secret traditions, in this case from oral teachings preserved from time immemorial and given to him in outlying rural areas in Sweden. Again, while Scandinavia offers greater potential scope for enduring folk customs than mainland Europe or the British Isles, this probably refers to more recent revivalist movements; investigations of similar claims by Wiccan and Druid groups have often found them to be exaggerations.[9]

Meadows is concerned with reforming our understanding of the Elder Futhark Runes in several respects. First, he claims that the original order of the alphabet places *urox* first and *fehu* at the end of the script. Thus we would have to rename the system the Elder Utharkr! This theory was once touted by one or two Scandinavian scholars but has since been dismissed as being due to the weathering of the stones on which the "full" sequence occurs, rather than some older, alternative ordering of the Futhark. Meadows also expresses concern at the adoption of the Runes as a "Magickal" system—in the tradition of mainstream Western occultism—and its misuse for purposes of personal power. He draws a distinction between the sometimes dark sorcery of the runic magician who seeks to control natural forces and the runic shaman or shamaness who uses the system for reconciling him- or herself with the will of the cosmos. Some of his corrected significations for the staves of the Uthark (as Meadows renames it), though very readable, are hard to substantiate in the early sources. Shamanism is, however, as Meadows asserts, an excellent field for cross-fertilization with runes.

Whatever their individual strengths and drawbacks, the power of these commentaries, mediated by the magic of synchronicity, has touched the minds and hearts of many, including me, and will doubtless continue to do so.

Nor are these the only authorities of note. There are now dozens of books of interpretation, and alongside the published works, a vast web of commentaries attached to the runic signs, including hundreds of Internet sites, many of them offering on-line readings. I do not find the Net as conducive to oracle reading as a good rune set, but to each his or her own. Personally, it seems to me there is far more magic in the nameless and numberless "workbooks" of individual practitioners or used by "rings" of Odinists and other contemporary Pagans that arise from study, contemplation, and ritual involving the Runes.

Finally, we must regard the "runic oracle" in total as a multitude of commentaries rotating around the central column of the signs of the Elder Futhark alphabet. As you develop the art of runecasting, your own interpretations have an important place within this web world, for all the threads of meaning generated through the Runes have a vital place within this vast and unfurling tapestry.

Π⊙TES

The Origin of the Runes and How to Use This Book

1. Nigel Pennick, *Secrets of the Runes* (1992; reprint, London: Thorsons, 1995), 11 (page citations are to the 1992 edition).

Runelore

1. I am indebted in this retelling of the materials of *Runatal* and other Eddic materials to redactions by Kevin Crossley-Holland, *The Norse Myths* (London: Penguin, 1980), 15–17, and Clive Barret, *The Viking Gods* (London: Heineman, 1989), 170–71.

2. Edred Thorsson, *At the Well of Wyrd: A Handbook of Runic Divination* (York Beach, Maine: Samuel Weiser, 1996), xvii.

3. R. I. Page, *An Introduction to English Runes* (London: Methuen, 1973), 107.

4. Thorsson, *Well of Wyrd*, 4–5.

5. Maureen Halsall, *The Old English Rune Poem: A Critical Edition* (Toronto: University of Toronto Press, 1981), 97–98.

6. Ralph Elliot, *Runes: An Introduction* (Manchester, England: Manchester University Press, 1959), 1–2.

7. Thorsson, *Well of Wyrd*, 5.

8. Elliot, *Runes*, 2.

9. Stephen Flowers, *Runes and Magic: Magical Formulaic Elements in the Older Runic Tradition* (New York: Peter Lang, 1986), 75.

10. Marijane Osborn and Stella Longland, *Rune Games* (London: Routledge and Kegan Paul, 1987), 97–98.

11. René Derolez, *Runica Manuscripta: The English Tradition* (Brugge, Belgium: De Tempel, 1954), 354–55.

12. Ibid.

13. Margaret Clunies Ross, "The Anglo-Saxon and Norse *Rune Poems:* A Comparative Study," *Anglo-Saxon England* 19 (1990): 23–39.

14. Thomas DuBois, *Nordic Religions in the Viking Age* (Philadelphia: University of Pennsylvania Press, 1999), 31.

15. Crossley-Holland, *Norse Myths,* 182.

16. Patricia Terry, trans., *Poems of the "Elder Edda"* with an introduction by Charles W. Dunn (Philadelphia: University of Pennsylvania Press, 1990), xxii.

17. Ursula Dronke, ed. and trans., *Myth and Fiction in Early Norse Lands,* Collected Studies Series (Aldershot, Hampshire, England: Variorum, 1996), 144.

18. From the introduction to Terry, *Poems of the "Elder Edda,"* xxii.

19. Terry, *Poems of the "Elder Edda,"* 3.

20. William Anderson and Clive Hicks, *The Green Man: Archetype of Our Oneness with the Earth* (London: HarperCollins, 1990), 25.

21. Mircea Eliade, *Shamanism: Archaic Techniques of Ecstasy,* Bollingen Series 76 (Princeton, N.J.: Princeton University Press, 1964), 271.

22. Terry, *Poems of the "Elder Edda,"* 10.

23. Ibid., 3.

24. Ibid., 15.

25. Ibid., 26.

26. Ibid., 31.

27. Joseph Campbell, *The Masks of God,* vol. 1, *Primitive Mythology* (London: Penguin, 1976), 257.

28. Terry, *Poems of the "Elder Edda,"* 31–32.

29. Ibid., 21.

30. Ibid., 33.

31. Ibid., 162.

32. Ibid.

33. DuBois, *Nordic Religions,* 124.

34. Terry, *Poems of the "Elder Edda,"* 66.

35. Michael Howard, *The Wisdom of the Runes* (London: Rider, 1985), 54–55.

36. Ursula Dronke, ed. and trans., *The Poetic Edda,* vol. 1, *Heroic Poems* (Oxford: Clarendon University Press, 1997), 14.

37. Terry, *Poems of the "Elder Edda,"* 7.

38. Ibid., 21.

Runestaves

1. Terry, *Poems of the "Elder Edda,"* 164.

2. Ibid., 14.

3. Ibid., 6.

4. Maureen Halsall, *The Old English Rune Poem: A Critical Edition* (Toronto: University of Toronto Press, 1981), 104.

5. Ibid., 105.

6. Campbell, *The Masks of God,* 293.

7. Terry, *Poems of the "Elder Edda,"* 68.

8. Crossley-Holland, *The Norse Myths,* xxxi–xxxii.

9. Ursula Dronke, ed. and trans., *The Poetic Edda,* vol. 2, *Mythological Poems* (Oxford: Clarendon University Press, 1997), 384.

10. Crossley-Holland, *The Norse Myths,* 26.

11. Ibid., 8.

12. Terry, *Poems of the "Elder Edda,"* 20.

13. Ibid., 13.

14. Flowers, *Runes and Magic,* 342–45.

15. Terry, *Poems of the "Elder Edda,"* 11.

16. William Morris and Eirikr Magnusson, ed. and trans., *Volsunga Saga: The Story of the Volsungs and the Niblungs: With Certain Songs from the Elder Edda* (London: Walter Scot, 1900), 42–44.

17. Kenneth Meadows, *Rune Power* (Shaftesbury, Dorset, England: Element, 1996), 50.

18. Crossley-Holland, *The Norse Myths,* 3.

19. Campbell, *The Masks of God,* 395.

20. Terry, *Poems of the "Elder Edda,"* 94.

21. James E. McKeithen, "The *Risalah of Ibn Fadlan:* An Annotated Translation with Introduction (Ph.D. diss., Indiana University, 1979), 148–49.

22. Terry, *Poems of the "Elder Edda,"* 20.

23. Ibid., 18.

24. Robert K. Barnhart, *The Barnhart Dictionary of Etymology* (Bronx, N.Y.: H. W. Wilson, 1988).

25. Terry, *Poems of the "Elder Edda,"* 18.

26. Ibid., 16.

27. Ibid., 37.

28. Elliot, *Runes,* 58.

29. Terry, *Poems of the "Elder Edda,"* 18.

30. Eric Partridge, *Origins: A Short Etymological Dictionary of Modern English* (1958; reprint, London: Routledge and Kegan Paul, 1996), 765.

31. Terry, *Poems of the "Elder Edda,"* 164.

32. Ibid., 18.

33. Ibid., 1.

34. Crossley-Holland, *Norse Myths,* 3.

35. Freya Asswyn, *Northern Mysteries and Magic: runes, Gods and Feminine Powers* (St. Paul, Minn.: Llewellyn, 1998), 44.

36. Halsall, *Old English Rune Poem,* 121.

37. Morris and Magnussonm, *Volsunga Saga,* 35–41.

38. Crossley-Holland, *Norse Myths,* 3–4.

39. Halsall, *Old English Rune Poem,* 123.

40. Ibid., 185.

41. Cited in Britt-Mari Nasstrom, *Freyja—the Great Goddess of the North,* Lund Studies in History of Religions, ed. Tord Olsson, vol. 5 (Lund, Sweden: University of Lund, 1995), 51.

42. I. Jean Young, *The Prose Edda of Snorri Sturluson: Tales from Norse Mythology* (Cambridge: Bowes and Bowes, 1954), 24.

43. Terry, *Poems of the "Elder Edda,"* 40.

44. John Grant, *An Introduction to Viking Mythology* (London: Apple Press, 1990), 29.

45. Hilda R. Ellis Davidson, *The Lost Beliefs of Northern Europe* (London: Routledge, 1993), 107.

46. Terry, *Poems of the "Elder Edda,"* 7.

47. Jones and Pennick, *History of Pagan Europe,* 144.

48. Davidson, *Lost Beliefs,* 69.

49. Terry, *Poems of the "Elder Edda,"* 2.

50. Ibid., 7.

51. Michael Howard, *The Wisdom of the Runes* (London: Rider, 1985), 83.

52. Nigel Pennick, *Games of the Gods: The Origin of Board Games in Magic and Divination* (London: Rider, 1988), 177–78.

53. Elliot, *Runes,* 52.

54. Terry, *Poems of the "Elder Edda,"* 32.

55. Ibid., 163.

56. Howard, *Wisdom of the Runes,* 84.

57. Terry, *Poems of the "Elder Edda,"* 1.

58. My own redaction, based on the creation-account section of the *Prose Edda.*

59. My own redaction, based on the account of Ragnaroc from the *Prose Edda.*

60. Terry, *Poems of the Elder Edda,"* 43.

61. Osborn and Longland, *Rune Games,* 75.

62. Elliot, *Runes,* 47–50.

63. Howard, *Wisdom of the Runes,* 86.

64. Howard, *The Wisdom of the Runes,* 45.

65. Davidson, *Lost Beliefs,* 93.

66. Quoted in Freya Asswyn, *Northern Mysteries and Magic: Runes, Gods and Feminine Powers* (St. Paul, Minn.: Llewellyn, 1998), 22.

67. Terry, *Poems of the "Elder Edda,"* 17.

68. Halsall, *Old English Rune Poem,* 142.

69. Arthur Cotterell, *The Encyclopedia of Mythology* (London: Lorenz, 1996), 178.

70. Terry, *Poems of the "Elder Edda,"* 33.

71. Howard, *The Wisdom of the Runes,* 45.

72. Hilda R. Ellis Davidson, *Myths and Symbols in Pagan Europe: Early Scandinavian and Celtic Religions* (Manchester, England: Manchester University Press, 1989), 116.

73. Davidson, *Lost Beliefs,* 106.

74. Terry, *Poems of the "Elder Edda,"* 37–38.

75. Ibid.

76. Ibid., 39–40.

77. Ibid., 7.

78. From *Völuspá* and *Vafþrúðnismál* in Terry, *Poems of the "Elder Edda,"* 7, 43.

79. I am indebted for these details to Kevin Crossley-Holland, *Norse Myths,* xvi–xvii.

80. Howard, *Wisdom of the Runes,* 91–92.

Runecasting

1. Jones and Pennick, *History of Pagan Europe,* 205.

2. Edred Thorsson, *Runelore: A Handbook of Esoteric Runology* (New York: Weiser, 1987), 55.

3. Nigel Pennick, *The Complete Illustrated Guide to Runes* (Shaftesbury, England: Element, 1999), 44.

4. Guido von List, *The Secret of the Runes,* trans. Stephen Flowers (Rochester, Vt.: Destiny Books, 1988), 1–12.

5. Ibid., 10.

6. Pennick, *Illustrated Guide,* 43.

7. Cited in Pennick, *Illustrated Guide,* 130.

8. Jones and Pennick, *History of Pagan Europe,* 218.

9. Page, R. I, *An Introduction to English Runes* (London: Methuen and Co., 1973), 12.

10. Davidson, *Lost Beliefs,* 162.

11. Quoted in Jones and Pennick, *History of Pagan Europe,* 218.

12. See the foreword to C. G. Jung, *Synchronicity: An Acausal Connecting Principle* (Princeton, N.J.: Princeton University Press, 1973), 3–4.

13. J. R. R. Tolkien, *The Hobbit* (London: HarperCollins, 1990), ix.

14. Ibid., 51.

15. J. R. R. Tolkien, *The Lord of the Rings: The Return of the King* (London, HarperCollins, 1997), 956.

16. Crossley-Holland, *Norse Myths,* xxvi.

17. J. R. R. Tolkien, *The Lord of the Rings: The Fellowship of the Ring* (London: HarperCollins, 1997), 351.

18. Tolkien, *Return of the King,* Appendix E, 1096.

19. Humphrey Carpenter, *J. R. R. Tolkien: A Biography* (London:

HarperCollins, 1995), 54.

20. Ralph Blum, *The New Book of Runes* (London: Angus and Robertson, 1994), 13.

21. F. David Peat, *Synchronicity: The Bridge between Matter and Mind* (London: Bantum, 1987), 140.

22. Flowers, *Runes and Magic*, 33.

23. Asswyn, *Northern Mysteries*, 95.

24. Tanya M. Luhrmann, *Persuasions of the Witch's Craft: Ritual Magic in Contemporary England* (London: Picador, 1989), 391.

25. Thorsson, *Well of Wyrd*, 87.

26. Elliot, *Runes*, 1–2.

27. DuBois, *Nordic Religions*, 124.

28. Details can be found in the chapter "Cults of the Northern Gods" in Davidson, *Lost Beliefs*, 87–106.

A Final Word: The Rune Revival

1. Osborn and Longland, *Rune Games*, 97–98.

2. Ibid., 22–23.

3. Ibid., 97.

4. Blum, *New Book of Runes*, 11.

5. Thorsson, *Well of Wyrd*, 8.

6. Edred Thorsson, *Futhark: A Handbook of Rune Magic* (New York: Samuel Weiser, 1984), 16.

7. For a discussion of this and associated matters, see Ronald Hutton, *The Triumph of the Moon: A Study of Modern Pagan Witchcraft* (Oxford: Oxford University Press, 1999), 371–72.

8. Pennick, *Secrets of the Runes*, 11.

9. See especially Hutton, *Triumph of the Moon;* Leslie Ellen Jones, *Druid, Shaman, Priest: Metaphors of Celtic Paganism* (Middlesex, England: Hisarlik Press, 1998); and Aidan Kelly, *Crafting the Art of Magic* (St. Paul, Minn.: Llewellyn, 1991).

BIBLIOGRAPHY

Anderson, William, and Clive Hicks. *The Green Man: Archetype of Our Oneness with the Earth*. London: HarperCollins, 1990.

Asswyn, Freya. *Northern Mysteries and Magic: Runes, Gods and Feminine Powers*. St. Paul, Minn.: Llewellyn, 1998.

Auden, W. H., and Paul B. Taylor. *Norse Poems*. London: Athlone Press, 1981.

Bammesberger, Alfred, ed. *Old English Runes and Their Continental Background*. Heidelberg: Carl Winter–Universitatsverlag, 1991.

Barnhart, Robert K. *The Barnhart Dictionary of Etymology*. Bronx, N.Y.: H. W. Wilson, 1988.

Barret, Clive. *The Viking Gods*. London: Heineman, 1989.

Bauschatz, Paul C. *The Well and the Tree: World and Time in Early Germanic Culture*. Amherst: University of Massachusetts Press, 1982.

Blum, Ralph. *The Book of Runes*. London: Angus and Robertson, 1982.

———. *The New Book of Runes*. London: Angus and Robertson, 1990.

Bradley, Daniel J. "The Old English Rune Poem: Elements of Mnemonics and Psychoneurological Beliefs." *Perceptual and Motor Skills* 69, no. 1 (August 1989): 3–8.

Bremmer, Rolf H., Jr. "Hermes-Mercury and Wodin-Odin as Inventors of Alphabets: A Neglected Parallel." In *Old English Runes and Their Continental Background*, edited by Alfred Bammesberger, 409–19. Heidelberg: Carl Winter–Universitatsverlag, 1991.

Campbell, Joseph. *The Masks of God*. Vol. 1, *Primitive Mythology*. 1958. Reprint, London: Penguin Books, 1976.

Carpenter, Humphrey. *J. R. R. Tolkien: A Biography*. London: HarperCollins, 1995.

Cotterell, Arthur. *The Encyclopedia of Mythology*. London: Lorenz, 1996.

Crossley-Holland, Kevin. *The Norse Myths*. 1980. Reprint, London: Penguin, 1982.

Davidson, Hilda R. Ellis. *The Lost Beliefs of Northern Europe*. London: Routledge, 1993.

——. *Myths and Symbols in Pagan Europe: Early Scandinavian and Celtic Religions*. Manchester, England: Manchester University Press, 1989.

——. *Pagan Scandinavia*. London: Thames and Hudson, 1967.

——. *Scandinavian Mythology*. London: Paul Hamlyn, 1969.

Davidson, Hilda R. Ellis, and Peter Gelling. *The Chariot of the Sun and Other Rites and Symbols of the Northern Bronze Age*. London: J. M. Dent and Sons, 1969.

Derolez, René. "Runes and Magic." *American Notes and Queries* 24, no. 7–8 (1986): 98–102.

——. *Runica Manuscripta: The English Tradition*. Brugge, Belgium: De Tempel, 1954.

Dronke, Ursula, ed. and trans. *Myth and Fiction in Early Norse Lands*. Collected Studies Series. Aldershot, Hampshire, England: Variorum, 1996.

——. *The Poetic Edda*. Vol. 1, *Heroic Poems*. 1969. Reprint, Oxford: Clarendon University Press, 1997.

——. *The Poetic Edda*. Vol. 2, *Mythological Poems*. 1969. Reprint, Oxford: Clarendon University Press, 1997.

Drucker, Johanna. *The Alphabetic Labyrinth: Letters in History and Imagination*. London: Thames and Hudson, 1995.

DuBois, Thomas. *Nordic Religions in the Viking Age*. Philadelphia: University of Pennsylvania Press, 1999.

Eliade, Mircea. *Shamanism: Archaic Techniques of Ecstasy*. Bollinger Series 76. 1951. Reprint, Princeton, N.J.: Princeton University Press, 1964.

Elliot, Ralph. *Runes: An Introduction*. 1959. Reprint, Manchester, England: Manchester University Press, 1989.

Flowers, Stephen. *Runes and Magic: Magical Formulaic Elements in the Older Runic Tradition*. New York: Peter Lang, 1986.

Grant, John. *An Introduction to Viking Mythology*. London: Apple Press, 1990.

Halsall, Maureen. *The Old English Rune Poem: A Critical Edition*. Toronto: University of Toronto Press, 1981.

Howard, Michael. *The Wisdom of the Runes*. London: Rider, 1985.

Hutton, Ronald. *The Pagan Religions of the Ancient British Isles: Their Nature and Legacy.* Oxford: Blackwell, 1991.

———. *The Triumph of the Moon: A Study of Modern Pagan Witchcraft.* Oxford: Oxford University Press, 1999.

Jones, Leslie Ellen. *Druid, Shaman, Priest: Metaphors of Celtic Paganism.* Middlesex, England: Hisarlik Press, 1998.

Jones, Prudence, and Nigel Pennick. *A History of Pagan Europe.* London: Routledge, 1995.

Jung, C. G. *Synchronicity: An Acausal Connecting Principle.* 1960. Reprint, Princeton, N.J.: Princeton University Press, 1973.

Kelly, Aidan. *Crafting the Art of Magic.* St. Paul, Minn.: Llewellyn, 1991.

Kocher, Paul. *Master of Middle-Earth: The Achievement of J. R. R. Tolkien.* London: Thames and Hudson, 1972.

Larrington, Carolyne. *A Store of Common Sense: Gnomic Theme and Style in Old English Wisdom Poetry.* Oxford: Clarendon Press, 1993.

List, Guido von. *The Secret of the Runes.* Translated by Stephen Flowers. Rochester, Vt.: Destiny Books, 1988.

Luhrmann, Tanya M. *Persuasions of the Witch's Craft: Ritual Magic in Contemporary England.* London: Picador, 1989.

Markale, Jean. *Merlin: Priest of Nature.* Translated by Belle N. Burke. 1981. Reprint, Rochester, Vt.: Inner Traditions, 1995.

McKeithen, James E. "The *Risalah of Ibn Fadlan:* An Annotated Translation with Introduction." Ph.D. dissertation, Indiana University, 1979.

Meadows, Kenneth. *Rune Power: The Secret Knowledge of the Wise Ones.* Dorset, England: Element, 1996.

Morris, William, and Eirikr Magnusson, ed. and trans. *Volsunga Saga: The Story of the Volsungs and the Niblungs: With Certain Songs from the Elder Edda.* London: Walter Scot, 1900.

Nasstrom, Britt-Mari. *Freyja—the Great Goddess of the North.* Lund Studies in History of Religions, ed. Tord Olsson, vol. 5. Lund, Sweden: University of Lund, 1995.

Osborn, Marijane. "*Hleotan* and the Purpose of the Old English Rune Poem." *Folklore* 92, no. 2 (1981): 168–73.

Osborn, Marijane, and Stella Longland. *Rune Games.* 1982. Reprint, London: Routledge and Kegan Paul. 1987.

Page, R. I. *An Introduction to English Runes.* London: Methuen, 1973.

Partridge, Eric. *Origins: A Short Etymological Dictionary of Modern English.* 1958. Reprint, London: Routledge and Kegan Paul, 1996.

Patterson, Jacqueline Memory. *Tree Wisdom: The Definitive Guidebook to the Myth, Folklore, and Healing Power of Trees.* London: Thorsons, 1996.

Peat, F. David. *Synchroncity: The Bridge between Matter and Mind.* London: Bantum Books, 1987.

Pennick, Nigel. *The Complete Illustrated Guide to Runes.* Shaftesbury, England: Element, 1999.

———. *Games of the Gods: The Origin of Board Games in Magic and Divination.* London: Rider, 1988.

———. *The Secret Lore of Runes and Other Magical Alphabets.* London: Rider, 1991.

———. *Secrets of the Runes.* 1992. Reprint, London: Thorsons, 1995.

Polome, E. "The Names of the Runes." In *Old English Runes and Their Continental Background,* edited by Alfred Bammesberger, 421–38. Heidelberg: Carl Winter–Universitatsverlag, 1991.

Ross, Margaret Clunies. "The Anglo-Saxon and Norse *Rune Poems:* A Comparative Study." *Anglo-Saxon England* 19 (1990): 23–39.

———. *Prolonged Echoes: Old Norse Myths in Medieval Society.* Odense: Odense University Press, 1994.

Sorrell, Paul. "Oaks, Ships, Riddles, and the Old English Rune Poem." *Anglo-Saxon England* 19 (1990): 103–16.

Stanley, E. G. *The Search for Anglo-Saxon Paganism.* 1964. Reprint, Cambridge: D. S. Brewer, 1975.

Terry, Patricia, trans. *Poems of the "Elder Edda,"* with an introduction by Charles W. Dunn, 1969. Reprint, Philadelphia: University of Pennsylvania Press, 1990.

Thorsson, Edred. *At the Well of Wyrd: A Handbook of Runic Divination.* 1988. Reprint, York Beach, Maine: Samuel Weiser, 1996.

———. *Runelore: A Handbook of Esoteric Runology.* New York: Weiser, 1987.

———. *Futhark: A Handbook of Rune Magic.* New York: Samuel Weiser, 1984.

Tolkien, J. R. R. *The Book of Lost Tales.* Part 1. London: Unwin, 1985.

———. *The Hobbit.* 1937. Reprint, London: HarperCollins, 1990.

———. *The Lord of the Rings: The Fellowship of the Ring.* 1955. Reprint, London: HarperCollins, 1997.

———. *The Lord of the Rings: The Return of the King.* 1955. Reprint, London: HarperCollins, 1997.

————. *The Lord of the Rings: The Two Towers.* 1955. Reprint, London: HarperCollins, 1997.

Toynbee, Arnold. *Mankind and Mother Earth.* Oxford: Oxford University Press, 1976.

Wells, Peter S. *The Barbarians Speak: How the Conquered Peoples Shaped Roman Europe.* Princeton, N.J.: Princeton University Press, 1999.

Willis, Tony. *The Runic Workbook: Understanding and Using the Power of Runes.* Bath, England: Aquarian Press, 1986.

Wilson, David M., ed. *The Northern World: The History and Heritage of Northern Europe.* New York: Harry N. Abrams, 1980.

Young, I. Jean. *The Prose Edda of Snorri Sturluson: Tales from Norse Mythology.* Cambridge: Bowes and Bowes, 1954.

INDEX TO THE RUNES
OF THE ELDER
FUTHARK

BOOKS OF RELATED INTEREST

Ogam: The Celtic Oracle of the Trees
Understanding, Casting, and Interpreting
the Ancient Druidic Alphabet
by Paul Rhys Mountfort

Gods of the Runes
The Divine Shapers of Fate
by Frank Joseph

The Secret of the Runes
Translated by Guido von List
Edited by Stephen E. Flowers

How to Read Signs and Omens in Everyday Life
by Sarvananda Bluestone, Ph.D.

The Way of Tarot
The Spiritual Teacher in the Cards
by Alejandro Jodorowsky and Marianne Costa

The Metaphysical Book of Gems and Crystals
by Florence Mégemont

Invoking the Scribes of Ancient Egypt
The Initiatory Path of Spiritual Journaling
by Normandi Ellis and Gloria Taylor Brown

The Secret History of Vampires
Their Multiple Forms and Hidden Purposes
by Claude Lecouteux

Inner Traditions • Bear & Company
P.O. Box 388
Rochester, VT 05767
1-800-246-8648
www.InnerTraditions.com

Or contact your local bookseller